Acknowledgements

First and foremost I have to give a very special acknowledgement to my precious children, they are my heroes and my life. Without the strength and courage of my kids and my love for them, I would have thrown the towel in a long time ago and never have made it this far.

I give special thanks to my brother David who had to listen to me, day in and day out, in the early years of disclosure. I never realised how deeply my talking and ranting affected him because he didn't tell me until a few month's ago but he was always there for me to talk to.

Now to a major influence in my life and a very dynamic guy, "The man who did," Steve Bevan, my very good friend. If you could bottle what this man has i.e. dedication, compassion, humanitarian, energy and a wealth of knowledge that he puts into helping fellow survivors, we would be billionaires!!
Love ya bro!

A special thank you has to be given to all the officers at the child protection unit. They deserve medals for the job they do and it must be so frustrating and soul destroying for them when they see the paedophiles either get off with the charges, or the judges give out pitiful sentences. I have to acknowledge one particular CID officer called Steve; he is what I consider to be a good cop and a doer. He also dislikes nonces more than villains.

MY TRIBUTE TO WOMAN

I have been lucky enough to meet some very brave and special women on my journey; men tend to be thinkers whereas women are doers. Whilst men are still thinking about it, women will already have it done. It will be mainly women who will be brave enough to read this book through to the end and it will be women that talk about it and pass the message on to others.

I joined an online community and met the most awesome women you could ever wish to meet. Despite their own individual pain at the horror's inflicted on their own most precious children, these women refused to be beaten and fought for their children and themselves.

I would like to say a very special thank you to the ladies of that community, because without their kindness, sympathy and unfaltering support towards me at a very traumatic stage of my journey, I most definitely would not have made it through.

I personally and thousands of others, who have been helped over the years, owe gratitude to Linda for starting the community in the first place. The assistant managers deserve thanks for overseeing the running and welcoming of new members to the site.

I have my special friends in there and my first mention has to be Grandma. She wrote me the other day to say she didn't realise how much of an impact she had made in my life. I had to laugh at that one. Grandma was like a real grandma to me and I'm sure to many others, she never went overboard with advice but always gave a gentle guiding hand and had the best sense of humour ever. You made a big impact on me Grandma!!

Lisa, I always saw Lisa as a-shoot from the hip-shining ball of light. She put so much energy into the community and its members. She helped me so very many times and once again it has to be said more than she will ever know!! I have to mention a fellow good guy and that's Wayne her husband. He has been her rock and has been there for her through thick and thin. They also have an awesome daughter called Deb's aged 13 who said she is going to be a lawyer so she can help parents protect other abused children. From what I know of Deb's "if she said it, she means it and it will happen."

Last but not least, my very good friend Kim who tirelessly kept me going, Kim gave me guidance, enlightenment and educated me in many ways. We'd spend hours talking via our computers and I learnt a lot from her. She will also be a dynamic and major force in getting this book marketed, especially in America. Kim is one of life's doer's!!

2

In my personal life once again I've met some special women, I owe special gratitude to Marisa who was with me through some very sticky times. She also helped me feel deeper love and emotions than I ever thought possible, she gave me faith that I could love and trust, and in return give love. We are both better people for having met and she will always be my princess.

Jo a woman with a big personality and an even bigger laugh, keep laughing Jo. She has been there for me as well and is helping me with the punctuation. I told her *"The next guy who gets you, is going be a lucky guy,"* because she is a diamond.

Kathie, who I met briefly, has also left a big impact. She is a woman who has made it to the top of her field and is a true survivor. She summed me up in a very short period of time and gave me something to believe in about myself when she said *"John you are more than qualified to be a counsellor."* Thanks Kathie.

Now for my good friend Charlie, who I consider to be another true survivor and a very special person; she can light up a room with her smile and although she's been to hell and back throughout her life, she always bounces back and continues to smile. It's Charlie who has asked me to write her life story and has allowed me some insight into her life. It will be my honour to be trusted to put it into words for her.

Another strong and courageous woman is Yvonne. She is better known as Myvonne to those who know and love her. She too has given me insight into her life and I have the utmost respect for her durability and the compassion she shows to those around her. She too has been to the school of hard knocks and survived. She has been very supportive and helpful to me at the later stages of putting all of this together and I'm very grateful. Stay just as you are Yvonne!!

INTRODUCTION

Here goes. My name is John; I'm a father to some great kids and fantastic grandkids. This whole story was only being written for myself to read, a way of keeping track on a whole crazy and painful sequence of events, that turns out to be my LIFE.

I can still remember starting it, my wife and kids had gone away for a few days and I had some peacetime for myself. My friend Jeffrey called to see me one evening over those few days; I got talking about what I'd been doing and Jeffrey being a playwright asked if he could take a look. I thought whoops he'll think it's crap, I'd only wrote it for me.

The first thing he noticed in big bold letters was the title and asked, *"Where did you come up with the title, its brilliant?"* I laughed. *"Well it just kind of came to me, it didn't require any serious thought, it just seemed an appropriate title"*. He got half way down the first page and turned to me and said, *"John I can work with this story, we can make a play out of it, your writing seems so natural and it's straight to the point."* He then continued to read the first four pages I'd done. That was it!! That was the moment I decided this was going to be a book.

Fate lent a hand there methinks, because he'd turned up out of the blue and I only mentioned in general conversation what I'd been doing.

I thought I'd have it done in a few month's, having no idea those months would turn into years and how many painful discoveries and changes would occur in those years to come.

I'm going to take you on a journey with me, a journey with many forks and crossroads in its path. Sometimes events and situations will go in all different directions but will all lead back to the same path eventually. I'll repeat myself many times throughout this book. Sometimes different situations will have the same affect on me but this was how it was and it has been written how it was lived.

I had full intentions that when it was written I would go back to the beginning and re-write it, making all kinds of adjustments but for me to do that, I don't think it would have the same impact.

You have to take into account that the last time I wrote a story was almost 30 yrs ago in school (I was also to find out I'm slightly dyslexic.) Presentation will probably be wrong and as I say I'll repeat myself many times (as I just did), promising to get back to things etc.

Also taking into account my typing speed in the beginning was probably half a page an hour, I was painstakingly slow. I used to sit on a small chair in front of the computer for hours, backbreaking hours, sometimes having to lie down to rest my aching back, lying in agony mentally and physically. Often having to close my eyes and go into a deep sleep because it was so exhausting mentally, then getting back up and deciding to carry on, or having to switch off for a while. Although you rarely fully switch off!!

If I was to do all the right things required in it to make it read like other books, by real authors, I feel would take the reality of the whole story away from it, the rawness. You must remember I was just a Dad, a very confused, angry, hurting and almost broken Dad on many occasions but I am "A DAD" and have stayed a Dad throughout it all, no matter what life threw at us!!

You yourselves will see me growing as you read along, how my writing skills improve slightly, speed never built up that fast. But with saying that, I could only ever do one or sometimes two pages at a time, because it was far too painful. Think the best I did was ten pages in a week and then didn't come back to it for months. I've not even read it myself for a couple of years, I just kept adding to it as I went along.

This is a journey that some of you may have already been on yourselves; some may even find themselves, or someone they know in the future, in a similar situation. But no matter what happens, you will know a lot more than you did, after reading this book.

To be honest I don't want my own kids to read it themselves, because they like me have lived it and are thankfully moving on.

I've also written this my way, a way that anybody can understand, without the need for big words that some people may have to look up in a dictionary, or not have a clue what they mean. Its simple, its real and easy to understand.

By the way there are also swear words but only where it felt appropriate to the way I was feeling at the time.

Hmmm I've just started off by reading the first pages and have no choice but to alter a few things, if only to make things clearer but I'll try to stick to the way I was writing back then as much as possible.

I've been back again and the weirdest thing has happened. It is like I'm re-living every moment. For the first time I can see things so vividly, even remembering some of the conversation. It's a freaky feeling and I've found myself adding so many things that I'd missed before. This is so very strange because so far it seems I'm detached from feeling any pain. It's like being there in person but without that inner gut pain.

Now what do I want from you as a reader? I'd like you to read through to the end if you can, trying to imagine and feel the enormity of the whole story. Not forgetting to allow for poor punctuation and my going off on a tangent. Also remembering that you yourself may get triggered by certain parts of it, or situations, so stay very aware and careful of that.

I also want you to talk about this story to your friends and family, in fact as many people as you can. The reason for this is "You never know who you might be talking to" because there are millions of us survivors out there. You may be talking to one of us without having a clue about it, in turn guiding them towards the book for themselves.

I would like you to buy it for someone as a gift if they are interested in reading it. Do not lend it because more often then not "You never get books back." By buying it for yourself or for someone else and they in turn buy for someone else etc, it is limitless how many people could be reached because you took the time and made the effort.

You are helping me to set up and maintain something that is so very much needed in the deprived areas of our country. I want to open up counselling offices that specialise in child abuse, I want to use my life and knowledge gained these last years helping others. I want to work with the parents of abused children as well as the children; the whole family needs help to adjust to the situation they suddenly find themselves in once child abuse has been disclosed and in turn everybody heals together.

The more people you speak to and they in turn speak to other people, that's a lot of people who can be reached through you and all the time awareness is being raised on what is normally a taboo subject for many.

Don't worry I won't be buying a big house with a swimming pool because I neither want that nor need it, besides I can't swim ha. I just want to make a difference in this sometimes very sad world and leave my mark upon it with what is probably not much time left on it. I want to leave something set up for others to carry on and you will be contributing to that.

Word of mouth is a powerful thing and even the predatory beasts will get wind of this book, *"the more people speak about sexual abuse, the easier it becomes for survivors to speak up."* People gain strength from knowing that others have walked in their shoes and can turn their lives around.

So now it's over to you, come walk with me into a very real part of my life and thank you very much for joining me.

John.

P.S., I've re-read it since writing the last part and am amazed at how close to the edge, I sometimes became. You may find yourselves thinking, I'm a total lunatic at some stages. I'm amazed at how very angry and so close to violence I was as well. Please remember "Nobody knows how they would cope with anything, until they've faced it". So with taking that into account please don't judge me too harshly and remember this story has been written over a very painful six-year period.

Part One

Chapter 1

Disclosure

I call him beast but once called him brother.

I 'm married with six children, Michael my eldest son isn't my biological son but I've brought him up since he was three years old.

The nightmare began several years ago. My wife Lillian had told me that when she was a child her older brother by eighteen months had sexually abused her. She didn't go into many details and I didn't press for more than she wanted to say at that time (This was something I later had to become an expert at) We talked awhile and based on the little she told me, I didn't see a problem when she decided she wanted to confront him on her own. In fact I even encouraged and supported her decision, thinking I'd be more of a hindrance. I felt my presence might intimidate him and in turn would be taking away her own moment of standing up against him and standing up for herself away from her.

Some weeks later she plucked up courage and chose the night to do it, she seemed confident and again I really didn't feel she had a problem doing it on her own. She took a deep breath kissed me on the cheek reassuring me she'd be ok and went on her way. I can still see her clearly walking off; and even remember what she was wearing.

About an hour or so later Lillian returned, she seemed calm and didn't give away the enormity of the ordeal she'd just faced. She told me that when she'd asked him, he said he didn't remember anything as it was a long time ago but if he "HAD" done those things to her? Then he was sorry.

After talking for a while she got up to leave, he walked her to the door and opened his arms and asked if he could hug her? She backed off and left, she knew then he'd remembered! He'd robbed her of her moment of confrontation and again he'd tried to manipulate her. He'd remembered ok but had given very little away.

All of this was discussed in front of his girlfriend Tina as well, although the relevance of this statement will be apparent later.

As far as I was concerned it was over and life went back to normal, or so I thought. Oh how naïve was I, BECAUSE OUR LIVES WERE NEVER GOING

TO BE THE SAME AGAIN.

If only she'd told me all the facts in the beginning, everything would have been so different. At least I'd have been able to form my opinions armed with full knowledge and had a greater insight into the enormity of what he'd done and WHAT he really WAS!

A little over three years later, our eldest son Michael came and told us that his uncle (my wife's brother, the same brother) had abused him when he was a child. Again he didn't want to go into details and once again I couldn't push for any.

Within a week my niece Michelle (the beast's daughter) phoned me, she was off her head on heroin and said
"John why didn't you stop him"?
I knew instantly what she meant and replied,
"What do you mean darling? What do you mean stop him"?
"Him, him, why didn't you stop him doing it to me, my Dad?"

She then went on to tell me that her Dad used to abuse her and her disabled brother Stuart when they were younger. I managed to stay calm, even though I found it so very hard to do so.

She said the heroin was the only thing that numbed the pain, when she smoked it all the pain went away. Even though she still remembered everything, it numbed the feelings for her.

That really cut deep into my soul hearing her say that, so very deep.

I told her that Michael had said the same thing about her Dad, her reply was
"Yeah and look at us, we're the most fucked up in the whole family. Now I know why he is so fucked up as well."

She needed to go but said she'd stay in touch with me.

Now my head was really spinning!!! This wasn't happening, this couldn't be happening, this only happened to other people? (Only the tip of the iceberg was being seen) my emotions were all over the place but so many things started to fall into place in my head.

I felt I was going crazy, having flashbacks to so many different situations, at so many different stages in my family's life. Michael had become an alcoholic and also been to prison. Every time he'd been in trouble with the police, he'd been drunk.

From the age of fifteen he'd gone from being a male model appearing in girl's magazines. He had done a few walk on parts in television programmes as well and in the space of a year, turned into a juvenile delinquent.

So many pieces of the puzzle were falling into place for me and it was so very frightening.

I decided to confront the beast myself this time!!

A few days later on a Sunday evening my brother David and myself went to the beast's house. All the way over I was determined to stay in control of myself, be cunning and sly but stay calm.

We got to the door and knocked on. Tina answered and said
"Hi John, are you ok."

She must have seen something in my face as I asked where Malcolm was (the beast). *"He's in bed, he's not well. Is everything all right John?"* I was already on my way up the stairs and her voice was miles away to me.

Out of the corner of my eye I saw David guiding her into the living room and calmly saying,
"Its ok he just needs to speak to him"

There he was, lay in his bed facing the wall, he must have heard my voice because he turned towards me as I stepped into his room; I looked at him feeling disgust and loathing, all the time trying to compose myself. He was looking at me and with a nervous voice asked,

"What's the matter John? What's the matter? Is it Michelle? Has something happened to Michelle"?

My only words were, *"Get dressed, I need to talk to you, come downstairs and I'll tell you."*

I had to say it a few times and then turned away, not being able to stomach seeing him climbing out of bed, with panic written all over his face.
I wonder now after re-living that moment whether he had some idea as to why I'd called? I think he did!!

Before I knew it I was stood in his living room and he was coming down the stairs, Tina was standing behind me near the kitchen door and David between her and me. His eldest brother Stanley was sat on the sofa. The beast walked in the room, still panicking and asking,

"What is wrong"?

Before I knew it, I was punching him in the face screaming.
"You know why I'm fucking here, you know why"!!

Tina ran at me but my brother blocked her off and pushed her onto the sofa and told her to stay out of it. The beast was covering his face and I realised what I was doing and snapped out of it, pushing him into the chair. I was raging and trying to bring myself back. I was shouting inside my head that I wasn't supposed to do it this way, furious with myself that I'd lost control.

Over the next hour or two he denied and denied it, he denied everything, even though I told him everything Michelle and Michael had said. He was staring directly into my eyes, trying to not only convince me but also intimidate me. It was a very strange feeling, almost hypnotic and I had to break away from his stare and shake my head.

For just a moment I was starting to believe him and somewhere deep inside I felt a fear of him! A fear I couldn't understand, I was bigger, stronger and as I thought totally in control. But I felt a deep gnawing fear inside. Once I shook my head I'd regained my composure but he'd touched something deep, very deep inside me.

Tina was listening to every word; I even mentioned he'd probably done something to her own son who'd lived with them a few years earlier. Her son ended up a heroin addict as well and I remembered the beast being very close to the lad whilst he lived with them.

I was saying so many things for her to switch sides including "Tina every time he touches you remember where his hands have been, remember what he's done to kids" but she kept sticking up for him, denying he was capable of such things. At one point she was wavering and asked him point blank as he was getting up and putting his coat on, he ignored her and asked us to take him for a drive. You could tell he didn't want her to hear anymore! He was panicking but he was also very cunning. I know this was either because he wanted me to deal with him in a violent way, or he was being clever and after we'd gone, Tina could phone the police? David and myself could have found ourselves up on kidnapping charges if we'd taken him out of the house.

Either way I wasn't going to give him that satisfaction and laughed telling him,
" If you think I'm going to kill you? You are oh so wrong! You can wait for the police to knock on your door. You're going to have to face the courts and eventually prison."

I really felt I was in control and he was so weak and I also knew full well how paedophiles get treated in prison.

Before I left I said,
"Every time you close your eyes, I want you to see your mothers face, because Lillian told her before she died what you'd done to her. Your mother knew before she died what you are! Wait for that knock at your door Malcolm, wait for the knock"

I then spat in his face and walked out (the spitting later became my way of not physically attacking him.) To see him sat there with my spit slowly dripping down his face and making no movement to wipe it away became a regular thing.

I believed in the justice system and how it would/should deal with these animals. Once again, I was being very naïve, never for one minute realising what we'd face and what was going to come into our lives in the future.

If I'd known then, what I was going to later find out, I'd have snapped his neck like a twig, with my bare hands!

I must also add that we lived in a rough area and violence was the main way people dealt with things, dishing out their own form of justice, especially for something like this! The police were rarely called for anything!

David was a club doorman so he was used to dealing with people, sometimes in a physical and violent way. For us to be able to walk away, without harming him let alone maiming him, was a major achievement for both of us. Especially faced with such an atrocity!

Lillian contacted the police about herself and Michael. She had to go in and make a statement and we let the police take it from there. Michael wasn't ready at that time to make a statement but the officers in the case were aware of what had happened to him

In the meantime Michelle got back in touch, I told her we'd contacted the police and after a few phone calls she too wanted to speak to them. She said she'd talk to the police because she wanted to show support to Michael and she thought they could both help each other through the whole ordeal. I arranged for the officer dealing with us to go to Bradford to see her but she didn't answer the door and I didn't hear from her for a while.

Now this was where I found out how cunning and devious the beast could be! I'd made one of many more mistakes to come. I'd practically told him everything we knew the night we'd confronted him.

The beast had mentioned on that Sunday night that they'd been getting strange phone calls with nobody speaking? I later found out it was Michelle plucking up courage to speak to him. By then he'd realised it was Michelle and managed to lure her back to Manchester to live with him. So of course she no longer wanted to speak to the police.

The beast had always come across as weak and feeble and totally reliant on us to help him with his family. He was a single parent, as his wife had left him when their kids were very young. He'd lived next door to us from day one of his wife leaving and had already become an alcoholic.

Numerous times he'd been in and out of rehab leaving us to look after his kids, cleaning his house and even once decorating it before he came home.

We'd always had keys to each other's houses. The only thing that separated us from living, as one big family unit, was the separate front doors. THE ENEMY WITHIN! THE BEAST IN THE FAMILY!

The year before Lillian's disclosure we'd both been out for a few drinks to a local pub. When we got home, we'd only just sat down when we heard an almighty commotion going on next door. There was shouting, screaming and lots of banging noises, so Lillian went next door to find out what was going on.

I didn't bother or want to get involved, as by this time I wasn't really interested in what went on next door anymore. He'd had Stuart his handicapped son put into care, which I despised him for! Although I must admit I'd found that strange at the time, considering the amount of benefits he'd been getting because of Stuart's disability.

Thinking back though? There was another night I'd heard a lot of shouting coming from the beast's open bathroom window, I let myself in and ran upstairs to find the beast in the empty bath. He'd told me that he'd been trying to dry Stuart after his bath and Stuart freaked out and threw him in the bath?

By this time Stuart was six foot tall and very strong! Obviously he was becoming too big to handle and was probably fighting him off?

Michelle had also gone completely off the rails and the beast and his girlfriend were both heavy alcoholics. Those were a few of the many reasons I had little to do with him by that time!

I was sat listening to all the shouting and decided it was getting out of hand and that Lillian was next door in the midst of it all. I decided I'd better go and see what the hell was going on. Although very reluctantly!

Just as I'd got through my front door the beast was walking down his path saying he wanted to fight a man, he wanted to fight with me. He'd pushed me to fight with him many times over the years whilst drunk. Many times I'd laughed and told him to grow up. This time it felt different, I don't know why? But it did! I'd let him off too many times. This time I was going to make sure he'd never ask again!

I walked out and said, *"You don't really want this do you?"* Still trying to give him a chance to back out of it but he was all worked up with himself and promptly replied, *"Yes I want to fight you,"* so I obliged him.

I'd learnt Thai boxing a few years earlier and was fairly good at it; I kicked him up and down the close with just enough force to hurt him, without finishing him off. Leaving him in no doubt that I was fully in control of what I was doing, toying with him like a cat with a mouse. The entire time saying, *"you asked for this"* as I swung another roundhouse kick to his thigh or his waist, allowing him in close to throw a punch, blocking and countering, mauling him and pushing him away.

I was really starting to enjoy it and he didn't know what to do, nothing he threw at me was hitting the target. I was smiling and following him all the time, with the roundhouse kicks, saying, *"You asked for this"*.

Looking back I'm so glad that when I finished him off, it was with a massive kick to his crutch! The part of his anatomy that I'd later find out had been used to rape children.

Michelle told me years later that on that night, whilst Tina was in a drunken sleep he'd come into her bedroom to molest her! By then she was 15 and she'd started to fight back! She'd turned the bedroom upside down throwing things at him, that's what all the commotion we'd heard was. Sooner or later kids get older, stronger and do fight back!

What I didn't know was that whilst we were fighting, a police car had driven past and the officer had seen what was going on. The policeman had hidden behind a tree waiting for back up to come. Next minute the close was full of police cars and vans.

I personally couldn't see what the problem was; all that had happened as far as I was concerned, he'd got a beating that he'd asked for!

I went on to complain to the police officers, that if they responded the same way to the burglaries going on in the area around that time, maybe the old people wouldn't be terrified in their own homes!

I'd acted as a guardian on our estate for a number of years, always the first out to investigate if somebody's alarm went off. I'd threatened the burglars because the older people would come to me for help. I'd even had words with the young kids if they were upsetting the older folk. The kids had respect for me because I never shouted or spoke down to them. I 'd just explain things as they were, appealing to their better nature and treat them with respect, so in turn they were respectful back to me.

Another night I'd chased and caught a pervert flasher and took him to the police station. The officer I handed him over to told me later
"I don't know what you said to him? But he's admitted everything! So your daughter and the other girls won't have to testify in court."

I just grinned and said, *"Oh that's good."*

What had happened was, when I caught him I'd thrown him in the back of my work van and told him if he didn't tell the police everything, I'd take him to the moors to kill and bury him. Ha, he must have believed me.

Another time a flasher came on to the estate two nights running, the kids didn't run to their own parents, they all came running for me. I chased this guy for two nights but he was fast and got away both times. He never came back again though!

Even drug dealers didn't work on our estate back then, as they knew better and more than once I'd moved them on.

I'm not a violent man unless extremely provoked! But my Dad had brought me up to stand up for what I believed in! Also to remove anything or anybody who got in my face, *"The world was a tough place and only the strong could truly survive"* was his motto.

One of my strongest beliefs was to stand up for the weak and people should be able to live without fear in their own homes and area. I also believed in a strong community spirit, love thy neighbour! We'd even tried to form a home watch scheme but the people were too scared of the new breed of thugs on the streets! I've got to admit I was getting a bit unsure myself, as one local gang had become a lot scarier by this time. I also felt I was getting a bit too old to take this particular gang on. Around the time of the fight people were getting mugged and burgled on a nightly basis. One poor old man died two weeks after being mugged and thrown into a wheelie bin.

The police and the whole community knew it was members of the gang that had killed him!! Proving it was another matter though!! "What goes round, comes around theory" definitely stepped into that set of circumstances though. The gang leader and main evil one of the lot died within a few years in a car accident, he lost control smashing into a barrier. The rumour went round that he was beheaded? Karma caught up with him!

I voiced my opinions to the police very strongly, insisting that the officer came into my home and sat down. I felt there'd been enough drama in the street for one night; you'd have thought there'd been a major incident with the amount of police that had responded. Instead of the simple fact the beast got a beating he deserved. That really grated on me.

The beast stood there, battered and bleeding begging them, saying he didn't want to press charges against me. I'd got their backs up by refusing to stand on the street explaining what had gone on. They wanted me, so arrested us both, so much for freedom of speech!

At the police station I explained to the custody sergeant about the beast wanting to fight me while I'd been trying to mind my own business. He seemed to see things from my point of view and asked if I'd admit to being drunk and disorderly and accept a caution? The alternative was a breach of the peace and an appearance in court, so I had no choice but to say I'd accept the caution. Then he told me, I'd have to spend a few hours in the cells until I'd sobered up, I laughed and said *"But I'm not drunk"* The Sergeant laughed back and said *"I know you're not drunk but you have to stay awhile as that's procedure"*

So that was it, I had to spend a few hours in a cell with a blocked toilet full of diarrhoea. Every time I needed to use the toilet I'd have to cover my mouth and nose with my shirt, the stench was terrible! The blanket I was supposed to cover myself up with stank as well, so I opted to sit in the corner freezing cold waiting for them to release me.

I had to be up for work at 7am and at the time was working seven days a week, so much for having a quiet drink on a Sunday night and trying to mind my own business!

Why was I stuck in that cell? All because the beast wanted to molest his daughter and then fight a man! How can anyone work out what makes a perverts mind tick??????? I've only been arrested twice in my life and both times had been because of the beast!

The first time was a few weeks before I got married. The beast and myself had just walked out of a nightclub and a mass brawl was going on. The police came and everyone ran off in different directions. An officer asked us to move on but the beast got cheeky with him, so he arrested him. I asked the officers at the back of the van if I could speak to the beast, to find out what to tell his wife? They agreed, as I hadn't been causing trouble, the next thing I knew the officer who'd arrested the beast had come up behind me and grabbed me by the hair, then threw me in the van as well!

A massive brawl and we were the only arrests. The case was thrown out of court as the policemen had tried to say I was ripping the doors off to let him out. It was complete fabrication and after I'd stood my ground in the witness box, the judge knew it was! The beast had completely crumbled in the witness box that day; and he kept tripping over his words.

That was another thing I'd remembered about him, which had kept me going, thinking about his new day in court that was to come. If he'd been a nervous wreck on the stand over such a trivial matter, how much would he crumble on so many much more serious charges!

I forgot to mention after the nightclub incident at the police station the beast got cheeky again and there was only one cell. After being slapped a few times in the face with a pair of leather gloves, in he went. I was told I'd have to stay in the waiting area and sleep on a bench. He was crying out so I looked through the spy hole. He had his hands together in a praying position pleading with me, *"Please John get me out, please get me out."* He has claustrophobia! I explained this to one of the officers but he just laughed and said *"So what, that's what he gets for being a cocky bastard"*

This was another reason I wanted him to go to prison all these years later! A claustrophobic alcoholic in prison! In my darkest moments as time went on, that picture in my mind was the only thing that kept me going! Death was too easy, too quick! Prison for him was the only punishment that would fit the crime! I knew a day would be like a week, a week like a month and a month like a year for him and waiting before appearing in the courts, would have filled him with terror.

The thoughts of how many other children may come forward to expose him for the animal he was! His mind must have been tormented! Like he'd tormented so many innocent children's minds and wracked their bodies with pain. Now it was his turn!

Oh how miserable his life became! But so did mine, I was being eaten up by it all! Anger, despair and thoughts of revenge were eating me alive. I was drowning myself without even realising it; sending myself demented.

Not long after that crazy night he upped and moved leaving Michelle who was soon going to prison, to survive alone. Did he realise that his game was almost up! What might Michelle have said that night, to frighten him enough to move out so quickly?

This hurts me so much to think, there was I helping to protect the community we lived in and the beast was an abuser of children right under my nose!!!! MY CHILDREN!!

Proving how manipulative and cunning paedophiles are!!!!
My mind has been tormented; my heart has been laden with pain, pains that nobody, except somebody who had faced the same things, could even begin to imagine. My soul had been savaged; my very being has been thrown into question!!! Who am I? Who was I? How did I not see? I hated myself!! How could he? Why did he? Questions, questions, questions to which there are no answers.

Even he couldn't answer! How could he! To answer he would have to face his own demons! To face what he is! To accept he was a monster out of control! He'd raped and abused children's bodies and minds! He'd done these terrible things without any concern to their future! As had been done to him as a child!
Did he think they wouldn't remember? Did he think they would never talk?
Or did he just take their bodies regardless of the consequences? Who will ever know? Because he just denies and denies and denies!!! Torturing them all over again!!

BUT HE KNOWS WHAT HE REALLY IS!! HE KNOWS WHAT HE'S DONE!!
And like the cowards he and all perverts are! They can only think "How do I get out of this"? And he used many tactics to get out of it! He'd learnt how to lie! How to scheme! How to scare children into silence and how to manipulate them for his sordid, perverted pleasures! THE BEAST WAS A MASTER OF DECEPTION!!!!!!! THE DEVILS DISCIPLE IN DISGUISE!!!!

Chapter 2

How We Met

I met Lillian in a nightclub when we were eighteen; Michael was only three years old at the time. We'd known each other at school and had been good friends and for one of those years we were in the same class. We secretly fancied each other but never admitted it to the other back then.

We started courting and one night I stayed at her flat. The next morning she asked me if I wanted to meet Michael? He was staying with his aunt and uncle around the corner and I remember the day most clearly.

It was sunny and we were laughing as we walked to collect him. She was laughing at me because I was nervous about meeting a three-year-old child! What if he didn't like me? What do I say? I was a nervous wreck!

We went into the flat and there was the beast sitting on the settee, feeding his baby son Stuart. I'd remembered him from school, although he looked very different from back then. At school he was very popular with the girls and lots of them fancied him. When I met him in his flat that morning he looked drawn and very ill looking, a shadow of his former self. We only talked for a few minutes and it seemed a strained conversation. Then I asked to meet Michael. This cute blonde haired kid came walking into the room and smiled straight at me, I introduced myself to him and we chatted for a few minutes, laughing and joking together.

When he'd come into the room, I was curious as to why he wasn't in the main room with the beast and his wife in the first place but I dismissed it. He also had breakfast cereal round his mouth and I could see he hadn't been washed. We left with Michael and went back to the flat and he and I both got on really well throughout the day.

That evening after he'd gone to bed I voiced my opinion! I said that I didn't like the idea that Michael hadn't been washed and that he'd had food stains on his clothes. I also said that I didn't really like the idea of taking her out, if it meant Michael having to stay with them. Quite a lot to say considering we hadn't been seeing each other for that long but it didn't feel right. I felt they were neglecting him and he just didn't look happy being there.

Obviously I was already showing paternal instincts and a sixth sense, If only I'd stayed that way and trusted my instincts! Again the blame and shame we carry because of a beast's behaviour!

The next time I took Lillian out Michael stayed at her Mum's and again I stayed overnight at the flat. The next day we were sat at the front of the flats, as her Mum walked up the road with Michael. He saw me and ran excitedly towards me, I opened my arms and he ran and jumped into them hugging me.

That was it! That was our moment; a bond was sealed! I felt such a love for this child and it melted my heart!

Lillian's Mum couldn't believe what she was seeing. She told us afterwards that Michael couldn't wait to get home, as he knew I'd be there. This child needed a Dad! And from the way I felt I obviously had gained a son and a very impressed future mother in law.

I did all the Dad things with Michael, we went to parks, we flew kites and I bought motorboats for bath time. We also spent lots of quality time together reading, writing, laughing and talking.

I had strong protective feelings for him, which seems really strange. Little did I know we were kindred spirits he and I, and those strong feelings were going to be needed, for what we would have to face in the future.

A few weeks later I moved in. After a week or so, one morning before I went to work Michael called me Dad! He called me Dad! I couldn't believe it, I didn't comment but asked Lillian quietly after he left the room,

- *"Did you tell him to say that?"* when she answered, *"No I was as surprised as you"* I was so overjoyed I almost cried and didn't want to go to work it had had such an affect on me! That was it! I was a Dad! It didn't matter to me that I wasn't his biological Dad! I was his Dad! He'd claimed me!

What I didn't know was, the beast had already claimed Michael! And how much this wonderful boy was going to change and we'd be clueless as to why. How cunning paedophiles are! How cunning they are! There was a whole chain of events that would follow and the beast would have more access to him. The beast abused his body and controlled his mind and all under the guise of loving uncle.

When Michael was aged five his behaviour changed drastically, he became moody and very naughty. He was wetting the bed and had also started bullying other kids in school. He got suspended from school dinners and we had to go into the school, to monitor how his behaviour had been on a daily basis.

Social services were contacted and we had somebody visit us a few times, they observed us and we talked. Had they given us any inclination as to what they may have felt was possibly wrong? i.e. classic signs of sexual abuse, maybe our nightmare would have been known back then but alas that wasn't to be!

By this time we'd married, had a baby girl and a son on the way. We were a classic example of kids bringing kids up! We were so very naive!

The beast had left his wife and asked if he could stay with us for a while.

We'd brought Michael's worst nightmare into our home for the horror to carry on and his behaviour got steadily worse over the coming months. When I'd get in from work the beast was always ready to tell me how bad Michael's behaviour had been.

Lillian was under stress, more than just the stress of raising a family. She too had her own nightmare living under her roof again and of course I punished Michael, he'd be shouted at and sent to his room. It seemed like he was constantly naughty.

Little did I know this was the beast's way of showing him how much control he had over him and us! He was manipulating us through our ignorance! And showing Michael that if he spoke up, WHO WOULD BELIEVE HIM?????? WHO WOULD BELIEVE THIS POOR VULNERABLE DEFENCELESS CHILD????

He was stealing his childhood! He was abusing his body! He was torturing his soul! How can we begin to imagine the horror and torment going on in Michael's mind? How cunning and twisted paedophiles are! The beast came across as such a nice person! THE DEMON WITH MANY FACES!!

The beast was always so willing to baby-sit our children. He'd even offer to look after our baby son Anthony, whilst Lillian took our daughter Elizabeth to play group. Anthony had developed a problem with his penis that was continually red and sore, so much so that the doctor recommended circumcision. This didn't seem untoward, as I'd been circumcised myself as a baby but we will never know for sure whether the beast had been molesting him then? That is a thought so abhorrent for me! But based on how twisted we were to find out the beast was, its most likely the beast was responsible.

How horrific for a baby boy only a few month's out of his mother's womb, to end up in the hands of a monster! Again under the guise of caring uncle!

Anthony seemed to cry all of the time; Michael was misbehaving and I was working all the hours God sends, leaving the house at 5am. The cracks in our relationship started to show! The house was like a powder keg and the atmosphere wasn't nice at all.

I've since read in the bible *"the devil causes chaos and confusion"* and it seems we had one of his disciples living with us! Lillian left me and moved back to her mothers but the beast stayed.

She came back after a few weeks and things seemed to me to be working out for us. I then decided that we needed the beast to move out so Michael could have his own room. I remember using the spare room as an excuse! The strange thing was, as much as Lillian didn't want him there any longer, she seemed scared of me telling him to go? I just didn't want him around anymore, instincts again I suppose! He wasn't happy when I told him and after a big argument he moved out.

Christmas came and went and as far as I was concerned we were getting on ok. It seems for Lillian things weren't ok at all. (But that will become more apparent in her story)

After a few months' she left again and moved back in with her mother, I'd tried everything to persuade her to stay but she was adamant our marriage was over. I felt, that time, it really was over and decided to make a new life for myself. I started going out and meeting other people and a few weeks later met a really nice girl called Jessica. She worked in a bank and came from a good family, who didn't like the idea of her getting involved with a married man at all. Looking back, I can't blame them in the slightest!! But she liked me a lot and it didn't matter to her that I'd been married before; all that mattered was what we had then.

Throughout the whole time Lillian used to bring the kids up to see me and stay over the odd night. The inevitable would happen and we'd sleep together occasionally.

The more I got involved with Jessica the less I wanted to sleep with Lillian, that's when she started asking could she come back home. I told her that she'd left too many times and I'd started making a new life for myself and was happy being with Jessica. Then came the bombshell!!! Lillian came to see me and told me she was pregnant! She'd been to the Dr's and he'd confirmed it, she said because I wouldn't take her back, she'd taken an overdose and fallen down the stairs, which had started her bleeding. She said she couldn't keep the baby because we already had three kids and the overdose might have damaged the baby? The Dr had given her time to think about it and if she wanted him to, he'd arrange for her to have a termination.

I knew I couldn't go back with her but was so confused as to why I felt so strongly about it?

A week later she had it all arranged and I took time off work to have the kids. The day came, she dropped the kids off with me and went to the hospital and I said I'd visit her later when the kids settled. When I got to the hospital she seemed ok and we talked about how it was the right decision to make etc.

As I was walking towards the door to leave, my brain was screaming at me to turn around and say "come home we can make it all work out." I glanced backwards before turning the corner, she was sitting up on the bed and she seemed so small and desperate looking. Although I wanted to lift her off the bed and carry her away, this very strong thought, voice in my head, whatever, said, "Keep walking and don't look back." It felt right with my gut feelings to keep walking as well.

(I really didn't understand it back then but have realised it for what it was since. I've kept this part brief. But don't judge me until you get to near the end of the book.)

I picked her up the next day and brought her back to the house, she was ill and stayed the night but couldn't wait to get back to her Mum's the following day. She lived with her Mum for a couple of months until the local council offered her the house next door to the beast.

I continued to see Jessica, until one weekend we'd been out and had a row when we got back to the house and she had left. On the Monday Lillian came to see me with the kids, nothing unusual with that until she said,
"Listen John I know you don't want to get back together but I can't stay at my Mum's any longer. We keep arguing and she's told me to get out. I'm moving into my new house soon and if its ok with you, can we stay for the two weeks while I sort everything out?" And of course I said yes.

A bit later there was a knock at the door, which Lillian answered and I heard her say, *"Is it John you want to speak to"*? I went to the door, Jessica was stood there, she said "I've felt ill since we argued and just had to come and see you" Like an idiot I told her Lillian was back and we were going to make a go of it again, Jessica just looked at me and burst into tears, then turned and ran to her friends in the car.

I've felt so guilty since then and have vowed if I ever saw her again, I'd apologise for doing that to her. I walked into the living room and Lillian had what I see now as a very smug look on her face, at the time I'd confused it with a smile. Over the next two weeks she was being so nice and understanding, occasionally she'd mention me moving into the new house but I'd say no each time.

She left the kids with me for the weekend whilst she sorted her house out and I'd said I'd bring them down on the Monday. Monday came and it was a bright sunny day and I'd had a great weekend with my kids. We walked into the new house and she was in the hallway mopping the floor, she turned and smiled as we walked in and had such a nice look on her face. I stood there looking around and heard the words coming out of my mouth

"It'll look nice once we do it up, eh!"

She looked at me and her face lit up *"So your moving in with me then?"* she said throwing herself into my arms, I hugged her and said, *"It looks like it doesn't it"*

That was it, we were back together.

The beast's wife, who was still living next door at the time, had let him stay until she'd sorted herself out, as she was going to leave him with the kids. She'd had enough of everything and wanted to make a fresh start for herself in Bradford.

This was to seal his and my children's fate!

Michael continued to misbehave and wet the bed; in fact he didn't stop wetting the bed until he was fourteen years old.

Chapter 3

Going To Jump Forward Now

When Michael was aged fifteen and after me being called into the school numerous times, he was expelled. He'd started his modelling career and was earning money of his own. With his looks and physique he'd have done well in modelling and I wasn't unduly worried that he'd finished school a few months earlier than he should have.

By this time I'd started my own business and was again working long hours. I 'd take him to work with me a few times a week, this kept him occupied in-between assignments and I was paying him, so he was doing quite well for money.

By the time he was sixteen he'd started going out and staying out, sometimes for three and four days at a time and we'd be frantic with worry searching for him.

What I didn't know was, that when he was at home, he'd be sleeping all day and he'd also started getting into arguments with his uncle. Lillian would shout at him and tell him he should have more respect! More respect! What did she know! She didn't know what the beast had done to him!

Most of the early pages were written 4-5 years ago, I've found out so many things since those early years, one of which was that Lillian asked Michael around this time, if her brother had done anything to him? Michael told her that he hadn't.

A lot of things were kept from me but had I known, I'd have followed things through because I was no longer a kid bringing up kids, by then I knew what drugs were about and would have known some of the signs.

His moods got worse and he stopped doing the modelling. I later found out that somebody had called him gay because he was a male model. Michael was heterosexual and had many girlfriends but the confusion for him, having been raped must have been tremendous. Male survivors of rape and sexual abuse often have problems working out their sexuality. He really went off the rails getting into trouble with the police, fighting, drinking and taking drugs.

One evening he came home and collapsed as he came through the front door, I picked him up and dragged him to the settee assuming he was just drunk again. I lay him down and looked at him with such disgust. After a while Lillian started to get concerned and felt something wasn't quite right?

26

We tried to wake him but he was comatose, she phoned an ambulance and he was rushed to hospital.

Whilst he was in the emergency room, he actually died for two minutes and had to be brought back by electric shock to the heart. Thank God for mother's instincts eh.

Later whilst Lillian took a break from his bedside, I sat squeezing his hand really hard, watching for a reaction and willing him back. After a couple of hours he eventually came round and the only thing he complained about was a sore hand. I smiled, as I was the only one at the time who knew what I'd done and realised maybe I'd squeezed a little too hard.

His life continued on a downward spiral, he started stealing from us, money; jewellery, clothes, anything he could sell. He'd go missing and turn up drunk all the time.

We felt it was our fault somehow and he was punishing us. We were looking into any reason that could be causing his behaviour? Looking at our own shortfalls, never suspecting for one minute, the real reasons for his self-destructive behaviour. We decided that as we hadn't told him, I wasn't his biological father, somebody else must have done. That was the last reason we could think of.

Oh how wrong were we! One night it came to crunch time!

We'd been to our local pub one Sunday night, Lillian was standing at the bar and she had noticed a dress the girl next to her was wearing. She mentioned that she'd got the same style dress. The girl said she'd bought it from her brother's mate. It was Lillian's dress; Michael had sold it to her!

This had gone too far by now and for far too long and although we dreaded it, we had to confront him and ask if he knew I wasn't his biological Dad. That night we got home and after arguing with him over the dress, Lillian asked him if his behaviour was because of my not being his biological father? I'll never forget the look on his face; he was screaming and wanted to run out of the house, I had to stand in the doorway to stop him from going. He was horrified and had no idea! He was totally shocked! We were so very wrong and once again he was robbed of a part of his life! We felt even worse, so guilty but we couldn't think of another reason for it at the time.

He later told us that were one of the worst things we could have told him at that time. He felt that we'd taken his identity away from and added even more to his unbearable pain.

By this time he had a girlfriend Pauline, who had a child from a previous relationship. She became pregnant by Michael but miscarried, he blamed himself. He thought it was because he'd taken drugs. I explained that it had nothing to do with drugs and he was only sixteen years old and far too young to be a father.

I'd since realised as much as I'd felt mature enough at eighteen to take on responsibilities of a family. I hadn't really been! In no way was he mature or stable enough, to do the same thing but of course my advice fell on deaf ears and she became pregnant again.

He continued on his downward spiral without any control over himself, he was getting drunk more often and in trouble with the police over and over again. The courts had been very lenient with him up until then. There was one judge who should really have sent him to prison. The judge told him the only reason he wasn't going to send him away, was because he'd read in the reports how much family support he got from Lillian and myself and the fact I employed him. The judge actually laughed at that and nodded to me, commenting, "it probably wasn't easy for him to work for his Dad!"

Not long after that lucky escape, he'd pushed his luck too far and just before his eighteenth birthday he was sent to prison on other charges. It was also just before his first baby was born. He spent his eighteenth birthday in a police cell because there was no room in the prisons at that time.

I can still see him as clear as day. There was a match on and the police had let him and the other prisoners lie on blankets behind the iron gates, watching the match through the bars. He was also missing that very special once in a lifetime moment, the birth of his first child.

He made all the promises while in prison, *"I'm going to change, I'm going to get a job"* and most importantly to me, he swore he was going to be a good Dad. I'd send him ten and twelve page character building letters, giving him advice on how he could turn his life around and there wasn't a visit that was missed. We did whatever we could for him. We told him all the past was forgiven and he could start with a clean slate when he came home. We helped Pauline set up a home for her and the children, believing he would come home and they could rebuild their lives together.

During his sentence he had a home leave, whilst on the home leave she became pregnant again. We couldn't believe how stupid they were to have not taken precautions. It was like history repeating itself with his Mum and me, having one child after another.

What could we do? We had to just accept things again and adjust to the situation. I felt deep inside we were going to have many problems in the future but chose to believe he'd prove me wrong and would really sort himself out, once and for all.

He came out to a Champagne welcome, I took Champagne and blew up balloons to let out of the car as he walked towards us. We held a big family party for him. It felt like the prodigal son's return but our joy was only to be short lived though!

He soon went back to his old ways but the major difference now being; he had responsibilities of his own.

I'd sacrificed so much for him and his Mum when I met them and found it hard to understand why he couldn't be more like me. I'd brought him up with strong morals, as had my Dad with me but nothing seemed to get through to him. He'd move back home with us on a monthly basis, backwards and forwards between their home and ours. Always after alcohol binges, very heavy and violent binges. We rarely had any peace and our whole family was suffering over and over again.

We had five other children but nobody else could get a look in! I later realised how much of my children's growth we'd missed out on, because all of our attention was on Michael! We fought constantly to save him from himself! As time went by we tried different approaches. We had no more ideas left and were being worn out completely.

We stopped supporting him and putting him up after he'd been on his regular binges. Instead we let him go through the hostel system and he ended up in some really rough hostels. Sometimes he even slept rough but as always, after the binges Pauline would take him back.

It was a constant cycle of drug dealers after him, getting into fights, leaving him with scars. He was once slashed from his ear down to his chest, just missing his jugular vein, he'd been beaten with baseball bats and one time somebody ran him over. Then he started to mutilate his own body, he once slashed his inner thigh so deeply he was lucky to have not ended up with a permanent limp. His model looks were going out of the window, along with all of our lives.

And still he couldn't tell us why? Why this cycle of self-destruction? If only we'd known! If only he'd had the strength to fight the real enemy, instead of himself. The beast had destroyed him!

Time passed by in a blur of fear and worry for us. We shed tears, I lost my business and life was totally miserable. I was on the verge of a nervous breakdown but was too proud and stupid to seek help.

We started to pick up the pieces of our lives, I got a job and things started to look up for us again.

Then came the bombshell! He only told us a bit at first.

We'd gone to a hostel to see Michael; it was the first time I'd been there, although Lillian had visited him there once. We walked into the entrance of this converted church, the place was run down and stank horrible. There were a lot of down and outs sitting around, one of which recognised Lillian and said he'd go and get Michael for us. I had to go and wait in the car, I couldn't bear to be in that place, it made me feel so sad, not only for the people in there but the depths Michael had sunk to, to end up in such a place.

Lillian and Michael came out to the car and when he climbed in I instantly smelt him; it was the same smell from inside the building. We talked for a while and then he asked us to drive away from the building because he wanted to tell us something. We drove off and parked around the corner. He sat for a few minutes and then just came out with,

"When I was young Malcolm used to do things to me." My heart sank and I felt physically sick but stayed calm.

Lillian started to ask him questions but he said that was all he wanted to say for then and asked would we please take him out of that place and home. He promised he'd turn his life around if only we'd give him another chance. I couldn't leave him there after what he'd told us, I also thought because he'd reached rock bottom, that the only way would be up from then on. We drove back to the building and I went inside with him to explain to a member of staff that we were taking him home. I walked into the office, an elderly lady with the sweetest of smiles and mannerisms was sat there, I told her that we were taking him home and she said,
"Michael is such a troubled boy but he doesn't belong in here and I'm so glad you've come for him"

We spoke for a few minutes whilst Michael got his things together and I couldn't help but have admiration for her for the job she was doing and thanked her sincerely for looking after him whilst he'd been there.

From the time he told us about the beast, his life became even worse. His mood swings and depression became unbearable. He was having counselling but it didn't ease his pains and he'd still go on his binges of alcohol and drugs.

We'd be so worried, knowing the states he got into, that we expected the police to call to say they'd found him dead, or in one of his drunken rages he'd killed somebody else. He seemed to be constantly lashing out. Even the beast's safety worried us. So much so, that one night we had to phone the police to tell them we thought he was on his way to take the beast's life.

To listen to your sons pitiful soul wrenching cries on the phone in his darkest moments of grief, to hear him say he was going to end it all to make the pain stop, to hear him saying he wanted to kill the beast and to kill himself. It was all too much for us. We were dying inside! We felt powerless and useless! We were powerless to stop it or take his pain away. We'd brought him home so many times and we'd cleaned him up. We'd reassure him things would be ok. He'd seem to gain some strength but it was never enough.

He'd then go back to Pauline for the whole cycle to start again. It was a monthly cycle and if we were lucky it would skip a month. But it was always the same, questions that couldn't be answered. When will it stop? Will it stop? Is it possible to stop? Will he kill himself? Will he kill the beast? Will he ever get better? Questions?????

This was our son who was turning into a monster before our very eyes. The alcohol fuelled his pain, he drank to forget but it never went away! He'd swallow ecstasy tablets to try to make him feel good, speed so he wouldn't go to sleep and have nightmares! Nothing would work. The only thing that was guaranteed was he'd self-destruct and the cycle would start all over again! It was always looming! How could anybody get better? How could any of us heal? With all of the chaos and confusion Michael was creating! The son we loved! The son who may have had the world at his feet, if only it hadn't been for the BEAST and his perverted ways!

We tried everything but nothing seemed to work. We tried love! We tried tough love! We tried to tell him we could no longer cope. We would have to tell him to stay away from our home. Nothing seemed to work for long. We had periods of calm and believed the worst could be over but it never was! It went on for years.

Somewhere in between all the chaos, Michael told us the beast had raped him and one of Lillian's other brothers, Alex had abused him, when he was young, as well.

In Michael's worst moments the BEAST would be there to welcome him in and give him a place to stay. He would try and convince him that it was somebody else that had raped him when he was only 5 yrs old. The beast would tell him it was his dead uncle, his dead grandfather and even his uncle Alex that had raped him.

The beast was still playing with his mind! Oh how cunning paedophiles are and the beast was no exception!

Throughout all of this there was no energy left for anyone else. Our strength was constantly being drained from us! The beast was winning! The beast was so cunning and still manipulating him and in turn Michael was manipulating us.

If he'd only realised that all he had to do was TALK!!! If he'd talked to the counsellors, they and we could have helped him to cope and help him heal his pain. If he'd talked we'd have known so much more. But that was his problem; he carried the shame and the blame that wasn't his to carry, it belonged to the beast!! He carried his own shame and blame for many things but we weren't to find out the full extent until much later.

This is the problem with cases of sexual abuse. The facts come out so painfully slowly. It 's like trying to put a jigsaw puzzle together but somebody else is holding most of the pieces and the pieces only get delivered here and there. Waiting constantly, waiting all of the time. We could see a lot of the picture coming together and would be told certain things but we had to learn patience, constant patience.

Patience and love are the main things that can get you through but knowledge of the affects of child abuse is most important! Leave nothing to chance, read books ask experts and contact agencies dealing with it. If they can't help you ask for any other agencies they might know of. Use the internet for information if you have access to a computer, there are plenty of online communities that will be more than willing to offer help, guidance and support. You have to sometimes put all of your own pain to one side and literally fight for survival! You have to arm yourself with the knowledge that is available, if you're to stand a fighting chance to reclaim your child!

I wouldn't wish this pain on my worst enemy!

The beast convinced him on one of his drunken binges to retract his statement in front of his solicitor and Michael did just that. We weren't to find this out until the day of the court case and Michael's case was dropped. He'd never even told us! We felt defeated and deflated.

We hadn't got to see Michael just before the court case as he'd ended up back in prison for his third time. He'd betrayed himself and us. Could we ever forgive him? YES we had to, we had to once again put our pain to one side and try to understand!

How cunning the beast had been yet again.

Chapter 4

Our Stories

Michelle's story (The Beast's Daughter)

She was a cute and quite loud child, who seemed to always want to be the centre of attention but she never seemed to want to grow up. The beast would spoil her all the time with sweets and money. On their birthday's he'd take Michelle and my eldest daughter Elizabeth out, as they were born only seventeen hours apart it was a double celebration for them both. Elizabeth seemed to envy their relationship because Michelle got so much more attention from him. I was working and he wasn't! I was working but he had more money! I had more children; he had only Stuart and Michelle, he was also getting a lot of money because of Stuart's disability. I always felt guilty for not being able to give Elizabeth more time and money.

From an early age Michelle wore lots of make up and looked like a little woman in a child like body, she doted on her Dad and was very protective of him. We put this down to the fact he was an alcoholic and her Mum had never been around for her.

One sunny afternoon when Michelle was about eight years old, I'd let myself into their house and seeing nobody downstairs shouted and went upstairs. I could see his bedroom door was open as I reached the top of the stairs. As I entered the bedroom Michelle was getting up from his bed and walking around towards the bedroom door, she only had a nightgown on but it was the look on her face that has always stuck in my mind. It wasn't a nervous look just strange, so much so I can't even put it into words but I now know what would have been going on. I commented
"She doesn't still sleep with you does she?" how stupidly naïve was I? His reply was *"Yeah sometimes she doesn't like to sleep in her own bed."* Although it seemed strange and I felt totally confused, I didn't really question it, even though it was the afternoon and neither of them looked like they'd just woken up.

Looking back my gut reaction must have been there, I just didn't see it for what it was. How much I've hated myself for not questioning that time more. He'd always have a conversation to distract you! Looking back at that scene etched in my mind I'd go so far as to say he looked excited! Maybe it was the thrill of almost getting caught? Who knows how their minds work?

When the girls were about twelve years old and boys had started hanging around them, I had a conversation with the beast about them getting older and how much I was dreading the thoughts of boyfriends.

My Dad had been fiercely protective of my sister Sharon, as had I when she was growing up and I remembered well the worry of her going out with boys and some of the disastrous relationships she had. The thoughts of somebody hurting one of my daughters were enough to put me on full alert and make me even more protective.

The beast's reaction was to laugh at me and say he didn't see it as a problem, Michelle would end up sleeping with boys and he'd allow it to go on under his own roof! I was shocked and couldn't understand it. I was glad that Elizabeth had started to play with other girls around the same time; Elizabeth and Michelle had started to drift apart a little. In fact from that time on I encouraged Elizabeth to move on, scared that she'd be influenced by such a relaxed attitude coming from him.

Michelle seemed to prefer the company of younger kids and they'd always play in his house, unfortunately one of those kids was my younger daughter Denise, my nieces and a few other kids off the estate. They'd dress up, play house and Michelle would put make up on them! Yes she'd put make up on them; he had his own personal little beauty pageant under his roof, day in and day out.

He'd also had a Wendy house for them to play in and they'd always had pets including a dog that was forever having puppies!

The beast knew the tools to use for drawing kids into his lair!!!!!!

They forever had sleepovers, all the girls would stay the night and us like fools never objected! After all he was their uncle wasn't he and only next door, they were safe!! So we thought!!

His most common ploys were used here! He'd go into the girl's room and say they were being too noisy and they'd have to go and get in his bed. They'd do as he said because he was the adult, leaving Michelle in her own bed.

Michelle told me one night she lay in her bed, listening to my eldest daughter Elizabeth screaming from his bedroom. That night we were watching television when we heard Elizabeth screaming and running down the path. I opened the door and she ran straight past me, going upstairs hysterical. Lillian chased up after Elizabeth whilst he kept me at the door, telling me that he didn't know what was wrong with her. He said she must have had a nightmare. I was worried about Elizabeth but being polite, I listened as he was continuing to talk (I now know he was again distracting me.) I finally got rid of him and followed upstairs, still confused.

I can still remember and sense that feeling of confusion! I'm sitting here now re-reading this part. I am feeling so very sick and so very angry with myself for being thick, naïve and downright ignorant.

I was such a trusting person and even gullible, the only things I knew back then about child abuse was what was in the newspapers. I could never bring myself to read the stories though; maybe if I had I'd have known more? Who knows? I lived in my own little bubble without a clue as to what was going on around me.

Lillian said that she kept repeating, *"She didn't want to sleep next door again"* but wouldn't say anything else, so we assumed she must have had a nightmare, like he'd said.

Again the arrows were pointing but I just couldn't see them! So many signs that were not being picked up, so many children remaining silent about his beast like behaviour. How did he silence so many children??

To this day Elizabeth will not talk about him or anything that happened as a child but for a whole year after having her own daughter she would cut herself in times of distress. A typical symptom of child abuse is self-mutilation but again we have to be patient and watch and wait for Elizabeth to reveal things in her own time. She promised me she wouldn't cut herself again, a promise she has thankfully kept, as far as I know?

Leading up to the court case Michelle told me about a friend of hers, with whom he used the same ploy. Her name was Toni. I decided to go and see her Mum. As I walked down her path Toni was in her garden and I asked if I could speak to her Mum?

I assumed I could tell her Mum and leave it to them to work out for themselves but at least her Mum would know. Toni told me her Mum had died, which made me feel terrible. What should I do? I decided to take a chance, as she seemed old beyond her years and really quite grown up. I told her about the beast and what Michelle had told me, about the night he'd made her get in his bed. She remembered but was a bit vague. She said she thought it was strange that he'd told her to get into his bed but once again he was the adult so she did as he said. After she got into his bed he'd said that the t-shirt she was wearing as a nightgown was his and she should take it off. Other than that she didn't say anything and once again I had to back off. I told her I'd let her know what was happening, as I found things out and asked was it OK for me to inform the police about her? She very bravely said that I could and she later gave a statement herself.

Michelle was giving me pointers but wouldn't go up against him herself at that time.

As I said Michelle stayed childlike for so long. Aged about fifteen she started going around with the older girls and then got a boyfriend. After that her life started to go completely downhill! She started doing street robberies with these other wild girls she'd met and they were particularly violent. Eventually she was caught and ended up in prison.

She'd changed from a sweet innocent looking child, into an unfeeling monster almost overnight, although she did tell me at a later date, after robbing an old ladies bag she started thinking about her own Nana and it did make her feel guilty but she still took the money and dumped the bag.

When she left prison she had nowhere to go and I said she could stay with us for a while. She later told me as much as she loved us, she couldn't stay because she wanted her freedom. What a freedom that was to become.

She'd told me when she was younger, she used to hide in a cupboard in the bathroom and draw pictures on the wall of my family and me, pretending she was our daughter. She used to pretend I was her Dad and I loved her as my own.

That poor tormented child, how she suffered at his hands, adding to my guilt again. How stupid was I, and how powerful was he to keep so many children from exposing him!

I asked the new neighbours if I could look in the cupboard and yes the drawings were still there.

Michelle and the friend she went to prison with moved to Bradford to stay with Michelle's mother. She'd phone every now and then to let me know she loved me and that she was o.k.

Michelle's life was to go on an even worse path of destruction. She'd started taking heroin and working in massage parlours. It was on one of her heroin binges she phoned and told me of her abuse.

After the beast had lured her back to Manchester, she started to sell her body on the streets because she had a very heavy habit by then. The parlours would no longer let her work because of her addiction.

She always did and still does keep in contact, phoning just to make sure I'm still there and still love her.

One night last year I got a phone call from Elizabeth saying the police were at her house and wanted my phone number. Michelle had gone to the police station to make an allegation against her father. We'd moved house and Michelle didn't know our new address and new phone number at that time but we knew if and when she needed us, she would contact Elizabeth.

The officer spoke to me on the phone and explained that Michelle had come to the station but unfortunately she was drunk and he couldn't take a statement from her until the next day. He knew all about the case that was building against the beast and said he'd arrange for Michelle to stay at a girls refuge that night and asked would it be possible for Lillian to come into the station with Michelle, to make a statement the next day?

About twenty minutes later Michelle phoned me from the station, she said that he made her sick. She was twenty-two years old and had woken up from a drunken sleep to find him with his hands inside her top feeling her breasts. He thought she'd had heroin and wouldn't have woken up. His excuse was that his girlfriend was ill and he hadn't had sex for ages!

What a twisted pervert! What kind of logic is that! He'd not had sex for ages so it's OK to molest his grown up twenty two year old daughter, whom he had molested all her childhood!! In turn showing that nobody is safe from a beast and his perversions!!! She kept repeating that she'd had enough and how many other times when she'd been off her face on drugs, might he have done things to her? At that moment she wanted to stand up to him and make him pay!

The next morning Lillian picked Michelle up and she made a statement about the abuse she'd suffered as a child. After that we had a lot of contact and gave her a lot of support, also attempting to get her into a rehab programme. She continued to work the streets and wouldn't accept any help to kick the drugs. Eventually just before the court case the beast lured her back to live with him Even as adults the beast had the power to influence them, when they were at their weakest!

Michelle promised she'd still see the court case through though! But on the day of the case she didn't show up. She later told me the beast had said she could always stay at the house, if she didn't testify against him. Again we had to forgive and try to understand the effects of sexual abuse on the individuals.

Michelle still carried on working the streets; she's been raped, almost murdered and hopelessly addicted to heroin and crack cocaine. Michelle said she can't kick the habit and will probably die on the streets. All we can do is to love her and wait for that fateful day that is beyond our control.

I still go out and look for her just to give her a hug and let her know I'm still there for her but she has to want to stop for herself.

She was such a beautiful child but has become ravished by the effects of her life, all because she was born to live her life with a PAEDOPHILE!!!! A MONSTER!!!! If only I'd known? How different would her life be!!!! All the signs but I didn't have the knowledge.

Annette's Story

Janet's daughter Annette was only twelve when she fell into his clutches! She thought she was grown up and had started going around with Elizabeth and Michelle. What we didn't know at the time was that night an older boy had bought them alcohol. Annette was only twelve and she had a few drinks but it made her feel sick, the girls decided to take her next-door as the beast wouldn't question them whereas I would. She wanted to be sick and went upstairs to the bathroom, the girls were listening to music, making food and coffee when the beast came downstairs shouting for Elizabeth to leave. Michelle was starting to answer back by now and said they were eating first and then Elizabeth would go home.

He went back upstairs to where Annette was still slumped on the bathroom floor; she'd been sick and was covered in vomit and dog muck she had fallen into outside the house.

She said she woke up in pain with her trousers round her ankles and the beast was on top of her, he was raping her! He raped her on his bathroom floor whilst Elizabeth and Michelle were downstairs! How brazen and perverted!! When he'd finished he stood up and looked down at Annette and threw a towel at her and told her to clean herself up. Nothing else! She lost her virginity to her Mum's brother aged only twelve.

Elizabeth said Annette came downstairs upset and crying, saying she wanted to come to our house, so they left. They both sneaked upstairs and got into bed. Annette was crying for most of the night but wouldn't tell Elizabeth why. She just kept saying, "I'm sorry" over and over again.

Once again an innocent child whose body was wracked with pain and whose mind must have been so traumatised but she was the one saying, *"I'M SORRY"* OVER AND OVER AGAIN!!

Once again the beast had got away with it, another child raped and stayed quiet! Surely he must have had moments of panic that somebody would speak up? Or had he just believed he could get away with whatever he wanted, forever!

After that night Annette became very moody wearing baggy clothes and no longer went out. This went on for a long time. I remember the time well! She'd stopped looking after herself, allowing her hair to go unwashed and looking very greasy. She'd also put on a lot of weight, about four stone and was always depressed looking. I used to try and talk to her and encourage her to start going back out but she'd smile at me and say she preferred to stay in looking after her younger sisters and brother. Her Mum had split up with her long-term boyfriend, the father of the youngest two children and she worked a lot, so of course Annette babysat a lot. She'd stopped going to school and her Mum allowed her to stay at home, because it was so difficult to get her to go.

That poor child, she wasn't even thirteen and having to carry all that pain. If only she could have spoken to me I would have understood. I could have helped her.

What power and control did this animal have over so many people????

I even suspected child abuse at the time and mentioned it to Lillian; I thought it might have been the ex-boyfriend or the boyfriend from years before? The last person I would have thought of was the beast. Lillian told me she spoke to Janet and Annette but Annette didn't give any indication I was right. I have since wished I'd done the asking back then, just maybe I'd have picked up on something.

How cunning paedophiles are!!! How blind was I!!

Aged around fifteen Annette started going out again with different friends; she met a boy and slept with him and became pregnant aged just fifteen.

The night Annette was giving birth, Lillian went to the hospital to sit with her sister Janet. It was shortly after we'd found out about Michael's abuse. Lillian was unwittingly telling Janet everything we knew. Annette overheard the whole conversation and the memories of her own rape, that she'd managed to bury in the back of her mind for so long, came flooding back.

Annette later told me that when her daughter was born, she couldn't cope with even looking at her because she felt so dirty and violated.

The next day my other niece Carol, Annette's younger sister visited her in hospital. Annette told Carol what had happened to her when she was twelve; but nothing was ever said again between them after that.

A year or so later Carol babysat for us one night and told Sean our youngest son about Annette being raped. Why she did this we still don't know? Was it a way to get it across to me? Sean told us some weeks later but both Carol and Annette denied it when Lillian asked them about it. Again we had to play the waiting game, we knew that Carol couldn't possibly have made something like that up!! Once again that familiar waiting game of backing off and let them come to tell us when they were ready.

Annette became more and more depressed as time went on, we knew why but were powerless once again.

Eventually after Lillian had spoken to Janet and told her everything we suspected, Janet spoke to Annette and she agreed to speak to Lillian, because by then she was having recurring nightmares.

We knew she was going to tell us soon!! This is where Lillian made a fatal mistake!

Lillian was at the doctor's surgery. Whilst she was waiting outside his office the beast came walking out, she confronted him and he seemed to have a smug look on his face. In a moment of madness Lillian shouted that he wouldn't be so smug for long, because Annette was coming forward next to make a statement against him and at last Annette was going to speak up and stand up against him. He being the cunning animal that he is, got in touch with his solicitor and told him what Lillian had said. The saying is *"To be forewarned is to be forearmed"* and the beast knew how to fight his battle well!!

The fatal mistake was that Annette didn't officially tell Lillian until the next day! Although we'd known for a long time based on her behaviour aged twelve and what we'd since learnt about the beast. In Annette's statement the date she told Lillian was logged down but it was the day after Lillian's encounter with the beast.

Annette had even forgotten that she'd told Carol the day after her daughter was born, the poor kids emotions must have been all over the place at that time, having given birth to her daughter and the reminder of uncle BEAST!!!! All on what should have been a very special night for her.

Up until the court-case Annette went through many emotions and nightmares. She stood up well against them though, only to find out on the day of the court hearing that her case was going to be left on file, because the beast had agreed to a plea bargain. He agreed to plead guilty to seven counts of indecency against Lillian if the rape charges were left on file. The defence barrister had agreed because Annette's case was so weak.

Annette felt violated once again!!

I'll never, as long as I live, forget the look on Annette's face as we told her what the barrister had said and insisted we accepted. She was devastated to come this far and then be told he wasn't even going to be prosecuted for what he did to her. She fell to pieces and ran crying and screaming into the toilets of the witness suite.

Lillian's mistake and the fact that none of us knew Annette had told Carol years before, gave the beast a chance to slip through the net on yet another charge. The barristers and solicitors are just as cunning as the paedophiles!

All that time, all of the pain and only seven charges committed as a juvenile to answer to, almost thirty years before.

His luck was well and truly holding up!!!!!

The devil smiles upon and protects, those that he loves!!

Lillian's Story
Lillian's father was a violent alcoholic, often beating her mother and spending all of their money on booze. He was a builder but would often con customers by taking money up front and then not finishing the work. All of which meant they often had to move house at the drop of a hat and her early childhood was very sad as a result of all of this.

Her father would spend time in and out of prison but would always return to the family home and the cycle would start all over again.

Lillian was a sickly child having caught T.B aged about four or five years old; she had to spend long periods of time in hospital, mostly in an isolation ward. Her only physical contact was with the doctors and nurses, who would have to wear masks and gowns because the T.B was so contagious. Her family seldom visited, as they were poor and the hospital wasn't near to where they lived, adding even more to her loneliness and imposed isolation. When the family did visit they could only communicate through a glass window, surrounding the isolation ward.

Lillian felt very alone and had to sleep in a cot type bed, that she felt she was too big for. In the morning when she awoke, she and a little boy in the next isolation room would wave to each other.

My heart bled for her when she told me this story, it wasn't just the story but the deep-rooted emotions she expressed while telling me. She'd felt so isolated and abandoned.

In-between bouts of illness she was allowed to go home, her mother would leave her unattended for long periods of time adding to her feelings of isolation. She said she felt such a burden on the family, as when she coughed up blood she had to return to the hospital. She'd even blamed herself as a child for getting sick.

She had five brothers and one younger sister but only one of the brothers would pay her any attention. He was only eighteen month's older and she loved him dearly.

They were bonded and he was the only one in the house that ever showed her any affection whilst she was ill and also as they were growing up.

Even beasts may have been nice children once!!

The mother eventually threw the father out and started having relationships with other men, often staying out and leaving the kids to fend for themselves. From the age of nine Lillian took on the motherly role of running the house, shopping, cooking and cleaning. This made her feel needed and grown up but she still lacked love from anyone, except the one brother. She was like Cinderella and was rarely allowed out.

It was from her early childhood that Lillian would create fantasies about her life, because of so much isolation, she felt she could create a nicer world to live in for herself.

Around the age of eleven her brother started to show a much more sinister interest in her. She was a late developer and was so childlike and naïve. He'd start play fighting with her and touching her in ways she didn't understand. He started to become more aggressive towards her, which she found so confusing, as they'd always been so close. The beast's perversions were starting to emerge!!

Lillian's mother was very strict and would make her change out of her school uniform and hang it up in the wardrobe as soon as she got in from school. He would be waiting for her in the bedroom they had to share with a younger brother. This became a daily nightmare of him standing in just his underpants, fighting to pin her to the bed and attempting to molest her. His hands would be all over her, getting into her underwear and telling her that she liked it. He'd call her a slag and say she was letting everybody do this to her anyway, so it was ok for him to do it to her. She was too scared to tell her mother and would rush home from school to change, throwing her uniform in the wardrobe instead of hanging it up. Her mother would then shout and make her hang it up and there he'd be, sniggering and waiting for her. He'd started to masturbate in front of her and delighted in humiliating her.

This went on and off for the next couple of years.

He'd have times of being nice to her, taking her to the pictures but other times he'd be horrible. Her emotions were all over the place; she felt love and loyalty to him when he was nice but a terrible fear to the pit of her stomach when he was being abusive.

One time whilst Lillian was in the bedroom aged twelve or thirteen; one of the beast's friends came in saying that he'd lent the beast his bracelet. He told her that the beast had said he could have sex with her as payment. She got upset and started to cry and his friend backed off and left the room. Lillian sat there crying and so confused wondering how the brother she loved could be such a monster.

He was constantly getting into her head telling her she was a slag and that she enjoyed it. It felt like he'd been brainwashing and controlling her for years. The more it happened the more she'd escape into a fantasy world where none of it existed.

Another time and another friend of his came to her bed in the middle of the night, saying once again her brother had said he could have sex with her. Again she cried and he also backed off leaving the room. She heard his friend shouting at the beast and the beast laughingly saying, *"she's a slag anyway."*

Lillian's mother had a boyfriend called Joe living in the house who was abusive towards the kids; he was a big guy and used to bully the whole household. One night whilst her Mum was out, Joe came into Lillian's bedroom looking at her menacingly. She was only twelve and already suffering at the beasts hands, he grabbed her legs forcing them apart and was going to rape her. She screamed that she was on a period; he stopped, threw her legs to one side and left her crouching on the bed, crying and frozen with fear.

This poor child seemed to be surrounded by predators and sexual abuse seemed to be a constant threat in her life. Lillian would later use the same excuse, her period, to keep the beast at bay. Sometimes he'd pull her knickers down to make sure and on seeing a sanitary towel would leave her alone.

To this day Lillian can still see her mother's boyfriends face glaring at her.

By the time Lillian was fourteen the beast had started drinking. On occasions of being drunk he'd be even more violent towards her. He'd started to expose himself more and trying to force her head down to give him oral sex, or to try to rape her. She'd manage to fight him off and run to lock herself in her mother's bedroom. He'd then say he was sorry and blame it on the drink.

Her life was a nightmare but she could still escape into her childlike fantasy world, where even he couldn't reach her.

She started to go out more to avoid him but her mother was very strict about the time she had to be in for. She was hanging around with girls the same age as her brother who lived nearby and went to the same school, her friends had boyfriends and were already having sex by then as well.

The inevitable happened and they fixed her up with a boy aged eighteen, he was nice to begin with but even he took on a predatory role and became sexually demanding.

The beast was becoming stronger; Lillian was finding it harder to fight him off. The boyfriend was becoming more demanding and one night she gave in deciding, if she was going to lose her virginity, she didn't want it to be to her brother. The boyfriend then started to force her to have sex. One night the boyfriend's uncle told Lillian he'd been watching them having sex, through the gap in the curtains, the boyfriend had opened purposely for him.

This added to her already tormented mind and she refused to go out again but the boyfriend continued to call to the house even though she'd refuse to see him. He eventually gave up and moved back to Ireland.

Lillian started to miss her periods and had to tell her Mum. She was tested and found out she was pregnant. Her mother went crazy calling her all the names under the sun, one of which was so familiar to her, SLAG. She just retreated more and more inside herself. Lillian's Mum decided not to tell the other family members for a while.

One night a few weeks later the beast tried to rape her again, he'd pinned her to the bed ripping her knickers off and was about to penetrate her. Only this time she felt a mist come over her and fought like she'd never fought before. She bit, scratched and pummelled him with punches, she was beating him and he for a change was feeling pain! It was then she screamed, *"I'm pregnant."* He stopped and looked down at her calling her *"A fucking liar."* She told him she was pregnant and he stood up, once again calling her a slag and then walked out, going downstairs to his mother, telling her that Lillian had attacked him and she was a lunatic. That was it; he never touched her again after that.

The beast was working at a baby clothes factory and would bring home clothes for the baby that was to come. He changed completely towards her, almost taking on the role of expectant father. He'd become so good and supportive towards her; she said she buried all of the abuse into the deep recesses of her mind.

She had to leave school and again was running the house, her mother wasn't very supportive towards her but seemed to delight in the fact a new baby was going to be in the house.

Another predator was then to come out of the shadows! She was eight months pregnant and in the house on her own. There was a knock at the door. She answered it to a man who said he was there to read the gas meter. The gas meter was in the downstairs room her mother used as a bedroom. Lillian took the man into the room and pointed to where the meter was. He walked around the bed to the wardrobe that he said was in front of the meter. She told him it wasn't; it was in the cupboard. He again asked her to come around the bed to help him move the wardrobe. She felt uncomfortable because this meant she would be away from the door and alarm bells started to ring for her! He then asked was her Mum in the house? She quickly said her older brother was upstairs and she walked into the hallway to shout him! The guy then ran out of the house, as she stood there shaking and realised she had a lucky escape!

That pervert would have done something to a pregnant young girl! HOW TWISTED ARE THEY!!!!!!! THEY'RE EVERYWHERE!!!

They moved to a bigger house before the baby was born and for the first time she had a bedroom of her own. It was only a small room and used to get very hot and stuffy at night, so she would often leave the bedroom door open. One night she awoke to find her second eldest brother kneeling at the side of her bed, with his hands under her bedclothes, he was trying to touch her!! She jumped up and asked him what he was doing? He just Mumbled and left her room.

Yet another predator in her midst!!

Lillian was fifteen when Michael was born. She felt so confused and was neither mentally nor physically ready to have a child. She felt her life was a mess; a house filled with people but she still felt so alone and very vulnerable. Her mother seemed to claim Michael as her own, with the exception of the sleepless nights or the nappy changing; Lillian had to cope with the down side of motherhood alone. She no longer went out because she felt so ashamed of having a baby so young, an emotion her Mum never let up on, adding even more to her shame.

Lillian really started to resent Michael by this time and felt her whole life had been turned upside down. When she first found out she was pregnant, she'd considered an abortion. Her friends said that would be murder if she did and although the boyfriend wasn't around, they'd stick by her. Once Michael was born and the novelty had worn off, the friends inevitably stopped calling.

When Lillian was aged sixteen her mother started to allow her to go out to the pub with her. She met two different guys over the next two years, one of whom wanted to marry her but unfortunately for him he was too gentle and nice. She couldn't accept him because she considered herself to be undeserving and actually resented him for being so nice to her.

Lillian's brothers were protective (or jealous?) over her and gave him a bit of a hard time; he didn't stand up to them and before they were due to get married, she finished with him. I actually met this guy in the early years we were together and he was a very nice guy.

The other boyfriend came from a good family but he used her and treated her badly. She seemed to relate better to him though. That relationship ended shortly before we met up for the first time since school.

Once Lillian reached eighteen, she knew she had to leave the family home for the sake of her own sanity. Her mother dominated her life and between her and the brothers they were destroying the relationship she had with Michael. They'd encourage this young child to punch and kick her calling her names, Michael not knowing any different and being encouraged by the family's laughter and applause, would do all of these things.

Lillian put her name down on a housing associations list and a flat came up for her to move into. Although it was in a bit of a rough area, at least she'd be free from the family home. She'd still feel close to her family spending lots of time with them but could always go back to what she considered her own home.

Lillian was beginning to feel free and independent, even grown up. She had at last found her sanctuary and closed her mind to all the abuses she'd suffered.

My Story

I'm the son of an Irish immigrant and English Mum. My Dad's father died when my Dad was only seven years old and my Dad had worked from being a young child to help support his family. He was very loyal to his family and they were very close.

He had come over to England when he was fourteen years old and found work on the roads. His first weeks were spent sleeping rough in Hyde Park London until he got his first pay packet and was then able to afford to live in digs.

He'd send money home to his family every week and this carried on until he was sixteen years old. He wasn't a drinking man and lived frugally to help support his Mum and sisters back home in Ireland.

Because he'd lied and said he was sixteen to get work, when he first came to this country, as far as the authorities were concerned, he'd reached the age for national service. This was age eighteen. He had to leave England for a while, then come back and declare his real age of sixteen and start all over again. When he came back to England his family followed, after he'd found somewhere for them all to live in Manchester.

He was working on the roads when he met my Mum; she used to find any excuse to go to the shops, so she could walk past where he was working. He used to whistle at her and then eventually they got talking, they had a whirlwind romance and got married

They had three kids me first, my sister Sharon and my brother David, I had a fairly happy childhood surrounded by a lot of love. We had plenty of love even though my Dad was very strict and he enforced strict morals upon me. One of the most important to him was family loyalty!! His words were *"You must always stick by your family."* Another was *"Your wife and mother are to be cherished like the Madonna."*

His sisters still live together even now and my Grandma lived with them until she died in her sixties. Even though my auntie Kay got married and had three children of her own the whole family had always lived together. Family loyalty runs strong in my Dad's side of the family.

I remember one time driving with my Dad and we were listening to the radio, the news came on and one story was about a child abuser. My Dad's exact words were *"I would give a weeks wages for five minutes in a room with one of them."* or *"They should put them in a room full of mothers and let them beat the shit out of them."*

Little did I know I would spend much of my life living with and next door to one of them!!!

That news story and my Dad's reaction to it, has always stuck in my mind.

When he was thirty-one and I was aged thirteen he had had the first heart attack. He was a proud man and had always thought of himself as invincible. To see him lying in a hospital bed wired up to heart monitors broke my heart. I could see even at my young age, how badly he felt about it.

It was a sunny Saturday afternoon when he came through the door of the living room clutching his chest and lay down on the settee. He'd been doing overtime that morning and thought he'd pulled a muscle in his chest lifting something heavy in work. He told me at one point whilst driving home the pains had got so bad that he had been forced to pull the car over to the side of the road. He was groaning a bit and then went quiet. My Mum came bouncing in and jumped on his back giving him a big hug. I could see the panic on her face as he groaned aloud. She jumped back asking what was wrong? He told her about the pulled muscle and asked if she'd run a bath for him.

About half an hour later she came downstairs and told me that she'd phoned the doctor without him knowing, because the pains were getting worse. The doctor came out and immediately phoned an ambulance and rushed him off to hospital.

It seemed to me that from that time on, he was giving me a crash course on life. I can now relate as an adult as to how it felt for him; the fear of death and the thought that his family would have to fend for each other without him.

It was almost like he knew he'd be leaving us and he had to prepare me to be strong and able to look after our family.

Twelve months later he had his second heart attack. That one almost finished him off. My Mum came to me in the middle of the night and told me that Dad was having pains again and she was taking him back to the hospital. I said I'd get up and sit downstairs and wait for her to phone me to let me know how he was.

It was still dark, I sat there in the living room all alone and feeling very vulnerable, the house seemed to make all kinds of noises and I was really afraid. I let the dog into the living room and sat in the chair with two potato knives in my hands, praying and waiting for daylight to come. To this day I've no idea why I was so afraid that night?

We lived in a big oval shaped avenue that was covered by grass, as daylight came the whole avenue was covered by a three foot high layer of mist, making everything seem even more eerie. I was so relieved around 6 am when I saw a car drive down the avenue and both my Dad's sisters got out of it. My nightmare was over and I quickly put the knives back in the kitchen, pretending that everything was fine!!

A habit I'd keep for the rest of my life "Yes everything's fine" even when it isn't. I still didn't worry too much back then, as I believed my Dad was invincible but for him it must have been a nightmare. For the first time in his life he must have been questioning and realising his own mortality and vulnerability.

We were very close in our home and by this time he wasn't able to work so we didn't have much money but again we had love and a very special family bond with each other.

The night before Christmas Eve that same year, my friend Mike and I were playing cards. My Dad decided it was time for Mike to go and for me to go to bed. Mike left and I was really pissed off with my Dad, because he'd shouted at me. I was walking upstairs and gave him the V sign. I knew he was sitting on the other side of the wall and I was muttering swear words under my breath.

In the early hours of the morning my Mum woke me up to tell me Dad was having pains again and she'd phoned an ambulance. She asked me if I wanted to get up and say goodbye to him? I was still mad at him for shouting at me. The memories of the last time, sitting wide-eyed, scared, with the two kitchen knives in my hands came flooding back to the forefront of my mind. I said "No Mum I'll stay in bed this time" and went back to sleep.

The next thing I knew my Mum was coming back into my room it was morning and she sat on my bed. I woke up fully and looked into her face and knew straight away. I said, "He's dead isn't he" She didn't even have to answer as the tears rolled down her face. I'd instinctively known it and have some recollection of waking up during the night, feeling that he'd died.

She hugged me for a moment and I said I was ok; she then left me and went to tell Sharon my sister. I turned over in bed and one tear flowed from my left eye. I heard Sharon screaming like a banshee. She kept saying that she wanted to die but I couldn't get up to be with her and just lay in my bed, withdrawn into my own little world of pain and loss!!

It was Christmas Eve morning and my Dad was dead. It was only three days before his thirty-third birthday. There was I, only fourteen years old and scared. He had been my rock and now he was dead.

All the things that he'd taught me came flooding back and I was terrified. I'd thought he would always be there. I had to grow up fast. I tried to be like a man when relatives told me "John your now the man of the house" but inside I was still a scared little kid.

The house was full all day with a steady procession of family, friends and neighbours. The whole day passed in a blur for me. In fact that whole Christmas was a blur for me.

I already had a job as a waiter in a social club at the weekends and I decided to still go to work that evening. A lot of people had heard about my Dad but I just wanted to keep myself busy. The funeral had been arranged for the following Friday which was New Years Eve and once again I went to work that evening.

I was serving a table and had to hand the tray of drinks over to somebody because I nearly passed out. They took me outside for fresh air. I started to feel better but couldn't do any more work that night. Imagine a fourteen-year-old boy losing his Dad on Christmas Eve, the funeral on New Years Eve and still going into work! Suppose it gives an insight into my strength of character even for one so young, that same strength was conditioning me for a lot of things in the future.

With my wages I would buy my family small gifts of chocolate every Sunday. It was my way of brightening things up and it was something my Dad had done occasionally for us. I used to love it when he bought us all chocolate. It felt like such a treat and it was heartfelt from him.

My Mum didn't have to buy my clothes from that day on either, which took a burden off her shoulders. I'd find work labouring illegally during the holidays to earn some extra money as well.

We'd decorate the house together and we were happy for a while, despite our loss. I seemed to fall into my role as protector and breadwinner quite easily and seemed to be coping well with it.

A few months' later I met a girl called Susan, she only lived around the corner from me and although we'd known each other for years, we'd never been close friends. We started to go out together and I had the best puppy love I could have ever wished for. Having a girlfriend and being in love made me feel even more grown up.

Then the worst thing imaginable to me happened. It was only six months after my Dad had died when my Mum went out with Susan's Mum, Audrey. Audrey had been suggesting it for weeks, saying it'd do my Mum good to have a night out and maybe cheer her up.

I was sitting in Susan's house babysitting her younger brother with her, when Audrey came in alone. I asked, "*Where's my Mum*"? Her reply was "*Oh she'll be here soon.*" I was frantic but too polite to ask again for a while. Then I asked her again and her reply was the same. I had to leave the house. I was becoming more and more agitated, fearing something had happened to my Mum. I was pacing up and down the avenue with all kinds of scary and horrible things going on in my head. I guessed by the way Audrey had said, "*My Mum wouldn't be long*" that a man would be involved, adding even more to my fear that he might harm her.

After waiting outside for what seemed an eternity my Mum appeared in the distance. To my horror she was arm in arm with another man walking towards me. I was demented, screaming, I couldn't believe it!! The man ran off and my Mum tried to calm me down. I was devastated and had bouts of anger, anguish and shed many tears that night. The whole family had very little sleep because I was screaming and shouting for most of it. I called my Mum the worst names imaginable because I was so angry and then feeling so much guilt because she was my Mum, "THE MADONNA"

My whole world collapsed that night and my relationship with my Mum was never the same again. I loved her dearly because that's the way I'd been brought up. But because I felt it was a betrayal of my Dad and us, I couldn't overcome the grief of what she'd done. My Mum decided from that night on she was going to live her own life and started to go out with other men.

I still continued to help support the family but my life seemed to pass in a blur, I don't really remember too much about that time.

School seemed to be less interesting and I found myself staying away more and more. I went from being a good pupil in the top class to a truant. I used to go in to get my registration mark and then sneak out and go to Susan's. Susan and I were inseparable and used to be together day and night.

After leaving school I became a trainee ladies hairdresser and worked in the same shop for two and a half years, also attending college.

My friend Mike and I both agreed we'd serve our apprenticeships and then go to Saudi Arabia working for two years as labourers. The wages to be earned back then were really good and we had a contact that could get us the work. Our idea was to work and save as much as we could, then come back to England and start our own business. Entrepreneurs aged only seventeen.

How different to work as a ladies hairdresser and then go labouring in a foreign country. We had ambition and determination to work hard for what we wanted though.

By the time I was eighteen I felt so low for many reasons and I took an overdose. Susan had finished with me and she was getting engaged to my best friend from school. Apart from that there were so many other things going wrong in my life. I no longer wanted to be alive. I went to the pub, it was a Sunday afternoon and I got drunk. When I got home I went to Mum's bedroom and took her bottle of nerve tablets to my room. I sat at my dressing table and wrote a note for Sharon telling her that I was sorry and she could have all of my money to share between her and David. I even wrote that Mike still owed me £35. My eyes were blurred with tears, I remember a few dropping on to the paper and smearing the words of my suicide note. I folded the note and put it on my dressing table, sat on the bed and swallowed all of my Mum's tablets. I was crying after I did it but put the empty bottle under my bed so nobody would see it, then I lay down and went to sleep.

Luckily my Mum had sensed something was wrong with me and came into my room to check. She didn't want to try and wake me up because we'd had a big argument earlier. So she went over to Mike's house to ask him to wake me. She didn't know Mike & I had had a big falling out earlier as well. Because she was so worried, however, he came over. When Mike wasn't able to wake me up she looked under the bed and found her tablet bottle empty. I was rushed to hospital and the doctors told her I was very lucky, another hour and I'd have been dead but they were concerned I may have brain damage.

Fortunately I seemed to pull through without any brain damage. Hmm I suppose that's questionable ha!

A few months later I walked into a club and there she was, my old school friend who is now my wife of twenty-two years, twenty-four if you count the two years living together.

Within six weeks of being together I moved into the flat, six weeks later she became pregnant. Not long after finding out she was pregnant, I had to give up my career and my dreams of working away. I was now a family man with responsibilities and needed a better paying job.

As an adult, my Mum and I discussed what had happened after my Dad died. She bitterly regretted what she'd done and had always been sorry. She loved my Dad so much, his dying had devastated her life and she needed to feel the comfort of a man holding her. She explained it was more than a sexual need it was more of a need for comforting.

People behave in different ways with bereavement and as an adult I had a better understanding of life and forgave her. She'd always loved me and is proud of me for the ways I seem to cope. I don't let the traumatic times of life damage me beyond repair.

She also reminded me that in the early years of leaving home, I would go upstairs to use the bathroom and leave money in her bedroom to help her out. We'd never spoken about it before but she told me how much it had meant to her during hard times. I'd forgotten I used to do that but again my Dad had given me good morals to live by. I'm glad I did it and been able to help her out.

24.9.05

I was told it might be a good idea to write this next part to help clarify how the beast managed to get so close, this was the best I could do after writing this story for so many years.

My Relationship with the Beast

Now this is a tough one to write and an even tougher one to admit to myself after everything that has happened and everything I've learnt since. Nevertheless it has to be written, if only to clarify a lot of things in the early stages of this book. I have to go way back to the very beginning in my mind, of how the beast managed to become not only my one of my closest friends but close enough for me to regard him as a brother. I am so very sorry for my kids in that I was stupid enough to not see through him back then, despite so many uncomfortable feelings throughout those years of being close with him.

I am going to give it my best shot and see what happens.

When Lillian and I started to live together, we would visit her mother at weekends and often stay overnight. The beast and his wife had moved back to live close to Lillian's mothers by then. The brothers would all go for a drink together and of course I would go too. It seemed a natural thing to do because I was being accepted as a family member. At that stage of my life I had a need to be accepted, especially by my future in laws.

The beast befriended me and we became closer despite my early feelings, which I pushed to the back of my mind. Before long we started going out for a drink and a game of pool on our own, because it seemed the brothers were always arguing and sometimes fighting amongst themselves when they were all together. I sometimes had disagreements with them because I'd stand up for myself, unlike Lillian's previous boyfriends and the beast would always side with me, against them.

Not long after we found ourselves visiting Lillian's mother and then staying overnight with the beast and his wife and we all seemed to get on really well together. When we got married his wife Bernadette was chief bridesmaid because she was Lillian's closest friend. Looking back now I can see how much the beast was playing me and luring me into a false sense of security, as I've said *"Paedophiles are masters of illusion and manipulation"* and as sad as it feels now to admit, I was gullible enough to fall into his trap.

It didn't seem untoward to let him come and live with us because he had nowhere else to go at the time and once again we continued to go out together for a drink and playing pool. I was new to the area myself and although I occasionally went into the local pub, I didn't really know that many people in there. That of course all changed once he started to come in with me because he built up a circle of friends around us and again he was very popular with the females which meant Lillian got to meet new people as well. We both joined the pool team and became part of the local pub scene that goes on in England.

As I've said things were pretty chaotic back then, Lillian was forever coming and going but never telling me how much of an effect having him to live with us was having on her. I didn't see him for a while after he finally moved out but he managed to wheedle his way back in once Lillian moved next door to him and we became friends again. He would often baby-sit for us and we would baby-sit for him and obviously had keys to each other's houses. As I've said before, for much of the time it was like living as one big family and he was forever popping in and out on a continual basis.

When I first moved next door to him, I occasionally went out for a drink with him but one of the things I'd realised in the time we'd spent apart was how much of his life involved going out drinking. I'd also worked out that I myself had developed a drinking problem, or a need for going out socialising back then. I decided as it was a fresh start for Lillian and myself, I would drop out of the pub scene completely and did so for a number of years. The beast didn't and became an alcoholic!

He always seemed to be around at the house and wanted to be involved with anything I was doing, whether it be the gardening, or fixing the car etc. His son Stuart had a nervous breakdown and I seemed to be forever driving the beast around either visiting Stuart, or dropping him off at places he'd be staying for a while to give the beast a break.

The beast had also been into detox units to stop drinking, the responsibility for the visits and looking after his children were always left to Lillian and myself. Whenever anything was going wrong in his life or any of the family's life, Lillian's Mum was always quick to pass everything over for us to take care of. Once again my upbringing came into show of absolute loyalty to family and taking care of them. Again misguided behaviour but Lillian and I fell into the role easily. I became really close to his kids and worked so hard to try and keep him on the straight and narrow for their sakes.

To be honest I really can't write anymore about my relationship with him because it's too painful at the moment. I'm going to leave it at this now and hope that you as the reader can read between the lines and relate to how patiently cunning and manipulative paedophiles can be in gaining your trust, especially when you take into account he was involved in my life for almost twenty years before I discovered what a monster he really was!

I've been talking with my two sons Anthony and Sean tonight, Anthony reminded me about the death of his Uncle Robert sixteen years ago. I'll explain how the whole situation came about.

Some years earlier the beast was constantly going on to me about taking his own life. Thinking back now I wonder if it was because he knew he was becoming an even bigger monster. I got so sick of hearing it and in the end I said *"listen if you want to kill yourself then just let me know when your ready to do it and I will be the one to come into your house and find you. I'll then phone an ambulance and have your body taken away before your kids come in from school"*. I was so matter of fact about it that it must have shocked him because he never mentioned it again after that. It's funny because as I remember it, to me it seemed the logical thing to do rather than have him do it and his kids to find him. Obviously I'd called his bluff but even I was shocked at my blasé attitude to the whole thing. Thinking back maybe it was because I'd tried to take my own life twice before but didn't tell anybody beforehand. I just did it and went to sleep.

That last sentence has awoken another memory that I feel is relevant to this whole story, as always I will go off on a tangent and come back to this part.

Lillian and I had moved into a bigger house directly behind the house we'd lived in when we'd got back together. As it happens the beast ended up moving right next door to us there as well. Social Services had had helped make that possible because he needed us to support him with his kids. The beast was once again living with just a dividing wall separating him from his future and past victims.

I'd worked on the new house for two weeks decorating it from top to bottom, coming in from work, decorating until midnight most evenings and all of the weekends. I was worn out at the end of it but the house looked lovely. We couldn't afford to buy new furniture for the living room until a later date but it was decorated and carpeted for when we could.

Lillian had started taking Thai Boxing lessons at the time in a gym. It was doing her confidence a world of good and she was really dedicated to it. A couple of the instructors had fallen out with the owner of the gym and had decided to open their own place which was going to take a couple of month's to get up and running. She told me her instructor was willing to give her private lessons at our home in the meantime if it was ok with me. The living room was free, so I agreed and of course I also paid for the lessons. Oh gullible me!

Lillian's mother and sister had started coming over to the house on Lillian's training days, which had really started to irritate her. I told her to stand her ground and tell them not to visit on training days, I suspected why they were coming over but because I trusted Lillian I sided with her. They obviously knew her better than me!

Lillian's behaviour started to change towards me around the same time and after putting a few pieces of the puzzle together I decided to come home early on one of her training days. I let myself into the house and expected to find her in bed with him but was so relived to hear them laughing and training together, although it has to be said they seemed very close. The following week I did the same thing and once again they were training. Lillian had told me a few weeks earlier they'd discussed her Mum's behaviour and the instructor had said if it was a problem for me they could put off the lessons until the gym opened. Although my instincts were ringing out alarm bells I wanted to trust her at that time. By the time I'd come home the second time I'd decided I could no longer cope with the doubts in my mind and asked her to stop the private lessons, which she agreed to do.

Some weeks later Lillian told me she no longer loved me and wanted me to move out. She said I'd become boring because we no longer went out and I was working all the time to finish the house off. I couldn't believe what I was hearing and tried everything to make the relationship work over the next few painful months. I won't harbour on about it all because it would take too long. I became a broken man because I loved my kids so much and had worked so hard at being a good husband and father since the last time we'd split up and lived apart. Adding to that Denise had been born so we had four kids by then. In a bout of severe depression I decided I couldn't live without my kids and Lillian and stupidly chose to kill myself. I told Lillian I would move out the next day. She said she'd go out for the day while I packed my things. The next morning I kissed the kids goodbye before they left for school and phoned my boss to say I was ill and wouldn't be coming into work. I walked to two separate pharmacists in the pouring rain and bought two separate packs of a hundred paracetamol. I went up to my bedroom and managed to swallow the first hundred. Then I managed a couple of handfuls of the second pack before I started to feel sick and lay down to go to sleep. I lay there for hours but couldn't sleep. All the time I was feeling my stomach bubbling away as it was digesting the tablets. I lay there praying for sleep so I wouldn't hurt as I died. It had been so much easier the last time, I just went to sleep and felt nothing.

Lillian came back around lunchtime and I remember thinking she was meant to find me alive and everything would be fine. I must have been so very depressed and desperate back then. She walked into the bedroom and seemed surprised to see me still there and said *"Oh you've not gone yet"* in a disapproving tone, I replied *"No its not time yet, I need a bit longer."* My heart sank because she seemed so indifferent and said *"I'll go back out then and come back after picking the kids up from school."* She just turned around and left.

I lay there feeling so dejected and so very alone, deciding I was meant to die because Lillian didn't want me anymore.

My legs were aching so I went downstairs for a few minutes break; I sat on the settee looking around the room and the photographs on the TV and fire jumped out at me. There is a photograph of Denise's graduation and some beautiful photos of my smiling grandkids. The enormity of what I'd just written hit home! Had I died back then, I would never have been around to see my beautiful grandkids. I haven't thought about back then for a while now but for quite a few years afterwards I was very grateful to have survived.

It all seems so weak, selfish and irrational now looking back but that was how my state of mind was, back then.

I lay there for a while before turning onto my side and drifted off to sleep. I awoke at 2.45 pm leaning over the side of my bed and being sick. I looked at the floor and all that was there was a mound of white partially digested tablets and froth. I remember being gutted because I'd brought them up but knew they'd been inside me for almost six hours by then, so the damage was done and all I had to do was go back to sleep again. Besides I couldn't do anything else by then because I felt so ill. I couldn't even manage to get out of bed to clean the mess up.

Lillian came back after picking the kids up from school and saw the mound of tablets next to the bed and started shouting at me. She wanted to call an ambulance but I assured her I'd be ok because I'd brought them up. I didn't want the kids to see me being taken away and in my twisted but depressed state of mind thought I'd die later on that evening whilst they were asleep.

Well I'm sitting here now writing about it so it's obvious I didn't die. I wasn't meant to die and against all the odds *"I SURVIVED FOR A REASON"*

I was really ill for a few day's but Lillian was determined she still wanted me out of the house. In the end I stood my ground and told her I wasn't leaving and we went through the motions for a couple of month's before we both agreed I should leave after Christmas. She wanted me to go before then but I refused point blank. It was destroying me living like we were, not being allowed to touch her, even in bed if we accidentally touched in our sleep she'd pull away. I left and went to stay at my Mum's until I could sort something out for myself. Two weeks later Lillian decided she wanted me to come back home and like a little lap dog that I was back then, I moved back.

I worked really hard at our relationship and my co-dependent behaviour of being carer and rescuer to everyone around me continued. I had my doubts about her and the instructor's relationship but chose to believe her when she told me nothing had gone on between them. Yes you've guessed it *"I BELIEVED HER"* because as far as I was concerned she'd always been faithful to me and I neither had reason to believe anything else or wanted to.

Robert and I shared the same birth date of May 15 and he'd come over to wish me happy birthday. Alex who was my business partner at the time had bought me a bottle of Brandy that I opened to give Robert a drink as a toast. That was to be the last time I saw him.

On June 1st my sister Sharon had given birth to my nephew, so Lillian and I went to visit Sharon in hospital. An hour or so later we were relaxing watching the T.V when the beast walked in saying *"I think there might be something wrong with Robert"* I clearly remember the resentment and annoyance I felt towards him but can't remember how that resentment built up or came about. I looked at him and asked, *"What do you mean?"* He said Robert had been acting strangely in the pub earlier that day and when the beast had gone back over to the pub that evening, Robert had left two rings with the barmaid. These came with instruction to give the rings to the beast for him to pass on to his nieces Annette and Carol. (They'd always been his favourites because my sister in law Janet had lived with her Mum and him when she gave birth to them both.) I looked at Lillian and said, *"We better go over to check on him."* I then turned towards the beast and said, *"Why didn't you just go to his flat and check on him yourself? If this is a waste of time I'm not going to be happy with you"* I can really feel the resentment towards him as I'm thinking back now and can clearly see the panic in his face.

We drove over to Roberts flat and the beast let us in with a key. I didn't think too much about him having a key at the time but would find out at a later date why! We walked up the stairs and the beast went straight to Robert's bedroom and opened the door and stepped to the side. As I walked closer to the door I saw Robert lying on the floor in the recovery position and a dribble of blood coming out of his mouth. The beast suddenly turned on me pushing and screaming in my face *"You're not supposed to be here"* I threw him to one side and dropped to my knees rubbing Robert's chest because I really didn't know what else to do in that moment of chaos. I then stood up and left to find a phone box to call for an ambulance.

The ambulance men came and went through the motions. They put Robert in the back of the ambulance and Lillian and the beast went with him I followed in my car. When I saw no sirens or flashing lights I knew he was already dead. I also knew there was something most definitely not right about the whole situation. As always I was to find out at a later date!

The family seemed to start falling apart; Lillian and her mother took things really badly. I don't think she ever recovered from Robert's death; we'd lied to her and said he'd had a brain haemorrhage. The truth was that Robert had taken an overdose because he was so depressed at the time.

This is what I managed to work out from gathering information from people, in particular the beast, over the months. Once again there was a jigsaw puzzle with only the beast holding all the pieces of it.

Robert had been depressed for a while and had talked about killing himself, with the beast. The beast had come up with the same things I'd said to him but being the coward he is couldn't see it through and involved Lillian and myself on the night. They'd picked the day (that's why the beast had a key to the flat) also the rings were left with the barmaid. She'd told me Robert seemed depressed and she suspected something when he gave her the rings and the message for the beast. She told the beast to check on him because she was so worried. The beast did go round to the flat but Robert was sat up in bed and said he was fine (that was according to the beast.) I think he'd already taken the overdose but was still alive and the beast left him more time and went back to the pub. I think Robert changed his mind and put himself in the recovery position on the floor in case he got sick and choked. In his weakened state he may have even hoped and prayed his brother would come back to save him. But his brother was a beast and loved to play with and control people's lives, Robert paid the price with his life; Lillian and particularly her Mum's lives were changed forever.

Part Two

Chapter 1

Leading Up To The Court Case

We moved house and into a different area, hoping we could start again without so many painful memories, of what had gone on in our old house and the area we'd lived in for most our adult life.

The build up of shopping for new carpets, furniture, paper and paints kept us busy for ages and it was a very exciting time. It was also a distraction from everything else going on around us and it was something positive and happy to put our energy into.

Unfortunately it didn't change anything, the pain moved with us and another part of our past was about to catch up with us.

Within a few weeks of moving into the new home, Lillian began acting strangely towards me. She started going on about our early years together and the times we'd split up. I'd had relationships with other girls whilst we'd been apart but had always been upfront and honest about them. I'd even regretted them bitterly over the years, because I felt I'd really let Lillian down badly and it was being unfaithful, regardless of whether we'd been together at the time or not.

This odd behaviour went on over a two-week period and I'd had enough, I couldn't understand why she was dragging it all back up? The new house and everything in it was meant to be a brand new start for us.

She then told me the horror she'd carried for so long. In the first two years of our marriage she'd slept with two of my so-called friends!! I couldn't believe it; I'd emotionally beaten myself up for what I'd done in the past, for so many years. I'd also blamed myself for all the times she'd left me, as she'd always maintained it was my fault. It was too much for me to take on board on top of everything else that had gone on within the family. She told me she'd slept with them both on two separate occasions and was so ashamed of herself, she'd hated herself for years because she'd been so cold about it and over the years realised that all the things she'd blamed me for, were not really my fault.

We argued for weeks over it and I felt a new pain, a pain I hadn't experienced before, I felt so betrayed as it meant she hadn't been faithful. For all of these years I'd worshipped her as my wife, in the firm belief that since we'd been together she'd never cheated. I'd also had contact with both of these guys for years after they'd had sex with my wife, one of whom I'd offered a job to and the other I'd helped out financially more than once. It put a tremendous strain on our relationship, the fallout and devastation that followed was indescribable.

I was later to find out that some victims of child abuse follow these patterns, reaching out to people for comfort and love and invariably end up having sex. Or even go on sprees of sleeping with people out of feelings of disgust for themselves, or feeling in control of the situations. All of which is self-destructive behaviour.

It explained so much about our married life! I endlessly had to prove to her over the years how much I loved her but it never seemed to be enough. Many times when things had been going good for us, she'd gone on self-destruct mode and caused mayhem. I'd always been confused but now I could see the reasons for so many things. The weekends we'd spent talking, she'd told me so many things about the past, so many painful things and each time she said there was no more! That was it she'd got everything off her chest and felt so much better for it. She'd lied and she'd still kept destructive things in our relationship to herself.

Inside I felt dead and again it took a long time to try and get over it. This was another thing I had to try and bury to the back of my mind. I was starting to fall apart myself though; I felt my heart had been broken in two and everything I'd believed in my marriage, had been an illusion.

It's so important to make sure you haven't got any unresolved issues between you, as that is what weakens you when the in fighting starts! You'll carry unresolved issues but not be fully aware they're affecting you. They just nibble away and when things are bad they'll bite chunks out of you and you in turn bite chunks out of each other! They have to be dealt with and buried once and for all. You need to focus on the love for each other to survive! It will feel like you can only remember any bad moments in your life. You must focus on the good times as well, because in time they'll get you through the bad times.

As I've said life was hell over that period of time and people were falling to pieces including Lillian and I. Everyone was suffering terribly. The strain was immeasurable, so much so I'd started getting pains in my chest. I went to the doctors, given my family history of heart disease and the fact my cholesterol level was in the danger zone, the doctor sent me to the hospital.

Fear and panic was really setting in. I was put on monitors to check if I'd already had a heart attack, which luckily I hadn't. I was diagnosed as having angina. Angina and thickening of the arteries I was terrified. My whole life had been dedicated to my family life, now with so many revelations about the beast and how he'd traumatised so many people; they needed me more than ever. How cruel life seemed to be and I felt I'd been sentenced to death! But how soon might I die was the question in my mind constantly. I was put on medication to lower my cholesterol, aspirin to thin my blood, beta-blockers to slow my heart rate down, tablets to counteract the damage the rest of the tablets were doing to my stomach and glycerine tablets to open my arteries when I had pains.

I felt like I'd rattle as I walked.

I've lost count of the nights I've lain in bed hoping that I wouldn't die, leaving Lillian and the children to face life without me. It surprised me when I opened my eyes in the morning because I'd made it through another night of pains. I was terrified history was going to repeat itself and claim my life, as my Dad's had been claimed.

My kids were so concerned for themselves and me because, they knew how much my life had changed after my Dad had died and it made them feel even more vulnerable. They bought me a heart monitor between them for father's day, so I could keep a check on my heart rate. My doctor had said to not let it exceed 100 beats per minute.

We all lived in fear, the beast had turned our lives upside down and now the stress was affecting my health. And of course in my mind the worst would happen, I'd just drop dead with no warning!!

Chapter 2

My Babies

One evening our youngest son Sean then aged nine came into our bedroom; he sat on the bed but seemed troubled to me. He'd been fully aware that something serious had been going on in the family. We'd tried to keep things from the youngest two but kids pick up on so much more than we realise they are capable of.

Both Sean and Paige our youngest daughter were born around the time Michael had began his downward spiral of self-destruction. In their short lives they'd witnessed so much chaos in our home. Sean and Paige used to talk amongst themselves and had been very close since being babies; they were born only eleven month's apart.

He said he felt that something had been done to Paige by the beast. He kept saying, "I don't know what but I think something has happened to her" I tried to control myself but showed some anger in my face.

(This was to be another major mistake I made. I felt my whole existence collapsing around me, please oh please not my babies as well! I stupidly said that if anybody had harmed them, then I would have to harm that person. I didn't realise the enormity of my words even though I'd said them calmly. My facial expression must have given me away because he didn't say anymore other than "*I don't know what happened to her*")

We talked with him for a while and when he was ready he went back to bed.

We sat there in a daze the life force sucked out of both of us, I was desperate, frantic "*oh please not my babies as well*".

My thoughts were taking on a new direction; I wanted to kill the beast now! How far had things gone? How twisted and perverted was the beast? I was crying and trying to control my own animal instincts of protecting my young! I wanted revenge! Please, please not my babies. Lillian and I talked for hours and the only sensible thing to do was to contact the NSPCC who were counselling Michael. My anger by now was simmering in the pit of my stomach, I'd managed to gain some control but it was too late because Sean had seen it.

The next day we contacted the NSPCC, they agreed to see us to discuss our fears and the counsellor agreed to see our children. Once again we had to learn that painful lesson of patience and they'd both go to a weekly appointment for the next few months.

Enlightenment

Around the same Lillian opened a bible and read something in it, then passed it to me to read for myself. I hadn't been a religious person and hadn't read the bible since I was a kid. I read it for a few days and gained some comfort but had many questions to ask? One part I'd read said, *"The prayers of a man of God are powerful prayers."*

A couple that had moved next door to us in the old house were pastors. They used to pray and sing for hours on end when we were living there, I used to say hello and exchange small talk with them but never wanted to go any further than that.

I decided to go to see them to ask about what I'd read and ask would they pray for us. They seemed really pleased to see me and invited me in; they told me God had told them I'd be coming to see them. They said they'd been waiting for me and that God had a plan for me?

After spending a couple of hours with them I believed everything they'd told me, I was so hungry for more and was hooked. As time went by and the more desperate I became, the more they fed me on the word of God (As they saw it!) Their place of worship was a dining room attached to an old folks home, they invited me to a prayer meeting for the week after I'd been to see them, which I went to. When I got there all the tables had been moved to the back of the room and the chairs were set out in rows but nobody else was there except them. He was talking and preaching like the room was full of people. Which I must admit looked bizarre at the time but being in such a weakened and curious state of mind, I felt it wouldn't do any harm to see how things went.

I was welcomed in and told that people would come eventually "God had told them people would come" He said his wife was usually there but she was away for that evening. We spoke for a while, and then he continued to talk and sing again as if the room was full of people. I stood there feeling really stupid but felt obliged to clap my hands and join in. Then he sat and preached to me one to one, getting into my head. I was feeling really confused but I needed something, anything to take away the pain I was carrying around, like a ton weight on my shoulders. I was a broken man!

They'd been using this room for months and although I was the only person there, I continued going.

They'd have other meetings where people would sometimes come from other churches. By this time Lillian and our younger kids had also started coming. Everything seemed to focus on myself and my family and the troubles we had and I found myself being sucked in more and more. My eldest kids thought I'd lost my marbles as I was trying to convert them and my friends avoided me for the same reasons. This went on for months and I was handing over money every week.

My life seemed to pass by in a haze of reading the bible and them telling me the word of God. The kids on the estate were amazed to see me spending so much time with these people; the pastors said I was to spread the word in the area because people respected me. God had a plan for me and the devil was waiting to claim my family and myself! I of course swallowed everything they fed me and believed everything they told me.

My Mum and my sister Sharon thought they were a cult and would try to talk me into leaving them but I wouldn't listen to anybody other than him or her. They'd show me videos about the end of the world coming and how the devil was taking over the world. I was being brainwashed! Other videos would be American evangelists preaching and saying you had to give money to receive Gods blessings. So many things seemed to revolve around money.

An American pastor preached at one of their meetings and once again the focus was upon my family. The pastors had told her all about our plight. This woman said I was to become a preacher myself and that people would listen to me. She asked for our address so she could send me some literature over, when she got back home to America.

I never heard from her again.

Months went by and instead of feeling better I was getting more and more depressed and my family was suffering even more than before. Michael also seemed to be getting worse! We took him to their house because they'd said he was possessed by demons and they could banish them out of him. They were stood over him praying in tongues, he stayed out of politeness but he laughed at them in the end and of course the demons weren't banished out of him.

Our middle son Anthony then aged nineteen took an overdose; I'd been going on at him for a while, saying the music he listened to was evil! I was constantly at him to join the church. His own memories from the past were coming back and to this day he will not say what happened to him at the hands of the beast. That night I'd sensed something was wrong with him and went upstairs to talk to him, I couldn't wake him up, so immediately knew something was wrong, I looked under his bed and there were the empty tablet strips. We phoned an ambulance and got him to hospital and thankfully he recovered.

The pastors told me it was the devils work and I seemed to be relying on them even more but at the same time I was seeing more and more, how it was affecting my kids.

Two weeks later, to the day, my middle daughter Denise did the same thing and overdosed. It was two weeks before her eighteenth birthday and again we were lucky that she recovered.

I felt I was going insane by this time, I didn't trust anybody and even television programmes were a conspiracy. They said I was suffering because of curses my ancestors had been inflicted with and I'd inherited them. I was so confused, I'd only gone to ask for them to pray for us and in the space of a few months I was losing my family and most of my friends.

She was the more powerful of the two and was constantly preaching to me, in my ear all the time, sucking me in deeper and deeper. She'd been away to London for the weekend to an evangelist meeting and on her return she was so fired up, she was preaching on the stage in their church and constantly looking at me. By this time another family had come from a church outside of the area but the focus was still constantly on me.

Afterwards we'd all sit and drink tea and have biscuits, Lillian had left to drop the kids off at Elizabeth's. That was when she started in on me, telling me "*You have to forgive your brother-in-law, John you must take us to his house to meet him. We have to save him and he must come to our church*" I couldn't, how could I? I told her I couldn't but she kept insisting! Then he was in my other ear telling me "*John you have to let it all go, you have to forgive him, to save your own soul. If you don't you're not living in Gods light and by his word*"

My head was spinning; I couldn't believe what they were saying. The thoughts of him sitting in the same room as our babies and these other kids were too much for me. My loyalty to the pastors and their version of God's word was being compared to the loyalty to my family. I gave in and said that if they insisted I'd show them where he lived but couldn't introduce them. What a shock the beast would have got, those two turning up to save his soul!! He would have laughed in their faces.

They stayed on either side of me trying to wear me down, I felt myself sinking deeper and deeper into myself, shrinking and going over the edge into that pit of despair! Lillian came back and on seeing my face knew something was seriously wrong. She walked up behind me and put her hand on the back of my neck and I almost melted into her hand. She didn't speak but her presence brought me back to reality and broke the spell they seemed to have over me. For a minute they'd looked like predators on either side of me but as Lillian held me they looked nervous, they shut up and backed off.

They'd seen for a while that Lillian was becoming disturbed with the influence they were having over me and she'd started to disagree with some of the things they were saying to us. I felt that Lillian had awoken me from a dream and the enormity of what they were asking sunk in. I said goodbye and left with Lillian.

When I told her what they'd asked me to do, she was horrified and said *"In no way will I allow that animal in the same room as any of our children"* She started to tell me that she too felt it was like a cult and I was being brainwashed. She'd felt this way for a while but still came to support me and keep an eye on what they were filling my head with. She also said she didn't want either of us to go near them again and all of our kids had been going on at her for a while. They were worried sick about me and had noticed so many changes in me.

I persuaded Lillian to come to the bible study on the following Tuesday evening and I said we'd see how things went from there. When we got to the house he invited us in, she was sat there praying and moaning with her head in her hands. We sat for ages listening to her groan, all the time repeating the word "condemnation". I'd noticed her looking between her fingers to make sure she still had our attention, It was all very bizarre and I felt it was all an act for me; I was starting to see through her as well by now. She suddenly stopped moaning and without speaking put on a videotape for us all to watch. It was a tape showing a female preacher she'd seen when she'd gone to her meeting; she kept saying, *"How awesome this woman was"*.

On the Sunday when she'd been all fired up and preaching, she'd been repeating the same things the preacher was saying on the tape. One of the things the preacher said was *"a pastor had come to her, as he needed to seek Gods forgiveness because he'd abused his daughter! He'd told her that he had his daughter's blood on his hands and needed forgiveness"*. This caught my attention fully. How could somebody who was supposed to believe so strongly in God do such a terrible thing? That was it! That was the connection with child abuse and my family!! A fellow preacher had asked for forgiveness and was being given it!! *"Would God really forgive such evil, I ask??"*

I felt she'd exposed herself and that was why they'd tried so strongly to convince me on the Sunday. She looked straight at me and once again she said we had to forgive him! Lillian stood up and told them in no uncertain terms where to go and stormed out of the house.

They again honed in on me, telling me I had to forgive him and said *"If I had to give up my family to spread the word of God, then that is what I must do. Jesus gave up his family to spread the word"* I couldn't believe what I was hearing, they were supposed to be God's chosen people and they wanted me to leave me family.

They said "*the devil was working through my family to stop me from doing Gods work. The devil would be all around me waiting to consume me if I didn't listen to them*" That was it, their stronghold on me was gone, I had flashbacks of so many things that had gone on over the time I'd spent with them, doubts that had been there at the back of my mind, things I chose to ignore for a while but almost in the blink of an eye I was seeing them all. I turned around and left never to return! Leave my family? Not on your life!

They'd tried to manipulate me when I was at my most vulnerable and searching for something. It took me months to get over that experience, I thought I'd die and go to hell and the devil would claim my family.

I did gain something good from it though. I got a new insight into the bible but not in the way they'd have liked. I felt it was good to have a degree of faith in God but not an all-consuming faith based on fear that they'd tried to teach me. I feel that I became a better person and if God truly does have a plan for me it doesn't involve them. I've also found that people have trusted and related better with me since then. I feel I've been able to listen and help but in my way not their way. Their way was to control, not guide and be there when needed! My family were so relieved as I recovered and an even stronger bond was formed between us. My friends were also around me again, all of them. They said they hadn't known how to act around me while I'd been involved with the pastors but had respected I had newfound beliefs.

All the same everyone was happy I came out of it in one piece. I feel I could so easily have lost my mind if I'd stayed with him or her any longer. It was almost like I had to de-program myself, which took months with plenty of uncertainty and sleepless nights.

In the meantime Sean and Paige had been attending the NSPCC but hadn't revealed anything about the beast. The counsellor that had been dealing with them told us, although they hadn't revealed anything about the beast, it didn't necessarily mean that nothing had happened to them. She said it could take years to come out and we'd just have to keep an eye on them. She mentioned Sean had been getting bullied in the new school him and Paige were in, so we'd have to take care of that.

My instincts were telling me that things weren't right but we had to allow them to speak in there own time, once again burying our fears and keep patient!

Life Changes

I became hungry for knowledge of a new kind by then, knowledge about child sexual abuse and the effect it had on people.

One Sunday whilst reading the News of the World, I saw an article in the problem page about child abuse and a web page address for Survivors U.K. I've always thought they were the leading campaigners against child abuse, amongst all of the tabloids.

We had a computer for the kids but I didn't have a clue how to use one. Only one thing for it I'd have to learn! The address in the newspaper gave me the inspiration I needed to help me learn more about child abuse. For that I'll be forever grateful to the News of The World for printing that address.

I learnt how to use the Internet and went to the web page; my life was about to change completely from that moment on. I found a link to communities of people who supported each other, people who'd been subjected to child abuse themselves; at last I'd found a path to follow.

The first community I joined was a site for male survivors of sexual abuse; the manager there is a staunch campaigner against sexual abuse and has devoted much of his life to helping others. He's also a trained counsellor and an inspiration to me. The amount of effort one human being can put into helping so many other people, makes him a credit to humanity in my estimation. He runs a survivors hotline and is always there on Instant Messenger late at night as a shoulder for people to lean on. Him and a group of others tirelessly arrange marches and petitions every year in London; being honest I wish I had just half of his energy and devotion. He's also involved with managing a community for male and female survivors and invited me to join that as well. I was made to feel very welcome and given a greater insight about how sexual abuse affects people individually.

This was my lifeline, I found advice about books that were available over the Internet and felt at last I could achieve something, instead of fumbling aimlessly around in the dark. At that time I was there to learn about my children but things were going to take on a sinister twist at a later date.

One of the members suggested I should join another community she was in herself; this one was for parents and grandparents of abused children. I joined and found another safe haven and felt I belonged more in this community as the people had been through the same things as me. Their children had been abused right under their noses as had been done with mine, the support they give to each other is nothing short of a miracle. I made many friends from all over the world and the sense of love and belonging was awesome!

All of this came from one article in my Sunday paper!

Unfortunately for me I was so slow at typing, I couldn't keep up with the discussions going on in the chat rooms and to type out a discussion point or answer somebody else's on the message boards, could take me up to four hours of one finger typing. I had to improve my speed!

That same weekend I decided to write about my childhood because I had so many unclear memories from the time before my Dad died. It seemed like a whole chunk of my life was missing. I could kill two birds with one stone, improve my typing speed and fill in the gaps from my childhood.

I started to remember things from my early childhood and merrily typed away, it was fun remembering so many things I'd forgotten. Suddenly I remembered something very disturbing from my early childhood. I was at Sunday school when I was very young and kept having flashbacks of an old man. I couldn't seem to get past this old man and typed out *why must I remember the old man*? I typed it three times and then sat back. Nothing would come to me but it still troubled me. All I could remember was I'd been crying and upset when I got home that day. My Mum had asked me what was wrong? I told her I had a headache and wanted to lie down. I remembered tears rolling down my face onto the bible I was reading in the class. I could see a nun in the corner on the right. The old man was sitting on a small chair, at the small table to the left. The table and chairs were like the type nursery kids sit round and was in a circle, with all of us kids sat around it. I remember him asking me to come and stand beside him and me looking at the nun. She smiled and nodded towards me but I can't remember anymore than that. Although I remembered that was the one and only time I went to Sunday school.

I left it alone for a while and came back later but still nothing more would come.

I just carried on as I remembered other things, happier things and got as far as the age of eight years old, then another flashback disturbed me, only this one was much clearer and although I'd always remembered this one, not in the same way I'd remembered the day I was writing.

I remembered walking from the Doctors room down a short dim passageway and then I was lying on a bed naked from the waist down in an examination room, alone with the doctor and my Mum wasn't around. The Doctor was as I thought examining me and then I heard a noise outside the door. I turned and could see people in white coats through the frosted glass in the door. He then went to the door to let some student doctors in and carried on examining me. I'd always remembered focusing on one female Doctor and her looking straight into my eyes. I had a single tear running from my left eye. I can remember her clearly looking shocked at what must have been the traumatised expression on my face. Who knows, just maybe she'd been a victim of something in her own childhood and recognised something in me at that moment?

I'd always remembered lying to my Mum as we walked home through the park that day and I remember I was upset and crying. I spotted the swings in the corner of the park and told her a swing had bounced into my groin, as that was one of the questions the doctor had asked about the pain in my groin. Had I been kicked or banged myself? My Mum had taken me there in the first place because I had pain in that area and against everything I was brought up to believe *"I LIED RATHER THAN GO BACK AGAIN"*

As I've said this memory had always been with me but now it felt different, I'd always remembered being upset and lying about being banged. This felt all the more strange because twice I 'd lied to my Mum and yet one of the things I'd been writing about, was how honest a child I was and how much my Dad hated lies. The first lie was a headache after Sunday school and the second after being alone with the doctor. Both times had the same feelings of dread and trauma to me.

From an early age I knew it was better to own up to something I'd done wrong, rather than lie, because I 'd be let off with being shouted at by telling the truth but to lie guaranteed to be hit with the belt and sent to bed.

I sat back and had another flashback; this time I was aged twelve, Id never forgotten this particular incident and once again hadn't seen it for what it really was.

I'd had a fight with my friend after school; he'd given me a massive kick to my outer thigh. It had swollen up like a balloon and the next evening my Dad took me to the Doctor's surgery. He was my Mum's Doctor from being young and mine since birth.

He'd told me to strip to my underwear and get on the examination bed; this bed was in his room not the same one from my earlier memory. I lay there whilst he was rubbing my leg; he then turned to my Dad and was telling him it was o.k. It was only badly swollen and would bruise. He had his back to me and was facing my Dad but his hands were behind his back and he continued to stroke my thigh, moving up towards my groin!

I've always remembered being lay there frozen with shock and I've often asked myself why I didn't just shout to my Dad and tell him what the doctor was doing. I just froze and watched his hands, I'd remembered looking towards my Dad but couldn't see him properly because the Doctor looked so massive and was standing in front of me. All the time I was lay there he was talking to my Dad and touching me up! I even had flashbacks of his smug face when he turned back to look at me!

The three separate situations came together with the same feelings of helplessness I'd felt as a child. I had to face a new trauma, I too had been abused as a child and somehow managed to block the abuse side of things out. Although I'd always remembered the situations! I was in shock but so many feelings were falling into place for me.

My Mum had told me a few years earlier about the Doctor examining her and her sisters in an intimate and inappropriate manner when they'd been younger and also whilst they'd been pregnant. He'd always given them internal examinations and they all said the same things! *"It was the smug look on his face as he was doing it and the uncomfortable way they'd all felt"*. Apparently he kept my Mum's youngest sister on his books as a patient, right up until she could no longer have internal examinations, whilst carrying her twin sons and then told her because she'd moved house she could no longer be a patient. Seems odd doesn't it, because she'd moved house month's before but he kept her on until he could no longer give her internal examinations.

Now I knew I needed the male community, I left a message for Steve the manager on the message board. When he got back to me he explained how the mind worked with flashbacks, I'd already read about them and knew the mind would only open up when the person was ready to deal with the issues. I knew I couldn't deal with my own and all of the people around me, so I put my own issues to the back of my mind until I was stronger.

I phoned my Mum to talk about it but she said she'd been told the Doctor was dead. So it seemed there wasn't a lot I could do about it if he was dead. I knew I could cope with what had happened to me, as it seemed like nothing compared to what my family had been through. All the same though had he been alive, I'd have loved to have given him a rude awakening for what he'd done to me as a child! I felt so strongly that all abusers of children should have to face up to their crimes, regardless of how long ago the crimes were committed! Public awareness should be aroused and the only way that can be achieved is by people that have been abused, standing up and being heard! If he'd been alive I would have come forward and gone up against him!

Instead of being too upset by what I'd remembered, I found myself reaching a better level of understanding, the books I'd been reading about child sexual abuse became easier to understand for me. It was like the mental blockage I'd had whilst reading, was becoming unblocked.

Even the things I posted on the message boards and the replies I gave to others were so much clearer. I knew my own abuse and although very wrong; it felt like I'd almost been vaccinated against the effects of sexual abuse. The simplest way I could think to explain it is this and again it was my own personal theory at that time. Children are inoculated by having a virus injected into them, for the body's antibodies to build up a resistance against the virus and to fight it! I felt that the abuse I'd suffered was like an inoculation, enough to make me ill but my body and mind would be strong enough to recover and fight back! And boy had I had a fight on my hands throughout all of this but I always seemed to be able to pick myself up off the floor, dust myself down and get back on with what had to be done. I felt I had an even clearer insight into the effects of sexual abuse and how the mind of a child could be so traumatised; it could shut down and not allow the memories to come back until the person was ready to deal with them.

I'd always thought my lack of childhood memories was a barrier to block out the effects my Dad's death had had on me. It was like I'd shut out so much of my life to protect myself and at the age of forty-one my mind was ready to deal with my whole life.

The downside now was, the beast had taken away my whole family life as an adult, as I thought I'd known it. Now I had to deal with the fact, my whole childhood had been turned upside down as well, because of sexual predators! It wasn't easy to absorb but my love for Lillian and the kids and what they were going through gave me the strength to carry on, although I did feel we were in a war zone.

The communities were the best things that could have happened for us as a family, I found even more support and gained even more insight. I became even more grateful for the article on the problem page that Sunday afternoon and the web address I got from it. Was it fate again?

Christmas was coming soon, that had been the most special time of the year for our family when I was a child. My Dad had had always made an extra special effort for Christmas and it was always family orientated. This was a tradition I'd always carried on with my own children, although it'd always been a time of sadness for me because it was the anniversary of my Dad's death. I would still always make Christmas special in our home, despite my grief.

When the my kids were younger and we used to live next door to the beast, it would infuriate me when I went into his house, his kids would be downstairs opening their presents on their own, whilst he was upstairs in bed nursing a hangover. He'd then get up and go to the pub leaving them alone, there would be so much joy and laughter in our home and so much sadness in theirs. I'd wake him up and have a go at him, telling him to get up with his kids but he just didn't care! We'd end up bringing his kids into our home to at least make them feel wanted and to join in our festivities.

So Christmas was coming and I came up with a thought. I suggested to Lillian, as all of our children came every year with our grandchildren for dinner, we could also invite our nieces as well this year. We could make this last Christmas before the court case that had been booked for the following year, special for all of the beast's victims, we could give them an even greater sense of belonging. Lillian agreed and everybody was really enthusiastic and had something to look forward to. It meant there'd be twenty of us in all, twelve adults and eight children.

We had to make sure it was special and went to great length's to make sure it would be, we even bought father and mother Christmas outfits that we wore all day.

We'd arranged for me to pick up Annette, Carol and my great niece first, their faces looked a picture when I knocked on the door. People were laughing as we all piled into the car, with me shouting *"yo ho ho merry Christmas"* to everyone around.

Michelle was still staying in the hostel the police had arranged for her, she couldn't believe it when I turned up for her dressed as Santa. She was so excited she ran inside to bring the other girls out to see me; it meant so much for her.

As we all sat round together eating dinner, I couldn't help feeling saddened looking around at so many happy faces and knowing what we all shared in common! Knowing what the beast had done to all of these people I loved so much but even he couldn't spoil the experience we shared that day!!!!!!! It was magical!!! The grown up kids were like kids again and just for one day all bad memories were gone, they had no idea the sadness I felt in my heart. They were innocent children again and I felt like a Dad to them all. I had my grandkids and a great niece climbing all over me throughout the day and I couldn't think of a safer place for them to be! They were safe from all perverts, climbing on a man who only knew how to love children in the proper way.

I'd just wished I could have stopped him years before, if only I'd known, if only I'd trusted my instincts! If only one of them could have broken the evil spell he had over them and spoken up? The shame and blame we carry is immense, how cunning paedophiles are! How EVIL THEY ARE!!!!!

Over the next few months Michael got worse as did Michelle and again our lives were chaotic. The court-case was getting closer and the cracks were beginning to show as the pressure mounted on everyone. Elizabeth became depressed and one night we got a phone call from her boyfriend Eddie, telling us they were on the way to casualty as she too had taken an overdose. My God what was happening, four out of our six children had attempted to take their own lives, once again we were lucky and she too recovered. But could we ever recover???

Around late February- early March things were chaotic as usual and Sean once again came to the bedroom, by this time he'd been having many recurring night terrors. I was to later find out from him, that he'd lie awake at night willing me to wake up and come to his room. He said just hearing me cough or turn over in bed would reassure him we were there and if I got up to go to the bathroom he was ecstatic to know I was still awake. I didn't sleep much myself by then and always had restless nights. Sometimes he didn't go to sleep until he saw the light of morning, he kept thinking aliens were going to abduct him. He was suffering on his own; he couldn't even be in his bedroom without the light on, or the door closed. He was exhausted going to school and as a result his schoolwork was suffering.

He found he no longer fitted in with his friends and kept himself to himself, preferring solitude. It was then the bullies started in on him again. On top of his flashbacks and not being able to sleep, now he was being bullied. Night times were a nightmare and now his days became a living nightmare as well. He carried it all on his own because he said we were under too much pressure with all our other kids and he didn't want to add to our burdens.

Again I knew why the night terrors were happening but we had to remain patient and let him know we were there for him; nobody could do anything for him until he was ready to talk and he wouldn't talk because he believed he could deal with it himself.

This was another innocent child suffering in silent pain because of the beast!

What a hold these perverts have over children, they traumatise their lives so much but it never really goes away!! The memories are always lurking waiting to emerge.

I sometimes thought I was going insane and just wanted to curl up in a ball and let myself slip into insanity and not come back. For all the pain around me to just go away!

Back to the night he came to our bedroom.

He said he'd started to remember things and had been doing so for a while and that was why he was too scared to go asleep. Everything was in fragments and he couldn't make sense of it or put everything together. I gave him a cuddle and reassured him, that if he wanted to speak, maybe we'd be able to help him put it together.

Inside I was dreading what I was going to hear but I was also glad, at last, he was going to unburden his heavy load. I'd had to stand back watching him shrinking within himself, as it was too much for him to carry. It's a very painful thing for a parent to watch helplessly as so many of their own are suffering in silence, the overwhelming urges to say *"I know what he did to you, we can help you but you must tell us"* but we had to be forever patient because of so many mistakes already made, throughout this whole traumatic journey.

He told us he remembered playing at the front of the house and the beast giving him and Paige bottles of coke he'd bought from the shop. The next thing Denise who was minding them came out and said the beast told her to send him into our house and he would look after them both, so she could go off with her friends. She swung him around and then went with her friend (can you imagine how being swung by his sister could have been such a happy moment in a kids life and smiling happily as he walks into his own house to his uncle, totally unaware of what horror was waiting for him) He remembered being dragged upstairs and the next thing facing the bedroom wall with his trainers on, somebody left the room and he covered himself with the quilt.

Another time he remembered Michael minding him, he was in the living room watching videos and Michael was in the dining room. He saw the beast come in and go into the dining room. He said Michael came running into the living room slamming the door shut and trying to block it from being opened. The beast forced his way in and tried to fight with Michael. Michael ran around the coffee table and as the beast lunged at him he fell over the table. Michael ran out of the house leaving Sean on his own with the beast. Sean said he then knew it had happened to Michael as well.

An earlier memory was being washed in the sink downstairs in the kitchen; his Mum was dressed in green but that was all he could remember of that time. He was really upset because he couldn't put it all together; the picture and times were becoming clear to me though.

Again we reassured him, I said we wouldn't go to sleep until after he did and we'd leave our bedroom door open so he could shout us if he needed to.

We started to work out ages he'd have been, to fit in with his memories. This time we wrote everything down so nothing he'd told us would be forgotten. We later found out that was the best thing we could have done. You need to write everything down including times and dates as your child tells you. It can then be used as evidence; you mustn't try to commit everything to memory, because you will forget so many things, especially dates. If I'd known at the very beginning what we'd have to face, I would have written every single thing down and dated it as we were told. I can't emphasise enough, the importance of doing this!

Chapter 3

Twist Of Fate

One night while I was having a bath my sister phoned. She told Lillian to turn the TV over to a certain channel and to shout me. I came into the bedroom and there he was! My own childhood demon! The Doctor! He wasn't dead! He was there in front of my very eyes. Once again he invaded my life, not only that, he'd invaded my home and even worse, it was my bedroom via the television! I was shocked but the anger welled up inside me. I'd buried him in my mind for so long and there he was in my bedroom talking into the camera, without a care in the world. I couldn't believe it.

The documentary he was in had been covering his life over a number of years; he was sitting in his garden opening bottles of champagne with his family around him, talking about his career and how he specialised in distributing the contraceptive pill and fitting contraceptive coils in the 60's.

What a perfect position for a pervert Doctor to be in, giving him unlimited access to women's private parts! I wonder how many other women had frozen whilst he looked down with that smug look on his face?

I phoned my Mum and she told me she knew it was going to be on but had hoped I wouldn't have seen the programme. I felt so betrayed by her because she wanted to bury her head in the sand, as so many others do. She knew if I'd known he was still alive I'd go after him, in turn knowing she'd have to back me up. She'd betrayed me yet again.

I contacted the child protection unit and the officer who'd been dealing with our case. I told her what had happened and she arranged an appointment for me to go and see her.

I'd seen a programme on television about a case where a headmaster had appeared in a documentary. Eleven women had been triggered to the abuse they'd suffered from him and reported him to the police. I'd hoped the same would happen with the eminent Doctor and maybe other people would contact the police.

I told her what I'd remembered and what my Mum and aunts had said he'd done to them. She had to be honest and let me know that because he was an eminent Doctor, that without my Mum and aunts to back me up, I wouldn't have a snowball in hell's chance of going up against him alone.

From my Mum's behaviour I didn't hold out much hope she'd get involved and I was right! My Mum even tried to convince me that he was probably only examining me. That hurt more than the memories of the abuse, as one of the first things a parent needs to know is, if their child comes to tell them something like this, It is so very important the child is "believed"! No matter how crazy it might sound, you must listen to your child and remember many times it will be someone you know or may even love, the child is talking about. Get help immediately to learn how to cope, if you can't get help; get a book and learn anything to help guide you through.

I felt like a child again! Knowing what we'd faced when our children had told us and we'd supported them 100%, I felt so let down! When I asked why she'd allowed him to be our family Doctor, when she knew what he was doing to her wasn't right, her reply was *"I didn't think he would do it to boy's"*.

This was a double-edged betrayal, as he was also my sister's Doctor from being a baby. Sharon had told me when she was sixteen, she'd gone for an appointment on her own, he said *"Your Mum has asked me to examine you to make sure you are a virgin"* Sharon got a bit upset at the thought of that, the doctor told her to come around and sit on his knee, she did this and he was rubbing her back and said *"You are missing your Dad, you need some love"*, as soon as she heard those words she froze and knew what he was doing wasn't right and got up and ran out of his office. She didn't tell anybody about it and had always believed our Mum had asked the Doctor to examine her. I asked my Mum after Sharon had told me, my Mum said she'd never asked the doctor at all!

Another beast working his lies and perversions on generations of the same family!

Once again I have had to be patient and wait but I haven't given up hope *"The pervert Doctor's time will come"* when the time is right he will be as scared as I was as a child and as uncomfortable as he made my Mum and my aunts feel. If the past can catch up with us, then surely the predatory perverts deserve for it to catch up with them too!

Some month's later a friend of mine asked if I'd give him a lift somewhere. We arranged for me to meet him at his Mum's house, when I got there his Mum invited me in but said he wasn't back yet. This was typical of my friend; he's the type of person who would be late for his own funeral. We sat talking in general and somehow got on to the subject of child abuse. I was telling her what had happened with the Doctor and how he'd been on the television etc. She then said that years ago she had a Doctor who was like that and no matter what the ailment he would make her strip to be examined. She and a friend of hers would discuss him and how he'd made them feel, she'd told her husband at the time and all he suggested was that she should change her Doctor.

As she was talking I said, *"It wasn't -------------health centre by any chance was it?"* she looked at me and said *"Yes it was"* I said, It wasn't Dr -------------- *by any chance was it?"* again the same reply *"YES".*

What a small world we live in, when a conversation could open up something like that. Although we never spoke about it again, it seemed to bring us closer, now when we see each other we always hug and I kiss her on the cheek.

The world is getting smaller all the time for abusers of children! People are speaking out and the media is at last taking up the reins against them. Again the News of the World fights the good fight. Every time a story is printed or appears on television, it fills me with hope for the future generations. It should also follow that the perverts will start to get nervous, reading or hearing about cases going to trial dating back twenty-thirty years. Let's hope that for every story that comes out, so many of them will wonder *"When will it be my turn?"*

In May, the night before my birthday, Sean again came into our room because he couldn't sleep. He said he'd been lying in bed and more memories were coming back, only this time they were much stronger. He said he hadn't wanted to tell us, because he didn't want to spoil my birthday and he'd only come to us because he remembered us saying, *"No matter when you want to talk you must come to us and we mean any time of the day or night."* How sweet is that son of mine to even consider not talking because he didn't want to spoil my birthday but thank God he'd decided to no longer try and carry it all on his own anymore.

He remembered the beast taking him to the shops and buying a packet of Maltesers, which the beast's dog would carry home. This was a trick the beast had taught his dog. The beast then said he would kill me if Sean spoke about anything that had happened. Sean stopped talking for a moment and then said he'd hated the beast from an early age.

He also remembered when he was a bit younger his friend Robert would often go into the beast's house, Sean would then knock on the door for him to come back out and play but either Robert or the beast would answer the door, to say he'd be out later. The beast had another dog before the one he taught the chocolate trick to. That one was a bit vicious and Sean said the beast would sometimes set it on him if he went to the door for Robert and it would chase him growling and barking.

The beast would draw monsters for him and Paige and let them watch horror films, telling them the monsters lived under the bed and would get them if they told anyone about him. The monster for Sean had four heads and a dome over it. I realised what his obsession with being abducted by aliens was then!

All of this was coming out in bits like a jigsaw and all we could do was sit there and listen without giving anything away, we couldn't show reactions, just gentle encouragement that he was doing fine. He sat there searching his tortured little mind to remember. All the time just passing me the pieces to keep safe for him, until he was ready to put his puzzle together.

By this time Paige came to sit with us as well, she said, the beast would draw killer clowns for her and say they lived under her bed. One time it was raining and I'd taken them out to buy crayons and crayoning books. (This was something I often did as a means of cheering them up on miserable days.) They were sitting drawing at the dining room table when the beast came in. The beast walked over to the table and drew a four-headed monster on Sean's paper in pink. Sean then started to scribble franticly and the crayon had broken.

Now we had both of them talking and remembering things which I think encouraged Sean to open himself up more, knowing his sister was also remembering *"He didn't feel so alone anymore"*

Paige then added she'd remembered the Wendy house we'd bought for her birthday and that she and our two eldest grandchildren were playing in. She also mentioned the games the beast would play with them of pretending he was dead and when they climbed on him he'd come back to life and tickle them. He'd play hide and seek in his house and again tickle them when he found them and of course the puppies! Lets not forget the puppies; these were the classic textbooks grooming techniques used by paedophiles!

Now another generation of our family was involved, our first grandchildren by Michael.

Sean then went on to tell me about being in Lillian's other brother Alex's house, Alex lived with a woman who had three kids, two boys and a girl. Sean said *"I went upstairs to the bathroom and opened the door, Alex was sat on the bath with Colin stood in front of him. As I walked in Alex shouted at me to get out. Colin just looked at me and I knew straightaway what Alex was doing to him. I just turned and shut the door behind me."*

I have no idea of how many children those two brothers may have molested between them!

Sean and Paige seemed to be doing well and the subject was changed easily before they went back to bed. Once again Lillian and I sat and made notes of everything they'd said.

A week or two later I'd managed to find out where Roberts Mum had moved to and went to see her. I explained what Sean had told me about Robert being in the house alone with the beast. As the beast had abused so many children, it was highly likely he may have abused Robert. She looked at me with shock on her face and said *"John, the house the beast is living in now, is the same house where the man who abused me lived."* Now I was shocked, what are the chances of that happening!

She said her and her daughter would speak to Robert and that he was very close to his sister, so if anything had happened he'd be more likely to tell her. She then went on to tell me more about her abuser. She said, *"As I got older he tried it again. I stabbed him and he died two weeks later. He hadn't died as a direct result of the stabbing but the police tried to charge me with murder, I got found guilty of lesser charges and had to serve two years in prison".*

I said I'd call back in a few day's to see how they went on. Being honest, a part of me hoped they too would go up against the beast.

I went back to see her and she said, *"Robert told them nothing had happened to him and she felt positive he'd have told his sister if it had".* I have my own feelings on that one but no doubt Robert like all the others will talk when he is ready.

At least I forewarned her.

By this time Lillian was cracking under the strain and the court case was coming up soon. Her friend Christine had invited her to go away with a group of friends of hers. They regularly had girl's weekends away in Blackpool. I could see she was under pressure and although she didn't want to go, I insisted it would do her good. I thought it would be a good distraction for her, instead of worrying about the court case to come in the following weeks.

She went and did have a good time despite setting her hair on fire with the hairdryer and on the Saturday evening somebody stealing her handbag with all of her personal belongings and money in it. The most upsetting thing was, that in her purse were things that belonged to her dead mothers, little medals and Mass cards etc.

We did get the bag back a few days later after phoning the club it had been stolen in. The only thing missing was the money but at least her purse and everything else was left in it.

Even a weekend away couldn't be enjoyed without something bad happening?

Chapter 4

The Case

By now I was holding up well and looking forward to the court case, safe in my own little world that the beast was going to be convicted and sent away for a very long time. There seemed to be enough witness's against him and enough evidence. It didn't seem to matter how many times Lillian tried to tell me to expect the worst. I was adamant he would either plead guilty or be found guilty! I was so full of confidence, that justice would be served on him and he would feel the full brunt of the law. The judge would give him a stiff sentence and then we could pick up the pieces of our lives and at last move on.

The big day finally came; Sean and Paige made me promise that I'd be home as soon as possible to let them know how long the beast had got? I was so sure on the morning that the beast would have to plead guilty because the evidence was so overwhelming against him. Michelle had assured us she'd be there to testify against him as well.

We all arrived at the witness suite in the courts with slight fears but were so confident he was going to prison one way or the other.

Then the bombshells were dropped! We were told the bad news, he was only being charged with seven counts of indecency to Lillian!! Michelle hadn't turned up and Michael had retracted his statement on one of his drunken binges.

We were all so deflated, my anger started to build up again and my thoughts of taking the law into my own hands were becoming uncontrollable, especially after seeing Annette and how upset she was. And I couldn't believe the way Michael had betrayed us. It was all too much.

I wasn't allowed in the courtroom, even though I was no longer a witness but my sister was in there listening to the case. She told us that all the statements had been read out and even the security guard who had stood near the beast kept shaking his head, looking at the beast with both shock and disgust. When the defence barrister asked for time to prepare reports for sentencing, the judge had been dismissive and had said, *"Any reports submitted will not change my sentence."* He then adjourned the case for sentencing a little less than six weeks later.

This still gave us some hope, as the judge would have it in his power to give a custodial sentence. It wasn't as good as we wanted but something was better than nothing. We could still be optimistic. My anger subsided a bit and I had to stay focused and strong for the others.

84

I left the courts and headed straight home, as Sean and Paige would have just got in from school. I had to get my head round what had happened and was thinking how could I put on a smile and not show how I really felt inside, in front of them. As I pulled into the drive the front door was opened quickly and these two smiling faces came running out towards the car. I hadn't even managed to park before they were at the car door! That was it, my heart sank how could I try to be optimistic. I opened the door and put on a smile and said, *"Well we didn't get the result we wanted but the judge was mad at him."* Their faces dropped a bit but I'd seemed to allay their fears a little.

We got inside and I explained how it had all gone and told them what my sister had said about the judge, again trying to be enthusiastic. So much so I think I was convincing myself. Sean looked particularly disturbed when I told him about Michael and how he'd retracted his statement. When I asked him if he was ok, he smiled and brightened up but I sensed something wasn't quite right. At that moment Lillian phoned and said the whole family was coming to our house as everybody felt we should be together. This excited Sean and Paige, as we have such a good time when we all get together.

They all arrived and everybody seemed so bright and bubbly considering where we'd been that day. I was sitting on my chair, which means I can focus on the whole room and be able to see everyone in it. I often do this unaware to everyone else. I love to see all of their smiling faces and listen to the hub-hub of different conversations. It gives me such a buzz of energy.

I'd noticed Sean looking around and not joining in the conversations. This kid can hold an audience of adults captivated with his conversations usually but he just didn't look comfortable. It was more than that. I could sense even more strongly that something was wrong.

I decided to go to the shops and asked Sean if he wanted to come for the drive?

We'd no sooner got into the car, than he broke down crying. I knew what was coming next!! I'd known for three years this moment would arrive. My heart and soul were screaming out and I felt sick to the pit of my stomach. I felt so scared of what he was about to tell me. I stayed calm and let him speak. His first words were, *"Dad I remember everything. Denise had told me to go in and swung me around, I went into the house and the beast told me to go upstairs but I said NO. He then dragged me to my bedroom, he stripped me but left my trainers on and pinned me on the bed facing the wall and put his thing up my bum! Then he got up and walked out of the bedroom and I covered myself up with the quilt"*

He'd raped him; that bastard had raped my Sean!

His next words were *"I want to take him to court and Michael should back me up.*

He owes me that at least, Dad!" I suspected Michael had known it all this time!

Sean was so upset but seemed more determined than broken! He was showing strength of mind that would become even stronger as time would go by and I will be proud of him for the rest of my life!!!!!!!!!

We drove around until he felt ready to go back to the house. Only the two of us knew what we'd discussed but he still managed to join in with the family fun. This lifted me enough to actually enjoy our time together and I was able to put what he'd told me to the back of my mind until later.

Somehow I'd found a way of removing myself from the pain and detaching. He gave me that strength!

I contacted the child protection unit and told them what Sean had said. They told me when he was ready they would interview him. I mentioned it to him the next day. He didn't feel ready at that time but said he'd tell me when he was strong enough.

It was too much for Lillian to handle. She started drinking more and we'd both started turning on each other again *"The unresolved issues from the past had crept back upon us again"*

Less than a fortnight later Lillian went for a night out with Christine and stayed at her house. The next day we had a blazing row and she left us to stay with Christine for a while. She said she needed to get away from all the pain and she'd reached breaking point!

The beast was winning we were starting to fall apart at the seams.

Once again I had to explain to the kids that Mum needed a break and we could cope together on our own until she felt better. Once again I managed to remove myself from the pain and had to become Mum and Dad to them both.

The next evening after the kids had gone to bed, I signed into the communities on the Internet. I realised that this was what had kept me going for so long. It was the strength and support from people that were suffering and had suffered similar traumas to us.

I went upstairs to the toilet and both Sean and Paige came running towards me crying. They said they'd been talking and Paige had remembered what had happened to her. She was crying uncontrollably. Once again I found myself reassuring them both and asked them to come downstairs, so they could speak to me properly.

Paige kept saying she and our grandkids were in her Wendy house and she was with our youngest granddaughter Julie. She started crying again because she'd left Julie with the beast. She said it made her feel so guilty for leaving her with him. She was only telling me bits and I couldn't probe, I was again holding back and trying to be patient.

Again the beast had passed guilt on to the children! How cunning paedophiles are!

She was crying and kept repeating, *"I want my Mum! Dad I need my Mum!"*

I phoned Lillian at Christine's and told her what had happened, she wasn't able to drive home because she'd already started drinking. I told her to get a taxi and I'd pay at this end.

As soon as Lillian walked through the door Paige broke down, sobbing uncontrollably again. Lillian took her into another room to talk and Sean said he'd never seen Paige so upset like that before.

When they came back in and sat down Sean went over to Paige and wrapped his arms around her telling her, it would all be OK. It was so touching to see them together; it was so very tragic but so moving; at last Sean felt like a big protective brother.

Paige had also bullied Sean for a long time; she used to prey on his weaknesses of the fear of the night. He'd beg to stay in her room and depending on how she felt at the time, she either would, or wouldn't let him. She said that's why she'd been so horrible to him. She'd known for so long about herself but felt she couldn't love him, she couldn't connect with him. She resented him because he reminded her of her own trauma and she just wanted to forget it. She then said, *"What had happened to Sean was worse than what had happened to her."* He was looking at her and you could see how grateful he was to be able to support her and they were embracing in a common pain at last!

She'd remembered another time she was playing in the beast's house with Michelle. He called Michelle into his bedroom and she'd been gone for ages. Paige left it there and said she didn't want to talk anymore, at least for now.

Lillian just sat looking confused and I knew by her eyes she just wanted to run again. I felt so much anger towards her for it but kept it inside me. If only she'd been able to open up sooner, to let me know how much of an effect it was all having on her. I could have understood and supported her more but she'd kept telling me she was coping, when really inside she was dying. She felt so responsible for not protecting her whole family from her brother the BEAST! She just needed to get away from it all because she didn't have any fight left in her.

That night Lillian stayed. The kids stayed home from school the next day as they were in no fit state to go. Paige was very lethargic and lay around in a dream like state for most of the day. I hugged and reassured her throughout the day. She said she loved me and trusted me to know what to do about everything.

That afternoon Lillian explained she still had to go but she'd be back at the weekend. She said by then she'd be stronger in herself. We all had to accept that and have the strength to let her go, no matter how hard it was on us.

God only knows how deeply hurt and abandoned Paige felt about her Mum leaving them again though. A few nights later I asked Paige if she'd consider counselling but she said she'd rather speak to me when she was ready.

We had such a good time together that week despite what had happened at the weekend and were all looking forward to Mum coming home. We'd started to better understand how she was feeling and decided to make more of an effort around the house, in turn taking some of the pressure off her. The kids also agreed to not squabble as much and we realised how much we all took her for granted!

Lillian came back and we had a good weekend together. On the Sunday night, I was in the bath whilst Lillian and Paige were in our room talking. She was telling her Mum that the beast was in a tent, in his dining room with her and our step granddaughter Lorna, who was only a few month's younger than Paige. She said he had his hands in their knickers and was touching them.

That was all she'd say for then but later on that evening she became upset again.

She said she wanted to kill him! She was so angry with him and wanted to stab him. She then told us about the time Michelle had been called into his room. She said Michelle had been gone for a long time, so she went to see what she was doing. She walked into his room and he had his trousers down and Michelle was stood in front of him. The beast screamed at her to get out!

The time with the tent they'd been playing at the front of our houses when he called them in. He took them in the tent and molested them, telling them not to tell anyone because the boogieman under the bed would get them. They'd both believed him and stayed silent for all this time.

Once again abused minds and bodies!

She carried on talking about another time we'd put her three little pigs Wendy house in our back garden. It was a bright sunny day and she and the grandchildren were playing in it. She'd even remembered her Nana, the beast's mother was over for dinner and I was cooking curry. Nana had chased them around the dining room and they'd been using her walking stick pretending it was a hobbyhorse.

This was a typical family orientated Sunday afternoon in our home; little did we know how much damage the enemy within was doing!

The beast had knocked on the Wendy house door saying *"I'm the big bad wolf, let me in."* He came inside and was tickling Julie who was still in nappies. He then told Paige and Lorna to go and get a drink. Paige said they'd already had a drink and didn't want another one. (In her own young little tormented mind she must have known what he wanted to do.) He then shouted at them to go and get another, which they did leaving the baby with him. As they were leaving he was tickling her. When they went back to the Wendy house, he left and came into the house talking to all of us, including his own mother!

How cunning and twisted paedophiles are!!!!!!!!!!!! We'd have been speaking to him within seconds of him molesting our granddaughter, who wouldn't have been much more than a year old. And right under our very noses!

Writing that part has sent a shiver down my spine! I can clearly see the Wendy house and the sun, the whole scene of children's playful innocence, myself cooking dinner and all felt well around me at the time.

That bastard invaded all of that and destroyed so many lives. I feel sick to my stomach.

Paige then told us she was having recurring nightmares of him coming and raping her. She was only twelve years old and her uncle was raping her in her nightmares!

The strain on us was again becoming overwhelming but Sean and Paige were remembering so many details that gave us a better insight, into how the beast had worked his spells over so many children.

Sentencing

Sentencing day was coming and in our minds he was going away and whilst away would be charged again over Sean and Paige, meaning he may never see outside the prison system for a very long time. We assumed their case would happen whilst he was doing this sentence and with the time added, he'd be an old man before he came out. And hopefully no longer a danger to any more children.

I was so confident that we'd arranged a big family get together for that evening assuming he'd be sitting in a prison cell whilst we were all celebrating.

This could seem a weird thing for some of you to understand. Because so many people had suffered at the beast's hands, we would be paying the price for the rest of our lives. Somehow it was our way of dealing with it, to celebrate his downfall whilst all of us had bonded together and had the strength to SURVIVE.

The whole family was going to be in the courtroom to see him squirm. We'd arranged transport for everyone and were all determined to be strong and united. Showing him that now we were the strong ones and he was the weakling! I even phoned him that morning and asked if he wanted a lift to court? He was panicking and asking, *"Who's that?"* I laughed mocking him and repeated myself, then the penny dropped for him. He tried to appear confident saying *"I'll make my own way thank you very much"* but I knew I'd rattled him and actually gained pleasure from it too!

We all sat outside the courtroom including one of his older brothers, Neil. This time he would walk up the corridor and we'd all be sat waiting to see him. I could only imagine how he'd feel inside the minute he set eyes on us all and was pretty sure he'd feel very intimidated and scared. We purposely got there early so he'd have to face us all.

Time went by and it was getting later. I could have kicked myself for making that phone call, thinking I'd sent him over the edge. We all sat waiting until 11.30am, by then I knew he'd done a runner! I phoned a friend of Anthony's and told him to go to the beast's house to see if he was there, even though we knew it was a waste of time.

Neil then decided to tell us that the beast had considered running away to Ireland the week before the sentencing. I told the barrister about our fears. He said a warrant would be issued for the beasts arrest that same afternoon. He also mentioned we'd probably have more chance of finding him than the police did. My biggest fear was, if he made it to Ireland it could be month's before he was found.

Everybody looked crushed as we were leaving the courts. Once again we started the day so positively and once again the rug was pulled from beneath us!! The beast cheated us again!

Anthony and I started making phone calls and rallied the troops. We were now going on a mission! I'd promised all the family that he'd be found before that evening and we would still have our get together! I believed it because I felt it deep inside!

Now he'd cooked his own goose by absconding and this would anger the judge even more, in turn giving him the power to dish out an even harsher punishment! After all, the judge knew what the beast really was. He'd read all the statements and the reports and the fact that he'd put us all through the hell of having to come back again. Not forgetting the judge had said reports would not change his sentencing!!!!!!!!!!

Anthony and his friends went to stake out the beast's house while I went to the nursing home where his girlfriend Tina was staying. By now she'd become even more ill. (I was to later find out she had cancer.) They must have thought he was definitely going to prison because they both decided she should go in there, Michelle told me this later. I went into the nursing home and had a word with some of the girls working there and told them what he was and that he may come there. They told me Tina had said she wasn't going home that weekend, which made me believe even more his defence team had told him to expect a custodial sentence. The girls knew who he was, they mentioned that their kids sometimes came to the home and it really unnerved them to think they'd been there at the same time as him. I explained I had to go home to change and if he came while I was gone I asked if they would phone the police straight away. They were more than glad to help.

I went and changed into casual clothes and then parked my car in a spot that allowed me to watch the home but at the same time the beast wouldn't be able to spot me if he turned up. I walked over to the building to let the staff know I was back. A woman who seemed to be in charge met me at the door. She said she was concerned that he may make it inside before I'd caught him and was worried about upsetting the staff and the residents. I tried to reassure her that I'd catch him before he got anywhere near the door and then turn him straight over to the police without violence!

I've got to admit she irritated me with her lack of concern for what I was attempting to do but in a way I could see it from her point of view and gave up trying to convince her and walked back to the car.

It was a baking hot day and much too hot to be sitting in a car watching out for a pervert! Especially as he should have been sat in a waiting cell to be taken to prison, had he turned up for sentencing!

A young guy dressed in a chef's outfit came walking from the building towards my car. He said the matron had phoned the police about me and he was letting me know before they got there.

That was really good of him and not being sure of the legalities of what we were doing I decided to join the others outside his house, as obviously the police would have told the staff at the home to phone if he turned up there.

We hadn't been sitting outside the beast's house for long when a police van turned up and the officers asked what we were doing? I told them everything about the beast, they said they understood and were very sympathetic but explained Tina was on her way home. She was scared of us and that we'd be outside the house when she got there.

That seemed really strange considering she wasn't meant to go home that weekend but I kept it to myself.

As we were talking I assured them we weren't vigilantes and wouldn't harm him in anyway whatsoever. There was no way I going to jeopardise the case, I just wanted it over with.

Tina turned up in a taxi looking ever so weak and walking with the aid of a Zimmer frame. I agreed we'd move on if the officer would search the house first. I explained there was no point in us searching for him if he was already hiding in the house. The policeman agreed and searched the house. He came out and told us the beast wasn't in there. We then moved on to search all the pubs in the area. I told all the landlords and people in the pubs about him and they all said if he turned up they'd phone the police.

A few of us went to Moss Side where two of his brothers lived, we went in their houses through the front and back doors to make sure he wasn't hiding out with them. Both places were full of drunks as they were both alcoholics. The smell and the squalor they lived in were disgusting and we were gagging for fresh air when we came out! The best description I can think to describe them was "pigsties".

About an hour later we were back at his house and sat in the baking sun for hours just watching and waiting.

Hours later Michelle came out of the house and walked towards the shops Anthony phoned me to say maybe I'd be better off around the back in case she recognised my car. It was too late Michelle had already spotted me and came across to the car. She apologised for not turning up at court and said the beast had told her that if she didn't appear in court she could live there with him and Tina.

When I told her that although I understood what she was saying, she needed to know how much it was affecting everyone because he hadn't turned up. She smiled at me and said, *"He sneaked back earlier and is in the house now, John."*

I looked at her and gave her a big hug and said, *"Thank you darling, you have no idea how much that means to me."* I couldn't phone the police immediately as he'd have known Michelle had told us.

The beast and Tina must have arranged it over the phone and after she got the police to move us on he'd sneaked back into the house, which is what I thought would happen.

How clever and cunning. This also meant she was also involved. She was covering up for a paedophile!

I phoned Anthony and we all drove closer surrounding the house, in case Michelle had second thoughts and tipped him off. I then phoned the police and the same officers that had spoken to us earlier turned up. I laughed and said, *"I told you we only wanted to hand him over"* one of them laughed back at me and said, *"watch the back of the house until back up comes."* The police officers were knocking for ages before the door was finally opened.

When they went in Tina was on the phone to the solicitor, at the same time screaming at the police to get out. We stood outside waiting and out he came handcuffed with a jumper over the handcuffs. I expected to see fear in him or maybe even some kind of remorse? But he just smiled and said in an evil voice *"You think your clever don't you"* That shocked me but I wouldn't find out why until later.

Michelle then came out and said he'd taken an overdose; this was something she'd told me he'd do rather than go to prison.

That was another thing that had haunted me for a long time. He may choose death and in turn cheat us all again!

I drove straight to the police station and told them what he'd done. I was really scared they'd think he was drunk and just leave him to sleep it off in a cell.

I went home to the family and everyone was so relieved he was in custody at last. Sean and Paige then told me they'd been scared in case he'd came back for them. You could see the relief in their faces because we'd found him.

As the evening went on I still felt uneasy? I phoned the police station to check on him and the officer on the desk said he'd seen a doctor and was ok. He laughed when I said, *"Don't let him die on us please"* I still couldn't relax and felt a premonition of doom? It was his arrogance that was disturbing me; it was like he knew something that I didn't!

We all assumed he'd be remanded in custody until a fresh date was set for sentencing.

The next evening I got a phone call from a friend telling me the beast was back on the streets, I couldn't believe it after what we'd been through the day before. I phoned the police station and was told the warrant hadn't been issued on time, which meant when we'd caught him, he wasn't officially on the run or an absconder. I couldn't believe it because the barrister had told me it would be done the same afternoon we'd left the court.

That's why he'd been so arrogant and unconcerned. He'd known they'd have to release him and because it was weekend a warrant wouldn't be issued until the Monday.

That was it; we would have to wait again!

I found out he was to go back to court on the Tuesday morning. Those next few days of waiting passed very slowly for me.

Tuesday came and of course he absconded again! Michelle said that he'd asked her to go to court with him? This was the kid he'd been abusing all her life and he expected her to give him moral support by going with him. How the hell do their minds work???? Michelle said he'd cashed Tina's benefit books earlier on and not come back, which meant he had money and this time he could be anywhere?

The pressure was on again; we'd have to go through the whole process of searching for him, back to all the pubs, the dirty smelly houses and sitting outside in the baking sun.

We were out all day looking for him. Around 6pm I had a thought! I phoned Lillian and asked her to phone his house pretending to be from the solicitor's office and needing to speak to him. She phoned the house and then rang me back to say Tina was frantic on the phone because he'd run away again. Which meant he hadn't been in touch with her this time! So we went searching again, even though deep down I knew it was fruitless.

Later on we went back to the house and were prepared to be there all night if necessary.

Michelle came outside saying that Tina was threatening to throw her out if she didn't get rid of us. They must have spotted us watching the house. She said he wasn't in there and Anthony could go in the house to look for himself but he couldn't go in the living room because Tina was in there. We felt sorry for Michelle because she was in a bit of a state.

Anthony went in and searched; when he came out he was gagging and physically sick. He said the house stank and had made his flesh crawl. I could tell by then Michelle was lying by her body language and hence the reason Anthony couldn't go into the living room. Obviously because the beast was hiding in there!

I asked Lillian to make the same phone call pretending she was from the solicitor's office, this time when the phone was answered and Lillian spoke there was a pause and the phone was slammed down. They were on to us! The dilemma now was, we couldn't phone the police and say we think he's in there; the only way to prove it was to go in ourselves. But that would be trespass and would jeopardise the case, so our hands were tied. I then realised if he'd come back home, it meant he had nowhere else to run to and was pretty sure his brothers would have told him we'd been to their places many times. So obviously there was no point in trying to hide out with them.

After thinking it through for ages we decided to take a chance and left, in turn, hopefully lulling them into a false sense of security.

That night I thought up a plan to draw him out. I was scared that he may do a runner again but had to think of some way legal to catch him out. I thought if I got his brother Alex to ring the house, the beast might speak to him on the phone? Then we could phone the police and tell them he was definitely in the house. I had thought of driving Alex to the house to knock on the door for us but the thoughts of him being in the car with us made me feel sick. The stress was building up in case I was wrong though and my kids were feeling scared again.

The next day we went to Alex's place to get him to phone the beast but he'd done a runner as well. We now had to search for him as well as the beast. We asked around the area and somebody gave us an address he might be at. We went there and the back door was open, his face was a picture when he saw us at the door. It was another dirty smelly flat full of drunks!

I said to him, "*if you never want to see me again and I'll be out of your life for good. I need you do something for me.*" He was scared to death because we'd found him again and said *"Yes"* straight away. I told him what we wanted him to do and he agreed.

He made the phone call and Tina said she'd not seen the beast for four days? We knew for definite then she was lying, as he'd only run away the morning before. We headed back to the beast's house trying to work out a way to expose him. The phone rang as we were driving, it was Tina; she'd dialled 1471 and got our number. Anthony pretended to be one of the drunks, saying that Alex had used his phone before going to the shops. It seems Tina was definitely as cunning as the beast because she didn't sound convinced at all to Anthony. Which meant we had to get to the house fast in case he ran away again!

We got to the house and parked up hoping he hadn't left whilst we were on our way but had to accept the only way to know for sure was by going in, which of course we couldn't do.

We were sitting outside the house for a couple of hours when Anthony said he couldn't take the pressure anymore and wanted to kick the door in. It was so hard explaining that we couldn't do it. Not after all the patience we'd shown so far and the assurances we'd given to the police. I've got to admit I had to fight my own impulses to kick the door in, because by this time I was getting so angry, frustrated and mentally exhausted myself.

About fifteen minutes later a guy walked into the small car park we were in at the side of the beast's house. He looked straight at me and then shuffled over to a wooden post in the ground. I was looking straight into his eyes and wondered if he could have been a mate of the beasts, that Tina may have phoned? He tried to move the post with his foot, which made me think he was looking for something to use as a weapon. I was getting on my guard and preparing myself for him.

He than crossed the main road to some bushes on the edge of another car park, I usually sat in and was mooching around looking for something? He bent down and picked up an old cobblestone hidden amongst the bushes and started crossing the road back towards us. As he got to the centre of the road he dropped the cobblestone to the floor. I thought it was strange until I saw a police van drive past him. He picked it back up again and ran the rest of the way until he was just out of my sight. In that split second I realised he didn't have a problem with us.

We then heard a loud smashing sound; he came back into view and calmly walked away with his mate who'd been stood on the corner. It appeared he was a disgruntled customer and had put the cobblestone through the bookmaker's window, right on the corner from where we were parked!

I turned and smiled at Anthony and said, *"Watch what happens now"* Anthony looked at me confused. I laughed and said, *"now the police will come"* and they did!! I needed a way to get the police there and it seemed my prayer was answered in a very unorthodox way, *"but hey it worked."*

I went up to the officers and told them what had gone on the last few days and explained why we knew the beast was in the house. At first they said they couldn't just go in and search because I thought he was in there but after a bit of nice gentle persuasion they radioed through to the station to ask for permission. The sergeant knew who I was, as did half the police force for the area at that time. So many times officers would stop and have a quick word with us over those many weeks. All the time just wanting reassurance that we wouldn't hurt him. They also knew they couldn't spend the time we could searching for a paedophile!! To be honest there seemed to be a lot of respect coming from the police officers. Everyone hates nonce's, except nonce's!! The sergeant said if John felt sure the beast was in there then yes they had permission to search!!

That was it, they were going in and once again we watched the back of the house for them, because they didn't feel the need to call for back up

We went back to the front once we realised nobody was coming out of the back door and stood outside for what seemed like a lifetime. The front door opened and the handcuffs were on the beast again, only this time his hands were behind his back and he wasn't being treated so gently. Not by these officers!!

We were over the moon he was caught at last! Believe it or not we jumped up and shouted, like somebody at a football match does when their team scores! Such was our elation! I can't describe the feeling I had knowing that this time he wouldn't be let out! How could he? He'd absconded twice! This time he didn't even look at us; the fear on his face was obvious. He knew this time it was all over! We taunted him whilst they were taking him to the van, letting him know what to expect in prison. The officers even gave us a few extra moments before saying, *"O.K lads that's enough,"* and bundled him into the back of the van.

They seemed as happy as we were, as they told us what had happened when they went into the house. They had looked around the downstairs first and then went upstairs. As they got to the bathroom, Michelle opened the door slightly and said they couldn't come in because she was having a bath. The officer said he had to look but she was insistent he couldn't come in. He then pushed the door open and there was the beast hiding like a scared rabbit behind the bathroom door.

We were all shaking hands and slapping each other on the shoulders, the euphoria of the whole situation was indescribable. The officer's radioed through to the station and simply said, *"WE GOT HIM. HE WAS HIDING IN THE BATHROOM AND WE'RE BRINGING HIM IN."* They jumped into their van smiling, laughing and giving us the thumbs up as they were driving off.

We sat back in the car with mixed emotions, elated because at last it was all over. I felt like a ton weight had been lifted off my shoulders and exhausted at the same time because of everything we'd been through to catch him. It was worth it though as he could have stayed holed up in his house for months, safe as long as he didn't venture out. That would have meant our nightmare could have continued for months! He'd added insult to injury with his cowardice; by not turning up for sentencing, for the atrocities he'd committed and worse he'd prolonged our agony even further.

We'd achieved all of this in a non-violent way and staying within the law, despite so much frustration and fatigue. But it was worth every painful second, to see the look on his face, as he was loaded into the police van!

Anthony said, *"Dad I'm buying you a pint. Come on lets go sit and have a drink in the gardens of one of those pubs, we've been searching the last few days"* The sun was beating down and it sounded like a great idea for a father and son who'd gone though so much together, to go sit and relax with a cold beer.

I then phoned Lillian and told her everything that had happened, she was so relieved.

We went to the pub and I went to the bar as Anthony walked into the gardens (looked like pops was buying the beer that he'd been invited for, ha.) I followed him out and saw a local bloke who lived not far from the beast. He called me over and we shook hands he then asked *"John is it true what I've been hearing"?* I told him it was and that we'd just found him. He said, *" John I'll pass the word on and get messages to people inside Strangeways prison. Just leave it with me."* He shook my hand again and we both looked at each other and smiled, because we both knew what that meant!

Anthony and I sat and chilled with the sun shining on us in the garden for a while and talked about how hard it had been on us the last few days. Only we could know what we'd been through together!

When I got home and saw the relief and happiness on my families' faces, it was better than winning the lottery! They cheered as we walked in; the little ones ran towards me and we were all hugging and laughing together.

How could so much joy be felt among us?

This man had abused so many and we were in a euphoric state. He'd caused so much pain and heartache to us all, physically and mentally, yet we were celebrating!

In a nutshell even he cannot destroy us, unless we allowed him to! We took his power back from him! That's what it feels like when you're down; you still give the beasts your life force. He'd still been dictating our lives as long as he was getting away with what he'd done to us. But that night we'd won as a family and he was on his way to prison for a long time and a life of fear for him. I would have loved to be a fly on his cell wall that night!

18.5.05
I have to admit to crying while I'm re-reading this last part because no words can explain the relief I felt and how important it was for me to catch him back then. In many ways I was a lot closer to the edge than I realised.

Chapter 5

Things seemed to go well over the next few days as far as I could see. The beast had been remanded to prison for five weeks, until sentencing, meaning he couldn't run this time and cheat us.

I just couldn't see what was going on in Lillian's head, she was slipping away from us emotionally but I couldn't see it. Her barriers were going back up again, the same barriers she'd always relied on as her escape route from pain and misery. She kept saying she was ok but she was trying to kid herself and us.

Whilst writing this part, I found a mental blockage on what was going wrong and had to ask Lillian to tell me in her words what was going through her mind back then.

These are her words.

Misery

Her biggest fears were, after seeing the mental anguish I'd been through, to get him put away. The realisation of how the kids and myself seemed to work together as one unit left her feeling she didn't belong. Deep down she'd felt he wasn't going to get a prison sentence for what he'd done to her and was worried at how it would affect me. She felt I'd lose myself and go seeking my own justice, which would mean only one thing; I wouldn't stop until he was dead. She knew I wouldn't be able to control my rage; the rage that had simmered below the surface for so long, would reach a point of eruption like a volcano! Where would that leave us? I'd be in prison, her brother dead and she would be left to cope alone with the aftermath. The kids would be devastated and she knew she could never cope with the blame directed at her.

The enormity hit home for her, of how unsafe the kids felt whilst the beast was at large, compared to how safe they felt the night he was caught.

She then took upon herself the full brunt of the blame. He'd abused her and she'd allowed him near her own kids. If only she'd spoken up, none of this would have happened and it was all her fault. How could we all still love her or even want her, she felt she didn't belong because she'd caused so much misery. She felt dirty, a slag just like he'd said she was all those years ago.

Also because of the vulnerability she knew he'd feel in prison, took her way back in time, to the brother he once was. The brother she'd loved. The brother who'd looked after her when she was ill. The brother she'd looked after when he'd been ill. The good times they'd shared before he became the beast!

The enormity of the damage he'd inflicted on her beautiful children, his daughter and so many other children seemed to be invading our lives again and it still wasn't over.

We were still surrounded by sexual abuse!

The thoughts of facing him again in court, after the other times she'd managed to feel strong and positive, she knew she couldn't do it this time. Whilst he was on the outside and had then turned up for court, he'd have been weak through drinking. This time he had time to think in his cell without the booze. She knew him and she knew he'd be strong again and would see her weakness and vulnerability! He'd still manipulate her, through eye contact; breaking her down inside. She was a mess.

She needed to run again! The kids would be better off without her! She knew I loved them and would cope! She felt we all deserved better. We'd all be better off without her!

She'd betrayed me in the early years and it kept coming back to haunt us; it wouldn't go away, we'd argue again, so that meant to her that I didn't love her! How can he love me? I'm a slag! It didn't matter that she'd been faithful for over twenty years. He'd said it and she believed him! She had to go, she had to run. She knew where to run to, she ran to her past. She ran to where she'd ran when she was younger, where she knew she'd be safe, safe from him, safe from us and we'd never guess where she was!

19.5.05

The last part you've read was written over three years ago and were Lillian's words, I wrote it the way she told me and based things on what I believed back then. I've chosen to leave it, as it was written to show how trusting and naïve I was and for you to form your own opinions as you continue reading. John xxx

One Friday afternoon I came home and she was gone, I'd come back to say, *"Lets forget about the past because its destroying us."* I was coming home to say so many positive things but it was too late. She'd gone again and left no word.

That night was full of mixed emotions for me. I was livid that she'd left again but worried in case she'd done any harm to herself? I knew things had gotten on top of us and deep down I think I'd known this was coming again. But once again she'd told me she was ok. And once again I was meant to be a mind reader!

I put on a brave face in front of the kids and tried to be positive, they were also putting on brave faces for me, we somehow got through the evening talking and watching films together, none of us giving away to the others how much we were really hurting inside. I kept trying her phone but as usual it was switched off. That was it. I'd have to wait for her to contact us. We all had to play the waiting game again.

The following afternoon Paige went to get dressed and found a note in her underwear drawer from her Mum, it had been there all the time. Lillian promised she'd be ok. And would be in touch with us soon, she just needed to get away on her own to think. About twenty minutes later my sister Sharon phoned to say Lillian had just phoned her and was very upset. She asked Sharon to ring me because she didn't want to speak to me; she didn't want me to try and talk her into coming back. So at least we knew she was alive and hadn't done anything stupid, which was a great relief.

I'd just have to be patient and see how things went; once again my patience would be well and truly put to the test.

She phoned the following day and I blew it. She wanted to speak to the kids but I wouldn't let her until she told me where she was. That was it. She just hung up and didn't switch her phone back on.

I was well and truly fed up by now; I'd kept the kids going all weekend and had to decide what was best for them. They too said that they were fed up with the way Mum had been, for a long time; they felt she didn't love them anymore and they'd also seen how much her behaviour had been grinding me down. She shouted at them a lot and didn't seem to be involved with them anymore.

This made me realise how bad things had been for a lot longer than I'd realised. I'd been fighting so hard and for so long against the affect the beast had had on us all but not seeing properly what was going on around me. I also began to realise how much energy I'd been putting into her and nothing had worked. I had to protect my kids and devote all my energies into them and if that meant letting her go, then I had to put their welfare and feelings before my own!

The next night Lillian's sister Janet phoned to say Lillian was on her way to the pub she managed. She told me Lillian was really upset and sounded terrible on the phone. Lillian also told her that she didn't want to come home. Janet suggested she let her stay at the pub with her until she'd worked out what to do? She said at least we'd all know where Lillian was and she could keep an eye on her. It seemed to be the most logical thing to do. I agreed to not come to see Lillian, as long as she at least phoned to give me some idea of what was going on?

Lillian phoned later on sounding really upset; she'd decided she no longer wanted to be with me. She came up with all sorts of reasons and excuses, she wanted the kids to stay with me until she'd sorted out a house and a job and when she had, it was then up to them if they wanted to go to live with her? No matter how illogical the things she said, she wouldn't back down and that was it and I had no choice. Other than patience (maybe patience should be my middle name) I asked where she'd stayed for the weekend and at first she didn't want to tell me but then she said she'd stayed with the ex wife of her eldest brother Stephen. The one place I hadn't thought of, she used to spend lots of time there when she was younger; she used to baby-sit at the drop of a hat back then. That was her safe haven from the beast and she'd make any excuses to be there. After all these years she'd gone back to where she used to feel safe! This is the devastation perverts create. She was forty-two years old but had returned to her childhood safe haven.

She visited and we had phone contact over the next fortnight, she even stayed over an odd night but her mind was made up. She wanted to make a new life for herself. Twenty-four years together and she wanted a new life?

Whilst she'd been gone both the kids and myself had enjoyed so much quality time together. I felt it could work out for the best if we did split-up. We could still be friends but no longer married. Once again I had to put the survival of the family before my own feelings of despair and the fear of coping on my own. I liked being married and loved the security of being with someone, no matter how crazy and sometimes toxic that relationship had become. Besides hadn't my Dad instilled that fierce family loyalty into me and here I was facing the reality it was all falling to pieces around me. As far as I was concerned there wasn't a problem in the world that couldn't be worked through and overcome. We'd come so far and she wanted to throw it all away and run.

By the end of the fortnight I felt much stronger and a lot more optimistic about my future as a single parent and started to make plans of my own for the future. That's when she wobbled! She'd already started to have second thoughts but kept them to her self. Luckily I felt it and allowed things to take their natural course.

She'd again reverted back to when we were first married; leaving home for whatever reasons and then wanting to come back. It was the same cycle all over again. Those damn cycles of self-destruction! She wanted to come home but didn't want to lose face in front of everybody, especially me. If I hadn't sensed this in her I'd have thought it was all over and was what she still wanted. I knew then that she needed time to get out of this mess gracefully. I also needed to make sure before we got back together, whether it was what I really wanted this time. So I backed off and waited. I was very relieved though, feeling inside that we may still have a chance to work through this, knowing both of us could be stronger and closer as a result.

I WAS BEING TOTALLY NAIVE ONCE AGAIN!!

Life Changing
This is the first time in over 12 months, I've been able to read this whole story and start to put together the last months of it. It's been too painful and there has been so much going on, this had to be left until I had the strength to face it once again. Although I've tried many times to pluck up the courage to re-start it, many times even managing to read some or change a few things in the early pages but it had to be left until the time was right. You have to imagine writing all this gut wrenching, soul destroying and heart rendering story whilst at the same time living it with so many other things going on, that it would take a lifetime to write and a lifetime for you to read.

But today is different and I have the strength to face those demons once again, because I feel love and am being loved wholeheartedly once again. Life is forever changing and today I want to grasp onto it with both hands. You'll have to wait until later chapters to find out why I feel love though.

Over the next two weeks Lillian and I talked on the phone, she even came over and stayed the odd night but still returned to Janet's the next day. Once again I had to hold back and try to be patient, once again I was making sacrifices I didn't really want to make. Forever the rescuer and fixer, forever putting others needs before my own.

Half way through the third week Lillian mentioned the girl's second weekend away to Blackpool was coming up the following week. This was a weekend that had been planned for months. She said she wasn't going to go as money had become a bit tight by then.

The next day she went to stay at Christine's. Later that evening she phoned to tell me that Christine had offered to pay for her and she wanted to know what I thought? (Massive question mark on who actually paid for that trip based on the lies told about how much money she'd gone through whilst being away.) Once again putting her needs before the kids and mine, I said, "*Yeah not a problem, it will do you good to go away again.*" Inside my guts were churning and my heart sank. How insensitive of her after being out of the family home for almost four weeks and then wanting to go away for the weekend with the girls.

She came to stay the night before they were going and although I really wanted to ask her not to go, I felt I couldn't do it, as she had to come to that decision herself or she'd forever blame me, for her not going. The next day she did all the food shopping for us and then got her bag to go. I was sorting the laundry out in the kitchen as she kissed my cheek and said goodbye. I watched her through the window walking to her car, willing her to turn around and say she wasn't going, praying she'd put us before herself, trying to convince myself she needed the break, although deep down knowing she was being selfish. My heart sank as she got into her car and drove off without even looking back.

The last time she'd gone to Blackpool we were a happy couple, phoning each other all the time, happy she was having fun and I felt really content with our relationship. This time felt different because we weren't that same solid couple and I had terrible premonitions of doom.

That evening she phoned to let me know they'd arrived safely, also saying as far as she was concerned, although she was away with the girls, she was still a married woman. It didn't make me feel any better inside though and I tried to convince myself everything would be all right.

Around 3 o'clock on the Saturday afternoon, I got an uneasy feeling deep inside. All through the rest of the day it was there and wouldn't go away.

She phoned me that evening before she went out but didn't seem her usual self and we had a disagreement over something or other. That uneasy feeling stayed with me until bedtime, by which time I'd decided if she was up to something, not only was it too late to do anything about it, I also couldn't change anything.

What would be would be!!

I phoned her on the Sunday morning and she sounded fine and said they'd had a good night and had just been down for breakfast. She said they were going out for the day and she'd see me later that night. She phoned around 7 o'clock to say they'd left Blackpool and she was on her way back.

I went to pick her up on the Sunday evening at Christine's and you could tell they'd both been drinking and were being giddy. She asked if we could drop Christine off at a pub in the opposite direction to the way we were going, for Christine to meet her boyfriend. I agreed but really didn't want to because I still had that knawing uneasy feeling, I was also feeling pretty worked up with a simmering anger.

They were laughing joking and being really loud in the car on the way to the pub. I was smiling politely but couldn't join in, which was unusual for me. We dropped Christine off and drove for about fifteen minutes before we hit the motorway. Whilst on the motorway she turned in her seat so she was facing me and said, *"I bet you think I've been with men all weekend?"* It seemed a really strange question to ask and even though I'd had bad feelings since the day before, I said *"no."* She just laughed and said, *"I bet you do."* I remember looking at her and she had such cockiness about her as she was laughing.

We got home and had a few drinks and talked a lot. All the time I had this nagging feeling, even wanting to check her phone, which was something I'd never ever done, or even thought of doing before.

We went to bed and were making love when she said, *"John, tell me to come home please."* I was taken aback because of the way she said it and the words she used *"tell me to come home"* and not something like *"John I want to come home."* I felt a groan come from deep inside me and couldn't believe I was hearing my own voice saying *"I can't tell you because you have to want to come home for yourself, I can't make that decision for you."*

As much as I'd wanted to be back together as a family, this deep feeling of confusion, pain and shock at my reaction overwhelmed me. Why? Why? Why?

Those deep-rooted, protective, sensitive and sometimes inexplicable gut reactions; inner voice or spiritual guides that we often dismiss, were at work again. We talked for a little while longer and then went to sleep.

The next morning I awoke and still had nagging doubts about how I was feeling, I got up washed, dressed and went downstairs. Her suitcase was still open on the hallway floor and her phone on the kitchen side. I had such a strong urge to look through her case. At one point I moved something in it before I realised what I was doing and stopped myself.

I made breakfast and tried to rationalise what was going on in my head, I could hear Lillian moving around upstairs. My eyes kept going back to her case and then wander back over to her phone, which was still on the kitchen side. I'd never checked her phone in my life but with saying that I'd never felt a need too! A voice inside my head said, *"go through the phone and you'll know once and for all."* Before I knew what I was doing I had her phone in my hand. The screen had been broken a few weeks before, so you couldn't see the numbers on the screen. I pressed the arrow down for the last dialled numbers and let the phone ring out, my phone started ringing and with a sense of relief my doubts started to lift. I pressed arrow down and rang out again, the phone was ringing out and a mans voice answered, I asked, "Who's this" his reply was "Terry" my heart sank into a bottomless pit, I was gutted and said "Hang on a minute" as I walked up the stairs. Lillian was vacuuming the bathroom, her usual penance thing of cleaning the house when she'd done something wrong, she'd done that all our married life. I handed her the phone and said, "Someone wants to speak to you" the shock on her face as she spoke into the phone asking who is it? She

106

panicked and said "Terry who, I don't know who you are" and quickly hung up the phone!!

That was to be the beginning of three days of torment, anguish, pain and lots of lies. It was also the beginning of the end for our marriage and even more upheaval, pain and torment for our kids. (What drove her to keep running and lying despite the pain it was causing everybody close to her)

I actually ended this part of the story at this point more than two years ago; maybe because it was so very painful on top of everything else we'd been through? Maybe it was to be finished when I finally got to the truth of the whole situation or as close to the truth as I'd ever get with Lillian. Either way it's the 3.5.05 and I feel ready to write this part now.

For a year before this whole episode and up to present time I've read a few books, mainly self-help books to do with relationships and co-dependency etc. One book that opened up a particularly new way of thinking was "The Celestine Prophecy." It was to do with coincidences, spirituality and power struggle dramas between people. That's why in a lot of the reading to come I will go on about gut feelings, fate and belief in God etc.

For so long my instincts and even bloody common sense were telling me one thing but my ignorance, gullibility and trust in Lillian, always overwhelmed everything else and I forever doubted everything I felt. In turn, believing whatever Lillian was telling me about whatever it was that bothered me, at that time. I have been a total idiot but in many ways. I was just a very trusting and naïve man/husband/father. Mind you, with saying that, how many of us have believed the person we loved, because we loved them and didn't believe for one minute they would lie to us??????

Anyway here goes

She denied everything and said she had no idea who this Terry was. I couldn't get his number because as I said the screen on her phone was broken. I pressed the arrow for the last dialled number and his phone was switched off this time. I kept trying again throughout the course of the day and eventually his phone rang out, he answered it but denied that he knew her and said he hadn't been to Blackpool for years.

Lillian said she'd fallen asleep on the coach and one of the other girls must have used her phone, which did sound like a reasonable explanation. I wanted so much to believe her but my guts and instincts kept telling me otherwise. We'd been here before, with things from the past. Lillian would swap and change stories and often come out with things that were so unbelievable, they seemed believable at the time!! Add to that my wanting to believe her, despite nothing adding up, made for a very painful and toxic relationship.

We were going over the same things for days and things from the past were getting dredged up too, we were all suffering again because the atmosphere in the house was terrible and neither Lillian nor myself were getting much sleep.

Christine phoned to try and reassure me that nothing had happened. She even got one of the other girls to phone and tell me that she'd borrowed Lillian's phone to ring Terry, because he was her friend. I was starting to accept the explanation until she slipped up and said *"John can't you forgive her, you've both been together for so long?"* I picked up on that straight away and I immediately replied, *"Forgive her for what"?* She then went quiet and said she had to go.

This had been going on for days until I eventually phoned Christine back to tell her I was going crazy over the whole situation. She understood by now how badly it was affecting me and said, *"put her on the phone to me John."* Lillian got on the phone and Christine told her to tell me the truth or she was going to.

I think what swung it was, when I said I'd find out where her mate lived and confront her in front of her husband, to find out the truth. Christine said *"you can't do that"* and I replied, *"well if this woman phoned another man on Lillian's phone and its caused this amount of distress to us, then surely the distress deserves to go to her"*. I was a bit cunning myself saying that but it had the desired effect because Christine must have believed me and then threatened to tell me if Lillian didn't tell me herself.

Lillian then told me she'd exchanged phone numbers with this Terry whilst they were in Blackpool but nothing else had gone on between them. They'd only talked in a pub and got on together as friends. She then came out with such a stupid thing. *"I can even prove I stayed in my own room that night."* That was it again!! So typical of Lillian when I'd be part way there to believing her, she'd then add something to it. All my barriers went back up and all the doubts came back into my mind!!

I have to be totally honest and admit that at times she'd make me feel I was going demented and I was so paranoid, it was unbelievable. But by now she'd been doing the same things with me for years and had got very good at it.

The only way I'm going to get this part of the story to come across with anywhere near the enormity of the whole situation, is to digress and go back to what had happened in the past, to explain why our marriage was spiralling out of control.

I feel sick at the thoughts of having to go back into my mind to those times because it was such a traumatic and volatile period in my life. I was so very close to going over the edge and having a nervous breakdown. Lillian at one point wanted to get me an ambulance to take me into hospital, because she said I was so paranoid and that she was telling the truth.

As this story unfolds you and I for that matter will see how conniving, selfish and so dangerously obsessed with self-preservation Lillian was. She would and still will go to any lengths and at the expense of anyone around her, to maintain her own self-preservation.

I won't be able to express how bad things really got, because you'd have had to live in it to feel the enormity of the effects. I lived it and still bear the scars of it all. In many ways it hurt me for a very long time and still does to this day but to a much lesser degree now.

I'll have to refer back to situations in earlier stages of the story, the only difference now is that I'm not so naïve, trusting and neither blind nor gullible anymore!!

When we'd first moved into this house and she'd told me things about the past. One of my biggest struggles was my quest for the truth, as I've said I was brought up to be honest and to worship the woman you love. I was the type of person that could have forgiven Lillian for literally anything, because I've always looked at the broader picture in so many situations and with knowledge gained would have worked through absolutely anything, to protect and maintain that the family stayed together.

Throughout the bad years when we'd come close to splitting up, we'd both agreed we'd stay together until the kids were old enough to cope with it.

Lillian would tell me things that wouldn't quite add up and yes those gut instincts would play a major part. I then got to thinking about the termination she had when we were younger? Lillian really started flapping then and would come out with all kind of crazy things about the times she'd slept with those guys and cover up the time of conception. She was constantly changing the dates and names around the dates.

In my mind I kept going back to the time I left her on the hospital bed and I'd just kept walking. I'd hated myself for so many years because of that and when you add the fact that she told me it was my fault she'd taken the overdose that may have damaged the baby? This in turn meant that she had little choice but to terminate. I carried a lot of guilt for a very long time.

Now I was starting to really question things, Lillian would one week say it was possible the baby was Johnny's and then another time it was James's? I'd then forgive her and we'd work towards moving on and within weeks she'd slip up and the whole story would be changed.

The worst story she told me was that she been raped and she thought the baby was the rapists. She went into great detail about leaving a club on her own and how she was grabbed from behind and dragged into some trees. She then came to and crawled to the side of the road where a man and woman helped her into a taxi. I felt so sick after everything we'd been through whilst trying to find out the truth and because I hadn't been more supportive. I felt so guilty for doubting her but once again my guts were churning and a few things didn't add up? Lo and behold she was talking so naturally about something else a few weeks later and slipped up again!! She hadn't been raped at all, she'd only told me that to get me to back off and gain some sympathy.

She'd gone into such graphic details about the lie I can't even bring myself to write it.

All the time she'd make up more unbelievable stories and as always, I'd forgive her. In the end she swore blind the baby was mine and time and time again I'd believe what she was saying, for her to slip up and change the story round again. As I said earlier, you had to be in it to feel it. It was such a crazy time of my life and my head was all over the place but I gave in and tried to accept I was wrong.

In between all of the chaos and crazy explanations for things that have been going on, for all these years, we had to also deal with everything to do with the beast, as well as the devastating effects on our kids and so many others around us.

As you can imagine its not surprising we were going crazy.

For me there could only be one real explanation for so many lies and that was there had to be a third person in the picture? Not only a third person but also it had to be somebody very close to me and that's why she couldn't tell me the truth! I then started to suspect my brother and my really close friends from back then, which drove me even crazier.

It would take too many pages, far too much time and far to much of my energy for me to cover all the stories that Lillian told me back then but you can imagine how it felt when she first came back from Blackpool and I found myself in a similar situation again, made even worse after having spoken to another man on her phone. As I said the same kind of bizarre explanations and stories were coming out and as always my gut instincts were telling me something else.

Back To The Blackpool Episode

She said that her and the girls had gone into a bar on the Saturday afternoon and had all got talking to a group of guys. She hit it off with one in particular because he reminded her of me and was so nice. She went on to tell me that him and his wife had split up because he'd had an affair with a barmaid. His weekend away had been booked for a while and although he and his wife had got back together, she was ok with him going away with his mates. I found that part of the story questionable? When they were leaving he asked for her phone number so they could stay in touch as friends? Once again that seemed odd because of what he'd already put his wife through and there he was exchanging mobile phone numbers with another woman.

She then told me the reason his number was in her phone, was because she phoned him whilst on the coach coming home, to tell him she was going back to her husband and would not be contacting him again. She then ripped his number up and put it in an empty cigarette packet.

I couldn't understand, if everything was so innocent why she'd had to lie so much about it and of course the being able to prove she stayed in her room really struck a chord.

For weeks my mind was tormented and for weeks I tried to make myself believe her, sometimes I managed it quite well and we'd have some really good times together. Other times I'd ask something quite innocent and she'd go very defensive and say she'd run away again, if I didn't drop it.

One night I snapped and told her I was going crazy and couldn't take it anymore!! She then said the very next day; she'd sit down and tell me the truth about everything. I wanted to know there and then but she said something very strange. She said, *"John I give you my word I'll tell you everything"* I looked at her and said *"Lillian you do know what you just said?"* She replied, *"Yes John I give you my word."* Giving your word meant everything to me and had for all my life. She knew that as much as I did.

I knew it was going to be bad but trusted her because she gave her word and I fell into a deep sleep.

The next morning she woke me up with a cup of tea and said she was going to the Market to buy Sean a pair of shorts for P.E, then to visit Elizabeth and she'd see me later.

In the cold light of day she couldn't face telling me the truth and she ran away for the last time.
Neither the kids nor myself could believe she'd done it again but she had.

In the last few weeks Lillian has since told me some truth about the whole thing but is once again still holding something back, because the odd time its come up in conversation since then, as always she backtracks and gets confused. To be a good liar it's important to have a good memory, unfortunately for Lillian she hasn't. Fortunately for me when it comes to things effecting my families' survival, I have!

It's not really that important to me now but I only really want to know so I can put a few old ghosts to rest in my own mind and hopefully find a little inner peace from the whole thing. Unfortunately for me only Lillian has all the pieces of that particular puzzle.

She told me she met Terry the first time she went on the girls weekend and it was my fault for making her go because she was going on self destruct (once again it was my fault) and because of that she did sleep with him!! They kept contact by phone for all those months. He wanted her to meet him again, the next time she went to Blackpool but she told him no!! She made the phone call I found out about to tell him she was going to come back to me and wouldn't be phoning him again.

Whilst re-reading what I wrote about her first trip to Blackpool and so many little things about that time, I have to be honest and doubt very much that she slept with him then, because of the things that were going on between us and the way we maintained contact whilst she was away. I think she did meet him then and they did exchange numbers and as always like the past there was someone else there for her to run away to. Lillian did what she did for her own reasons and it explains why she was so angry and ran away not long after getting back from the first trip. Once again those old feelings of guilt were eating her alive.

I think the time she ran away and told me that she stayed at her sister-in-laws is the time she slept with him. Once again there are loads of reasons for me to reach these conclusions but I have not got the energy or inclination to go into them.

In a conversation the other night on the phone she was talking about the termination and was so relaxed whist talking that she said, *"When I found out I was pregnant I went to my Mum's and worked my dates out. I knew then it wasn't James's, it was Johnny's."* She carried on waffling and then I stopped her and told her what she'd just said. She instantly went back into her old mode and started telling me I'd heard it wrong and what she said was this, that and the other and *"I never believed anything she ever said etc."* The saying is that the truth will out and it certainly did in that conversation because once and for all Lillian had slipped up and not managed to convince me she said otherwise. For once I don't have to question my own sanity. I heard what I heard and she said what she said.

Even though hearing the truth did hurt and I mean it really did hurt me! The upside is that I can finally stop blaming myself for the decision to terminate a baby. It was Lillian's decision because she knew it wasn't mine and that would have been obvious once he or she had been born. Lillian has to live with her own decisions and the fact that she told me so many terrible things, to make me feel so guilty, for all of those years.

I sometimes think she can convince herself of her own lies.

The reality of the whole marriage was this!! As badly as the beast's atrocities affected our relationship, it was Lillian's lies and betrayals that put the final nails in the coffin!!

With saying that I have to tell the story of how we came to be married to show how our marriage was also based on a lie.

One Sunday night we'd gone for a drink with Lillian's Mum to a pub that she used to like to sing in. Towards the end of the night Lillian asked if I'd remembered her saying she'd been in hospital as a child? I said of course I remember. She then said, *"it wasn't T.B, it was cancer and its come back."* I looked at her in total shock and the pain in my face must have shown instantly because I saw the panic on her face when she said, *"John its not true I was only joking."* I couldn't believe what she'd done and became a bit emotional and told her that in that moment of thinking she was going to die, had decided to marry her and spend whatever time left together. (how very noble and romantic eh)

That night and the following morning her and the beast's wife kept saying, *"Well you said you were going to marry me/her so you might as well get married anyway."* Like a fool I said ok then. Six weeks later we were married in a church and had a full reception afterwards. She took care of everything. What a great way to get married, talk about shotgun wedding!

Back To Her Leaving
We were all shell-shocked and as usual her phone was switched off.

Later that evening Elizabeth phoned me to say her Mum had contacted her, she was ok and would be in touch soon but she definitely wouldn't be coming back this time.

Once again the kids and I sat and talked all weekend, Sean told me that things had got so bad with him, when he came in from school and her car wasn't there, the first thing he thought was that she'd left again. This was no way for them to live their lives, with a constant fear that their Mum was going to leave them, or at the worst kill herself. I had to make decisions for us all and this time there could be no turning back. As scary as it was for me to accept, I had to really let go of Lillian this time.

Over the next few months' Lillian would call to see the kids and she'd do some cleaning and ironing for us, even staying over the odd night. She put her name on a housing list and got herself a job working nights. She'd even come over and baby-sat if I wanted a night out for myself, on her nights off.

We'd still have the odd fallout but all in all we got on ok and the kids settled into the situation nicely. Lillian did seem to be drinking a lot though but there again she always had. It's just that I hadn't looked too deeply into it.

Chapter 6

Final Sentencing Day

16.9.05

I can't believe with everything I've written about the chaos that was going on back then, I actually forgot to write about the beast's final sentencing day. Once again as with so many things in my life maybe I was meant to be write it now, as opposed to earlier. In fact there are a few additions that I feel I should make and maybe now is the time to add them all in together at this point.

Lillian was still at her sisters and had arranged to meet me at the courts with our nieces. I was driving from our house with my sister and picking our older kids up on route. It did feel really strange to not be going together and united as we had so many other times before.

The beast had been on remand for five weeks by this time, five very long weeks for him I guess. The night before court somebody had approached him in prison and asked if he knew my family and myself. He of course denied it because he knew what was about to happen next. I have no idea who the guy that approached him was but I did hear he wanted to double check he had the right person before he gave some prison justice to the beast. He left him with the intentions of catching up with him the next day though. Unfortunately the beast was to appear in court the next morning.

We all sat outside the courts. Lillian was sitting on separate seats with our nieces and I was sitting with my sister and our kids. The divide was so overwhelming for me.

Another group of women were sat further along and their case was being dealt with before ours. Lillian and Sharon had walked into the courtroom mistakenly thinking our case was about to be heard. The doors were shut behind them so they had to sit through the other case.

After a while the doors burst open and one of the women ran out crying and screaming saying, *"I don't believe it, he raped my son and abused our daughters and the judge is letting him go."* One of the other women and my sister followed her and tried to console her. Apparently the case had been plea-bargained because he was willing to admit abusing his daughters if the rape of his son was left on file! He raped his son and it was being left on file! The judge had sentenced him to Five years on the sex offender's role, three years probation and rehabilitation. The woman was looking at me with disbelief and I asked, *"Where is he from"?* She told me the area he lived in.

As I was walking into the courtroom the paedophile was on his way out, I leant forward and whispered in his ear "I know where you live and will be coming looking for you." He gave me a frightened look and scurried out of the courtroom. I had no intentions of looking for him but did often go into the area he lived in. If I was to ever see him on the streets I wouldn't hesitate to get out of my car to intimidate him and tell anyone who happened to be around, what he was and what he'd got away with. I feel very strongly that people should know if a paedophile is living near them.

We all sat down in the courtroom, myself and Anthony sat right at the front and as near to where the beast would sit as you could get. Lillian, Sharon and all the kids were sat at the back and to the right of us and as far away from the beast as you could possibly sit.

He was brought up to the room and looked straight at me; I fixed him with such a glare he was forced to look away and in front of him. I sat staring at him, willing him to turn around but he stayed focused on the judge. He had changed while in prison. He looked bigger somehow, healthier and it had to be said, so much younger! He really did, it was as if years had been taken off him.

The charges he pleaded guilty to against Lillian were read out aloud, his barrister then said, *"These charges were committed when the defendant was fourteen years old and he hasn't committed any other offences since."* I looked in disbelief because even though the other charges were either dismissed or left on file, both the defence barrister and the judge knew how many other times the beast had offended but had managed to wriggle out of it! There was me sat there, the father of six abused children, uncle to abused nieces and was hearing, *"The defendant hasn't offended since he was fourteen."* It knocked me sick and made me glare even more at the beast. I could hear Lillian sobbing behind me; I looked around to see Sharon hugging her and Carol who was also sobbing uncontrollably. The beast looked in their direction briefly and with absolutely no emotion looked away. I couldn't move to comfort Lillian and felt really guilty at the time but had to stay focused on the beast.

I wasn't really listening consciously to what the judge was saying because as far as I was concerned it was a forgone conclusion the beast was going away! Until I heard him say, *"I don't want any dramatics from the family when I read out my sentence."* I looked towards the judge as he looked away from me and at the beast. I sensed somebody behind me and turned around to see two police officers stood on either side of me. In that split second of the judges words sinking in and seeing the look on one of the officers face, I knew I wasn't going to hear good news. The officer looked at me and mouthed, *"Are you ok?"* I looked at him and nodded as if to say, *"I will be and you have nothing to worry about from me."* After all he was only doing his job and I knew how much the police hated nonces too!

I glared at the judge as he delivered his sentence *"I sentence you to five years on the sex offenders register, three years probation and rehabilitation."* It was exactly the same sentence he'd given the other beast! I stood up and shouted to the judge *"You must be a fucking nonce yourself to give a sentence like that."* I turned on the officers and they stood back and let me walk through. I was fuming and once again turned back to the judge as I reached the doors and shouted, *"You must be a nonce yourself."* He just looked at me and said nothing. The realisation sunk in of what I'd just done. I actually stood up in a court of law and called a judge a nonce and got away with it. He could have so easily charged me with contempt of court. Not sure why he didn't but I did think at the time, when I'm stronger it would be interesting to find out for how many cases of sexual abuse that particular judge had given paltry sentences out. Something I will look into in the future though.

Everyone was devastated at the time and I have to admit it is very much a blur to me now, I do remember optimistically thinking that maybe he would get a prison term in Sean and Paige's case. Unfortunately after them both giving very painful and traumatic statements, the crown prosecution decided to not proceed with the case because it could be said that I put them up to it! Can you believe that? As if two young kids could go into a police station and be filmed breaking down crying whilst describing in graphic detail what had happened to them. Add to that the fact I'd dated and written down everything they'd told me, as they told it to me over such a long period of time! Even the officer interviewing them said they did really well. THE JUSTICE SYSTEM IN THIS COUNTRY STINKS AND ITS NO WONDER SO MANY ANIMAL ABUSERS OF CHILDREN GET AWAY WITH IT!!!

(Going to add this part here now as well, which is my relationship with the other brother Alex)

Here it is very briefly.

We'd been business partners for a couple of years but as he started to make more money, he also started to drink more. He had a bit of a breakdown and his drinking got worse. He turned on me terribly and as the business was going downhill I dissolved the partnership and left him to it, (absolutely so much more to it but I would rather leave it at that.)

He went on to lose the business, his long-term partner and his home and ended up living in the squalid conditions that I've described in earlier chapters. Suppose its worth mentioning one of the things he did say to me once, which definitely gave me an insight into not wishing ill on people and what goes round comes round, because he said, *"I want to see you in the gutter with nothing, I will make a success of this business and will be up there whilst you are down there,"* pointing to the floor. Hmm not very nice words are they and it was him that ended up in the gutter and died a very lonely man.

At some point leading up to the court case against the beast I came up with the brainwave of getting Alex on his own and trying to get information out of him whilst taping him. One Saturday afternoon I set off from home to try it.

I traced him to a house in the ghetto. I knocked on the door and the people made him come outside to me, because they most definitely didn't want me coming in the house, ha!

I sat in my car waiting for him; he came limping out of the house with a walking stick (the ulcer caused by the injury to his leg after throwing himself in front of a car, was to later become infected and kill him.) He sat in my car with his legs hanging out. I'd already switched the Dictaphone on as he opened the door. I started to ask him questions but he didn't want to speak to me. I stupidly lost my temper and slapped him in the face. He then got out of the car and walked back to the house. They wouldn't let him back in because I was still sat outside. I was so annoyed at myself for losing control and managed to compose myself. He'd set off walking/limping towards a main road. I caught up with him and walked alongside him for a while saying nothing. He was trying to walk faster but couldn't. It was a football match day and there were lots of fans walking towards the stadium that was just down the road. I started shouting out in the street that he was a nonce, to anyone who walked past. The football supporters were looking at me like I was crazy. I suppose it did look strange to an outsider looking in. A few local guys walked up and I said, *"This is a nonce here and I want everyone to know."* One guy looked at Alex and said, *"Yeah, man could die round here for being a nonce."* He then nodded to me and walked on. Alex wanted to cross the road but there were too many cars, he then said, *"Please John, leave me alone or I'll throw myself in front of a car."* I looked at him and smiled saying, *"Go on then, can I watch."* He must have seen something in my face because he half smiled back.

I carried on telling all the football supporters what he was as he crossed the road to get away from me. I, of course, followed and as we walked into the estate, one of the local guy's I'd told minutes before came walking towards us again. He fixed Alex with such a stare and shook his head in disgust. Alex was really begging me by then. That's when I told him I wanted him to tell me everything he knew about the beast. Another local came riding up on a mountain bike. I could tell this one was a gang member. I stopped him and pointed to Alex and told him what he was. Once again it was the look that was enough and he nodded to me before riding off.

That was it; he'd had enough and offered to take me somewhere to tell me everything he knew.

We walked back to the car and drove to his brother's house. I switched the Dictaphone on again and let him regain his composure before asking if he'd been drinking. He said he hadn't, so I started asking him questions about the beast. He told me the beast had admitted things to him and even gave me a name I didn't know about. We were talking for quite a while and I slipped into the conversation that in no way was I threatening him, nor should he feel threatened to say anything he didn't want to. He was quite calm and actually said he was ok a few times. He also told me the beast had abused him as a child and he would willingly volunteer to give a statement to the police telling them about his abuse and what the beast had told him about the kids he'd abused. I had it all on tape and when he said he knew no more I switched it off and decided to leave. I then made a massive mistake!! I asked if he was ok and he replied *"I'm a bit shaky John, would you do me a favour and buy me a drink, my nerves are shot now."* I looked at him with pity and knew he must be rattling desperately for alcohol. I went to the shop and bought him a bottle of strong cider. I then went home to phone the officer dealing with Michelle's case to tell him what I'd done.

He came to see me and collected the tape and laughingly told me I shouldn't have done it. A few days later he contacted me to say, *"John you have stuck a stick into a hornets nest and I've managed to do a forty two page report on what you gave me."* He wouldn't say anymore than that at the time though.

The next day the officer called to see me to tell me the bad news; Alex had contacted the beast to tell him I'd been to see him and what he'd told me. They then went to see the beast's solicitor and he made a statement. Apparently because I'd slapped him and bought him a drink when it was all over, it made everything on the tape inadmissible. The beast walked on water yet again!!

I must say that as much as I loathed and terrorised Alex for what he was, the very last time I saw him it was such a weird experience. I was driving through the ghetto and saw Alex sat on a wall to the right hand side of me. I wanted information on the beast because he'd been moved out of the area and thought Alex might be willing to tell me. I pulled over to where he was and climbed out of the car; he looked up at me and smiled as I walked towards him. He didn't show any fear and the situation seemed almost dream-like. I didn't feel anger towards him.

I told him what I wanted and he was more than willing to try to find out for me, even giving me his mobile phone number to ring him the following week. He then told me that one of his mates had beaten the crap out of the beast a few months earlier. He had a broad smile on his face as he said I kicked him myself and told him what a bastard he was for what he did to me as a kid. You could tell by his expression it was the first time he'd felt safe enough to stand up to the beast! I even felt some warmth towards him, maybe that was the kindred spirit of the survivors in us connecting for a moment, who knows but it was real. I walked back towards the car and he bid me farewell and also added, *"Don't forget to phone me soon John, I'll find out where he is for you."*

I got back in my car and looked towards him, he was staring blankly but still had a smile on his face. In that moment all my anger and resentment towards him seemed to lift from me and I decided to leave him in peace and despite what he was, I would never bother him again. I'm so glad that moment happened because he was found dead the following week.

Part 3

Chapter 1

Marisa

2.5.05

The lovely Marisa, start of a new phase in my life.

One Friday night I went for a drink with David and a few of our mates to a pub where we knew the landlord. As we walked in I noticed two sisters I knew from my old neighbourhood. We got a drink from the bar and I sat down to talk to them. They were pleased to see me and we all hugged and kissed. They introduced me to their friend Marisa who was sat quietly with them, I said hello to Marisa and continued talking with Sara and Margaret. We were laughing and joking together but Marisa didn't seem to be joining in with the conversation. I felt myself looking at her more and more, trying to bring her into the conversation and before I knew what was happening we were both talking directly to each other. There was no cheesy chat up lines or anything like that, just a very relaxed and natural flow of conversation.

She was struggling to hear what I was saying at one point and came to sit directly in front of me. That was it, we chatted for the rest of the evening about our kids, past relationships and she was giving me advice about coping with being single, because I admitted having spent so long with one person, it felt very strange to me.

The whole evening passed in a total blur and it was only the next day that I realised I hadn't even been to the bar, we were both so engrossed with each other, our friends had just kept bringing drinks over to the table and were all buzzing to see us hitting it off so well, talking and laughing together.

At one point I sat back and looked at her arm and for the first time noticed she was a natural blonde, I then looked into her eyes and realised how truly beautiful she was. That was it. I was smitten. Cupid must have saved his longest arrow for me that night and got me straight in the heart. We exchanged phone numbers before I left and I carried on talking on the phone to her, all the way home and into the early hours of the morning.

I left it for a day or two before phoning to ask her out for a drink but she said she couldn't make it that night and would phone me back later in the week. She didn't call me back and I was gutted.

I was telling everyone I knew for month's, all about this girl called Marisa that

I'd met. I spoke to a few other women on the odd nights I was out but couldn't get Marisa out of my mind.

Almost four month's later Sara walked into the same pub that we'd last met in and came straight over to me, she said, " *John I'm so glad to bump into you, Marisa lost your phone number and has been saying what a nice guy she thought you were.*" I smiled and told her how gutted I'd been because she didn't ring me back. Sara suggested I phone her there and then but I felt it'd be better for her to give Marisa my number and let her ring me. Which she did the very next night.

We spoke for hours on the phone every evening, really getting to know each other over the following few weeks. I felt so comfortable I could tell her anything and I felt so happy and alive for the first time in a long time. She admitted she found it so easy to open up to me as well.

We spoke on the phone for three weeks before we even went out on a date together. My friend Peter was having a party and Margaret and Sara were going to it. We both agreed it would be a nice first date together, at least we'd both have mutual friends around us.

I was so nervous when I got to the party. Marisa sent me a text to say she was on her way. I got butterflies in my tummy. (I felt like a lovesick teenager all over again.)

She walked through the front door and looked absolutely stunning. As she walked towards me smiling, our eyes locked on to each other and I knew I was in love. We kissed on the cheek and gave each other a hug; we kept our distance for a short while but once we got talking the whole night was swallowed up again, oblivious to anyone else around us.

She later admitted she'd fallen in love with me whilst we'd been talking on the phone but was worried sick the physical attraction wouldn't be there when we met. I asked her what happened? She said, "*Sweetheart I knew the moment I set eyes on you.*" Those words made me feel so special after everything I'd been through, to find somebody who loved me for being me, was heaven sent.

We had a whirlwind romance and it was a wonderful experience. We'd go to all kinds of length's to see each other and sometimes we got to spend four and five nights together by shuffling our time around.

Marisa shared my passion for food and I loved cooking for her, she'd come over to my house on a Saturday night and I'd love to spoil her with good food, candlelit baths, soft music and as always we had great conversation. It was fantastic feeling, so romantic and having romance in my life again.

My kids took to Marisa straight away as she did to them. My kids were so pleased to see me happy and it was so very important to me that they liked the woman I loved.

I met Marisa's kids and got on well with them too, especially Aaliya her youngest daughter.

There was one person that wasn't happy though and that was Lillian!! Marisa was the one thing Lillian hadn't counted on!!

When I first started seeing Marisa I was quite content that Lillian and I had become friends and were both moving on with our own lives. I felt comfortable enough to tell her how I felt about Marisa and how happy the kids were with the relationship. At first she seemed ok but within a few weeks she came to tell me that she'd started seeing someone from work. I won't go into all the details of why he was unsuitable but neither the kids nor myself were happy with her choice of partner!! This put a lot of strain on the kids and no matter how much they let her know, how bad an effect it was having on them, Lillian was not prepared to give him up. She was determined it was her life and she was entitled to see whoever she wanted, despite how her children felt!!

I will say our opinions were right, because he turned out to be a junkie and got her into drugs as well.

Lillian got a house and moved into it but she seemed to be drinking more.

The kids would go to stay with her but she'd have friends round and they'd all be getting drunk whilst the kids were there. We argued because I couldn't understand why she had to do it when the kids stayed.

Eventually she lost her job because she failed a drugs test and was drinking on the job. After that she seemed to get even worse.

Marisa, the kids and myself all became closer and closer but Lillian carried on drinking and in turn would try to make our lives hell. We'd get abusive phone calls in which she'd call Marisa all the names under the sun and say she was going to hurt her.

She'd throw all kinds of spanners in the works to upset our lives together, which kept us forever on our guard. Marisa was a great support to the kids whilst Lillian was at her worst and was always there for them; emotionally she became a surrogate Mum to them.

No matter what Lillian did we'd bounce back and stayed close. Then Lillian changed her tactics!!

I stayed at Marisa's one Friday night and Lillian knew about it. The kids had Marisa's house number so I was able to switch my mobile off. We had a great evening together and were lounging around in bed the next morning, both feeling really happy and content. I switched my phone on and within about 20 minutes it started ringing, Lillian's number came up. I remember looking at it with a feeling of dread and really didn't want to answer it. I heard heavy breathing and what sounded like a tablet container being shaken and then the line went dead. I looked at Marisa and told her what I'd heard. I tried ringing Lillian's number but it was just ringing out. I had no choice but to go over to her house, to check she was ok.

When I got there the door was locked, I knocked and waited but nothing happened. I walked to the window but the curtains were drawn, next second the curtain moved feebly, then Lillian came to the front door. She opened the door and started to stagger and then passed out on the settee. There were crushed tablets on the table and a half drank bottle of Vodka. I phoned for an ambulance but was told it would take a while, I decided it'd be quicker to get her in the car and drive to the hospital because I was terrified she might die and was worried sick how devastating that would be on the kids.

While I was driving I was begging her to hold on. Her breathing sounded terrible and I had to take chances driving too fast and overtaking other cars on the wrong side of the road. After what seemed like a lifetime I got her to the hospital and she was rushed into a recovery room. She managed to get sick and some tablets came up. The Doctor took a blood sample to do a test to see how much of the drugs were in her system.

After about half an hour or so she started to come round but seemed a little bit too well recovered for me, considering what I seen in the house and heard on the journey to the hospital.

She started picking arguments with me, blaming me for us splitting up and for why she'd become the way she was.

I had a word with the Doctor once the results of the tests came back. He couldn't tell me anything because it was confidential. I'd suspected the whole thing was a set up and when I suggested that to him, he neither denied nor confirmed it but then again he didn't need too, because I already knew by the look on his face.

I believe she took enough tablets to make her ill and drowsy but definitely not enough to kill her.

She had to wait to see a psychiatrist before the doctor would let her go, I stayed until he arrived and gave him a quick rundown on our relationship and about the things that had gone on in her life. I then went back in the room to Lillian and told her I was leaving. She couldn't believe it and started shouting at me. I tried reasoning with her but she told me to get out and she'd phone her junkie boyfriend to come to the hospital. I knew I had to walk away for my own sake.

How could she have done something like that to me??

It wasn't going to be the last time though because a couple of weeks before Christmas I got a call on the house phone from Denise at about 1am (my mobile is always switched off at night time.) She said she was out with her friends and had got a call off her Mum. She said Lillian sounded drunk but was also acting weird and saying how much she loved everybody etc. I asked Denise to hold the line while I switched my mobile on; it beeped immediately to let me know I had a message. There was a message from Lillian saying, *"By the time you get this message I'll be dead. You'll find my body in the back garden because I don't want Paige or her friend to find me in the morning. Goodbye John"*

Denise said she'd get a taxi and meet me at the house as soon as she could. I raced over and tried the front door but it was locked. I went to the back gate and tried to open it but something was blocking it? I looked over and there she was wrapped up in a blanket on the other side. I managed to push the gate open and bent down to check for a pulse and tried waking her up but she wasn't responding. I managed to half carry; half drag her into the house and phone an ambulance. Denise turned up before the ambulance did and her face said it all when she looked at her Mum. She was disgusted and really angry.

When the ambulance men arrived I explained that it wasn't the first time she'd done this. They checked her out but she wasn't responding. Being honest they were well pissed off with her and gave the impression she might be faking it again. They asked if I was going to go to the hospital with her? I looked at her and as horrible as it might sound I had to say, *"No."* I felt that by going with her, I was giving her a licence to keep doing this to me!! Maybe by waking up to find that I wasn't there, would send out a clear message!! Also I had to get back to the house because I'd left Sean asleep in bed. He would have been terrified if he'd woken up to me not being in the house. Denise didn't want to go either because it would have meant waking Paige and her friend, for me to take them home. The ambulance driver understood and said he didn't blame us at all.

I did still worry about her but felt deep down that I'd made the right decision and at 6am had it confirmed. Lillian phoned and went mad because I'd let her go alone in the ambulance. She was so annoyed when she came round and I wasn't there. She said she'd phone her boyfriend again, to get him to come to the hospital to pick her up and then she hung up.

Christmas was coming soon; Marisa and I were making all kinds of plans to make it special, with it being our first Christmas together. We thought my kids deserved it with everything that had been going on with Lillian and the upheaval of the whole year. We shopped for everything together, I'd have been lost without Marisa's help, especially when it came to sorting out all the sizes for pyjamas and slippers I was getting for the grandkids.

We both decided Christmas Eve we would all go to the cinema together and then back to Marisa's for a drink and loads of eats. Christmas dinner was going to be at my house and of course yours truly was cooking. Christmas night my kids were staying with their Mum and Marisa's kids with her Mum. We decided Christmas night was going to be for us and we felt we deserved it.

We'd even arranged News Years Eve and bought tickets for us all to go to a local social club that was organising a family night. It was perfect, being able to enjoy the festivities of New Years Eve and having our kids out with us. Everything was arranged completely around a family orientated festive season and we were all looking forward to it.

On Christmas Eve the kids wanted to visit Lillian on the way through to Marisa's, which wasn't a problem, until we got there.

Lillian seemed fine and made out she was prepared for the first Christmas that she wouldn't be at home to see the kids open their presents. Her words were saying one thing but her face was saying something completely different, the kids obviously picked up on it, as did I.

It came time for us to leave and she hugged the kids and we all said goodbye, we'd no sooner drove down the road when Paige said, *"Dad I feel so guilty leaving Mum on her own on Christmas Eve and also her not being with us in the morning."* Sean then added that he too felt the same way. Paige then asked if we could pick Lillian up on the way back home and let her stay the night with us, just for this first Christmas. I couldn't believe what they were asking but had to admit I felt a little guilty myself. Paige started to get upset and cried and like an idiot I gave in and suggested they phoned Lillian to ask her and of course Lillian was over the moon and said, *"Yes."*

My real dilemma then was how the hell could I explain it to Marisa? I knew for a fact it would upset her. We arrived at Marisa's and all the kids were buzzing. She'd organised the drinks, sweets and food for later on when we got back. I could see and feel how much it meant to her, from the amount of effort she'd put into making the night special and how excited she was about it all.

126

After all, it was our first Christmas together.

I didn't know what to say about Lillian and decided to leave it until we got back after seeing the film.

We sat in the cinema like one big happy family. The kids were all chattering away and eating before the film came on. I remember looking at Marisa as she was laughing out loud, in that moment my heart melted and I knew why I loved her so much. I also knew how much I was going to hurt her later, when I told her about Lillian.

We got back from the cinema and everyone was still lively. We stayed about an hour or so before I took Marisa to one side and asked if we could talk upstairs. She knew there was something wrong immediately and when I told her the expression on her face will stay with me forever. I explained how it had all come about and although she could see it from the kid's point of view, she really didn't like me spending the night with Lillian in the house. I have absolutely no idea how I would have coped had roles been reversed but I can guarantee that I wouldn't have been so accommodating, or so dignified about it.

As we were leaving Marisa hugged me and said, *"watch her, I don' trust her."* She had such a sad look on her face as she was waving us off.

As long as I can remember we've always lit a candle just before midnight on Christmas Eve in memory of the dead and we've always had a toast to see Christmas in. It's always something the kids have loved and they felt grown up because they got to have a glass of champagne or an Alco pop.

We were running a bit late and were cutting it fine to get back before midnight. Paige phoned Lillian whilst on route to let her know we wouldn't be long and to make sure she would be ready to leave straight away. Lillian's phone kept ringing and she wasn't answering. I knew what the kids were thinking because the same thought crossed my mind, *"had she done something stupid and killed herself"*? We got to the house and were knocking on the door for ages before she opened it. She was drunk and staggering!!! She hadn't answered the phone because she'd fallen into a drunken sleep!!

She pointed to the table and said, *"John I've made a drink for you to let the Christmas in."* On the table were two glasses of Bacardi and Coke and she was insistent that I at least drank some of it. I took a swig from the glass and nearly spat it out because she'd made it so strong. The kids stood there just looking at her in horror. We hurried her up and all got into the car but realised that we'd never make it back to the house before midnight and had to light the candle in the car. Normally we set up the photographs of my Dad and Lillian's Mum next to the candle.

She'd even managed to spoil that family tradition!!

When we got back to the house the kids were fuming with Lillian. They looked at me and said, *"Dad we're so sorry we asked her to come now, she's drunk."* They were so disappointed in her and also knew how much it had hurt Marisa and were really sorry they'd suggested it in the first place.

Lillian insisted we had a drink together and I have to admit my stress levels were going through the roof and I needed one to calm me down. Things settled down and we all started to relax a little bit until Paige asked Lillian, *"Where are you sleeping tonight Mum?"* Lillian's immediate reply was, *"With your Dad of course."* I looked at her shocked and Paige said, *"Oh no your not!"* at the same time as me. Lillian burst out laughing and said, *"Why what's the matter with you, there's nothing wrong with us sleeping together."* She then told the kids to go to bed whilst we had a chat, which they did.

Lillian and I talked for a while about how we'd come to split up and I told her that I was very happy with Marisa and had moved on with my life. I said I'd bring a spare quilt and a pillow down so she could sleep on the settee. I went to my room to get them and guess who was sat up in my bed?? My Paige was sitting there and said, *"No way is she getting near you tonight Dad. I'm sleeping in this bed and she'll get the shock of her life if she comes up here."* I burst out laughing, there was my daughter protecting me from her own mother. I took the quilt downstairs and told Lillian that Paige was in my bed. Her face was a picture, especially when I suggested she might as well sleep in Paige's bed, ha!

The next morning we all got up and opened the presents as normal but things really didn't feel normal. We'd always visited our older kids and grandkids on Christmas morning, Elizabeth had invited Lillian for dinner, so obviously she was going down with us in the car and then the kids and myself were going back to our house to prepare dinner for Marisa and her girls.

Lillian was being so loud in Elizabeth's and started drinking again not long after we got there; I looked at her wondering, *"How on earth had I managed to stay with her for twenty five years"* and I couldn't wait to get away from her.

We arrived home and I got the dinner ready, Marisa came over and our Christmas began. We exchanged presents, took photo's and all sat round the table to eat. The whole afternoon was fun and laughter.

That night we'd arranged for Marisa's Mum to have Aaliyah and Marisa's eldest daughter Lauren was staying with her boyfriend and his family. Sean and Paige were going to stay with Lillian for the night, which meant Marisa and I had all the whole night to ourselves and we were really looking forward to it.

We dropped Sean and Paige at Lillian's and then carried on over to see Marisa's Mum. Marisa's Mum made us a drink and we'd just sat back to relax when my phone rang, it was Lillian. She said that the kids were going to be bored with her and they'd said they wanted to come home. I looked at Marisa and she asked what was wrong? I then had to explain what Lillian had said and that was it again, all our plans had to change because of Lillian.

I found out later from the kids that it was Lillian's idea they came home, because she wanted to go out herself.

As it happens we had a great night, Aaliya was buzzing because she didn't want to stay at her Nana's anyway. We ate loads of goodies and played games all evening, so it was a really family orientated Christmas evening on top of the day we'd already had. Lillian had said she'd have the kids over to stay on Boxing Night instead, which meant Marisa and myself could have our night at her house alone.

Lillian phoned me the next afternoon and asked if I'd pick her up from Elizabeth's and drop her home with the kids. Marisa had gone to drop Aaliya at her Nana's and I was to meet her at her house.

When I got to Elizabeth's, Lillian was drunk and started arguing with me. She'd apparently been drinking all night and day. She said some terrible things that aren't worth repeating. The kids and I got back in the car and drove off, after witnessing lots of dramas from her and her drinking partner, which once again aren't worth mentioning!! We just reversed the car and watched her and her drinking partner ranting and raving. It felt really sad for me, so God knows how it felt for the kids.

When we got home Denise who was nineteen by then, Sean and Paige insisted that I went over to Marisa's and have our time together, despite what had happened with Lillian. I have to admit that a great big part of me felt she'd done it on purpose, to ruin my night and so I decided not to let her. I didn't really want to leave the kids but thought I had to make a stand to let her know that I really had moved on and the kids had promised they were fine with it.

I went over to Marisa's and we had the most romantic night. We put a quilt on the floor in front of her living flame fire, candles dotted around the room and a few drinks, it was lovely.

Lillian did phone a few times to hurl abuse and threats down my mobile phone but I'd switched it off and didn't get the messages until the next day!!

I could go on and on about how many bad things have gone on over the last few years with Lillian but that would be wasting time and energy! I'd rather write about some nice things for a change.

Marisa stuck by me through a lot of things and for that I'll be forever grateful. It was nice to have somebody to back me up and help me to pick myself up when times were bleak. I had so many great times with her over the next couple of years and it was so nice to find someone who understood me so well.

We even managed to get away on our own for a few romantic weekends, staying in log cabins, which was something I'd always wanted to do and so glad I saved it for the right person.

I managed to get in touch with myself, my inner feelings and my real emotions, during our time together and realised the beauty of a real love. The kids grew with us and I feel it was really good for them to see their Dad in a loving, nurturing and positive relationship.

This must have been where I stopped writing the last part, more than eighteen month's ago.

It's the 5.9.03 and months since the last time I was able to come back to this. I even got a complete block on what the next stage was after last time. A total block and now I'm back to do this once and for all.

So much has happened these last 12 months it's a whole story in itself, a whole story!! Going to bring this up to present day and then drop back at a later stage to fill in the gaps.

Chapter 2

Bringing Up To Date

The last months have been really happy for the kids and myself in many ways. The beast and all he did hasn't been at the forefront of everything for a quite awhile.

But a nagging curiosity is often in my mind, what is happening with him? Where is he living? What is he doing? Nagging questions? Trying to be happy and move on with our life but always a nagging feeling holding me back slightly.

Two weeks ago Sean and I went shopping, as we came out of the supermarket we decided to visit my older kids before we went home. The funny thing was, we weren't supposed to shop where we had, or be on the route to Elizabeth's, that we were on. Who knows why or what took us where we were going, destiny, twist of fate, or maybe a higher power??

As we turned a corner I glanced to the left and saw two drunks sat on a grass verge. I'd already driven past but found myself turning the car around in a trance like state, pulling over to the wrong side of the road and not for one minute expecting it to be the beast, so sure it wouldn't, couldn't be him. Thinking in my mind that the two guys' will wonder what the hell am I doing. I even pulled slightly past them. The one sat to the left lifted his head and looked straight at me!! I couldn't believe it, it was he; it was the beast, the rapist and defiler of children, the beast that had caused so much chaos in so many lives. The sheep in wolves clothing and there he was looking straight at me!!

I was out of the car in a flash before it had even fully stopped, everything in one motion like in a dream. As I ran at him he curled into a ball on the ground screaming *"Don't touch me, I've just come out of hospital, please don't touch me."* In those seconds it took to be standing over the beast with him rolled up in between my legs and totally at my mercy, something snapped me back into control. Somewhere in my rational mind the realisation that I was opposite a police station and there would be CCTV cameras watching my every move, brought me back to reality and stopped me from turning into an animal and throwing everything away for my family and myself, by pulverising him to death.

I came to my senses as I was screaming at him, then grabbed his full bottle of strong cider, opening it and pouring it all over him as I'd done to his brother before him, the one I call the pervert, then I walked back towards the car still ranting and raving. I then realised Sean had got out of the car to see what was going on. He had no idea who was on the floor before us. I walked back towards the beast and again he was pleading for me not to hurt him, with pure terror in his eyes. I started to lose it again screaming at him for what he'd done, screaming and pointing Sean out to him, letting the beast know who he was and at the same time saying to Sean. *"Look at this piece of shit on the floor, you have no reason to fear him again, look at him begging for mercy, he is nothing, he is the weak one now and can never harm you again."* I asked Sean if he wanted to do anything to the beast. The beast was just staring, pleading, no longer the one with the power, no longer being able to intimidate and silence children with stories of aliens and monsters! Sean was now almost a man himself! Sean looked down at the beast grovelling and spat his chewing gum at him; he kicked the beast's empty bag at him and said, *"No Dad he isn't worth it, he just isn't worth it."* I was shocked in a way because he'd always said, if we ever came across the beast how he'd love to beat him. I'd promised I'd make sure the beast couldn't stop him. It was primitive thinking but it worked for him and kept him going for a long time and that was all that mattered to me. Here he was with the beast totally at his mercy and Sean was showing compassion and maturity. I was so proud of him for that, so proud that he didn't want to mete out street justice, proud that he saw the beast for what he was, as he told me later, *"A pathetic old man."*

People were walking past looking and listening to what I was saying. I turned to the drunk that was with the beast and snarled, *"Are you a fucking nonce as well?"* He looked scared and said, *"No."* I carried on, *"Well what are you doing with him then, he's a fucking nonce."* He looked at me, his eyes fixed on mine and replied, *"I didn't know he was one."* I calmed down a bit then, because of something I sensed from him and said, *"I'm telling you now, I want you to tell everyone you know what he is! I want everyone to know he's a fucking nonce and if you don't, I'll come looking for you too."* He said he would and turned to the beast with a disgusted look and said, *"Move, move away from me now and stay away from me."* For those few moments the beast was looking at the drunk with a blank but fearful look. It was either a please rescue me from what is happening look? Or the look of a beast being seen for what he truly was, within his little community of street people, being exposed once again for the monster and abuser of children that he was. The drunk then turned and walked away.

It was something in the drunks face that made me sense that plenty of people were going get to hear about what happened.

I noticed the beast had some old bruising around his eye and a couple of scabs that looked like they'd been treated with paper stitches. It crossed my mind that maybe that's why he'd been in hospital, he'd obviously been fighting or been beaten up by somebody.

I asked him where he was living and his reply was that he was living on the streets. He did look dishevelled but not enough to be living on the streets though and I have to admit that I didn't believe him but he did look scruffy enough to be living relatively rough, which I have to admit gave me some satisfaction.

A policeman came out of the station and asked what was going on, saying he'd heard me shouting from inside the station, the beast said under his breath to me, *"We were only having an argument."* Maybe in some way thinking he was saving me from the police? Who knows but by this time I was past caring about the police, or the justice system anymore!! This predatory animal shouldn't even be on the streets; he should have been locked up so he couldn't harm any more children. The justice system had let us down badly! Before I answered him, I sent Sean back to the car, as I didn't want him to hear what I was going to say next. I shouted at the policeman that this was a fucking nonce (slang for child abuser.) He asked, *"What do you mean?"* That was it I started to lose it again and screamed for him to stop asking stupid questions, at the same time telling him about my family and adding that I hadn't hit the beast. He asked the beast if he was ok and then told him to be on his way. That was it for me I walked away myself.

I drove around the corner to see the beast scurrying through some trees to get away from us; he kept looking back, nervously thinking we may follow him. I shouted out of the car window to him *"You might as well slit your wrists tonight because now your back in Manchester I'm going to haunt you."*

Whilst driving away my mind was replaying the scene and things my gut instincts had picked up on during the whole encounter. Firstly it was the blank expression as he lifted his head to look at the car that had pulled up in front of him, with no idea his worst nightmare was sat looking down on him, **"ME"**!!!! It was the look of a troubled and broken (can't bring myself to use the word man or person etc.) The recognition and fear in his eyes as I launched myself out of the car towards him, automatically curling into a ball and offering absolutely no resistance whatsoever. Nothing like the arrogance this animal had had for such a long time in the past. The cockiness and air of superiority had all gone. His pleading for mercy like he must have done so many times since the last time I'd seen him, I'd been told about a few beatings he'd had over those last few years. The word on the street always gets around. The way he just laid there as I poured his drink all over him, it was all so confusing.

Somewhere deep inside I sensed he was not going to be in this world much longer, a sixth sense maybe but he had the look of a dying man to me. I didn't know how or why I felt that, it just came into my head giving me a sense of hope, relief or whatever? And he'd go straight to hell for what he'd done and although he hadn't been punished by the law of the land, if there was an afterlife he'd have to face up to his sins and be made accountable for the horrors he'd inflicted, on so many innocent children's minds and bodies. But that's in Gods hands to decide.

We carried on to Elizabeth's discussing how rough the beast had looked and how powerless he'd become. In the back of my mind I was worrying how this encounter was going to affect my Sean though. Would he again start re-living his old nightmares? I coaxed him gently, for him to say how he felt but it seemed he just wanted to push the beast to the back of his mind. That in itself was quite scary but I had to respect his wishes, allowing him to come to terms in his own way but at the same time reassuring him I would be there if he needed to talk to anyone.

Once again having to keep quiet and try to guess what was going on in his mind, once again that feeling of hopelessness and having to stay a patient observer. I even had to question whether seeing the beast had done more damage than good for both of us?

We arrived at Elizabeth's to find Anthony was there and told them all about what had happened. They had a sense of gladness for what he'd become and in a way it felt like I'd exacted some sort of revenge for them, as well as myself. Again I had to observe and second-guess what was really going on with them with the mention of the beast. All in all they seemed to handle it well though.

The next two weeks I had mixed emotions, slightly angry with myself, as the macho man inside me hadn't beaten him up. A sense of pride because I'd handled it the right way and looked at the bigger picture, in turn not endangering my liberty and therefore putting my family before some caveman mentality. Lillian could never, in a month of Sundays, be able to meet the emotional needs of our children, if I went to prison. She had by then become a total alcoholic wallowing in her own self-pity, sewer type mentality and lifestyle.

The worst of all was the feeling of being tainted by his very presence back in my life and mind, the wanting to go looking for him, wanting to keep reminding him I was still around and haunting him. I've a gut feeling those thoughts have seldom been far from his mind, the thought of me turning up one day and not being to show the same self-control, I'd had, on so many occasions before. I really hoped that had been so, him living in fear of me and his past catching up again to haunt him.

There were also a couple of other coincidences that struck me and felt quite strange. Firstly the place the beast and the other drunk had been sat, was the same spot that had once been a street many years ago, where the beast had lived as a child with Lillian. There is still a street sign but it is now a council work yard. The second was that it was around 25 yrs ago give or take a day

(I don't know the exact date) that I'd actually met the beast for the first time in his grubby flat when we'd gone to pick Michael up. Adding both of these coincidences to the chances of him and us being where we met, does raise a few questions to fate and destiny theories. It does seem very bizarre to me though.

Two weeks later I went shopping to the same supermarket and upon leaving found myself being driven to go looking for him again. I couldn't help myself, even though I knew the chances of bumping into him again were slim. That old hunger was back, a hunger that had been suppressed for such a long time, that avenging angel syndrome! It frightened me because I didn't want to risk becoming out of control. In a way it had started to feel like I'd have been better off not having bumped into him at all. I'd managed to start this new life with Marisa, leaving behind as a distant memory so much unresolved anger and pain. The kids were doing great, so many things had been going well for us, after the troubles and traumas we'd all been through these last twelve month's or more but now the beast was back in our lives.

The next night I got a phone call that was going to change everything for us all, especially me.

Denise rang me to say her Mum's sister Janet had received a phone call from one of her brothers, saying the beast was in hospital, after having had a blood clot removed from his brain but he wasn't responding after the operation. I could hardly contain myself and as bad as it may sound I was glad. I felt that my prayers had been answered and at last the beast was being punished properly. I phoned Janet myself to find out what was going on but she wasn't quite sure of everything herself and said, *"to be perfectly honest John he died in my eyes a long time ago."* She wasn't interested in anything about him but she gave me Neil's number to find out more for myself.

I rang Neil, trying to hold down how I really felt about the whole thing; after all, the beast was still his brother. Neil sounded tired and not really interested in the whole thing either. He did say his son was going to pick him up later and take him to the hospital to find out more and he'd let me know what was happening when I rang him back.

That was it, more time hanging around waiting for news, it was so frustrating!! I was like a cat on hot tin roof, trying to make the dinner, trying to appear calm in front of the kids but inside I was elated that at last something had happened to him. Hoping he might be out of our lives forever on a physical level, although mentally the beast would be around forever with the damage he'd done to so many people.

By pure chance Michelle had left a message on my answer phone only the day before saying she'd signed on at a police station and she was going to attend court that day. I knew it was going to be up to me to let her know about her Dad. I also knew that it would devastate her because no matter what he'd done to her and how miserable her life had become as a direct result of all those years of being abused, which in turn had been responsible for her addictions to drugs and the terrible lifestyle she now lived, he was still her Dad and she loved him. There was no point in trying to contact her until I knew more though but thinking it might only be a matter of a couple of hours before he may die, it concerned me to let her know as soon as possible.

Then something suddenly dawned on me. *"What if something had happened as a result of violence?"* The police had told me a couple of years before that if anything happened to him, I'd be the first person they'd come to as a suspect. The bruising on his face, flashed into my mind and could the blood clot be as the result of an old injury? Or could it be he'd been beaten up again that day? All these things started to play on my mind, also thank God I'd had the control to not hit him the week before, I could have found myself up on murder charges. The thoughts of being dragged into this were starting to scare me a bit. I knew I had nothing to do with it but would the police believe that I hadn't? Especially after the anger I'd shown outside the police station the fortnight before. Had my car registration been taken by the officer that came out? If so, they'd know it was I, behaving like a madman that night.

The waiting was getting to me so I had to phone Neil again. He answered the phone but hurried me off saying he was just going in and hung up. I then started to get paranoid thinking maybe he thought I had something to do with it? Some of the elation I'd been feeling was now being replaced with fear.

I phoned again an hour later and Neil apologised to me and explained he was just being taken into see the beast as I'd phoned him. I felt a bit relieved and tried to sound genuinely interested and concerned as to how the beast was.

The beast had apparently walked into the hostel, the eldest brother Stephen lived in and collapsed, he had a nasty black eye as well. My mind was ticking over at that point again wondering how it may all affect me. The people at the hostel called for an ambulance to take him to hospital. Neil got the impression that the doctors wanted to find a family member, to give permission to turn the life support machine off. He said he didn't want to get involved and if that was the case it was something only Michelle should do and not anybody else! He didn't want to be involved with Michelle and was very grateful and relieved when I said I'd take care of that side of things, which was good from my point of view as it gave him the impression I was doing it for him, when in reality I was doing it for Michelle and her alone. I also felt it would keep him open for finding out information and keeping me informed of what was going on

I started to relax a bit as well, working out it was probably a fellow alcoholic that had given him the beating and the police would hopefully assume the same. Although I was still scared that things could come back at me.

I contacted the police station that Michelle signed on at and gave the officer at the desk all the information for her.

The next night she phoned and was really upset over what had happened to him, she said he looked so peaceful lying in his bed and all the creases had gone from his face making him look young again. I felt guilty because she was so upset and all I could think was, *"how long before he dies?"* She then asked me to come to the hospital to see him. I couldn't believe what I was hearing and had to explain that it wasn't a good idea and as much as I loved her I just couldn't do that for her. She sounded so childlike but seemed to understand how I felt.

Chapter 3

A New Phase

Well once again it's been a long time since I added anything else to this story, which seems to change all the time. It is now 12.30 pm on the 31st of December 2003. 2004 is only hours away. A New Year and a new start and for me and it's the start of putting an end to this story.

I've come to realise that the biggest factor that's kept me away from finishing this book is, as much as I want to, I have to finish this book, for a thousand different reasons. It's not lack of time, motivation, tiredness and a dozen other different reasons, that the mind can con you into believing! The reality is a small word which creates such a massive impact on everybody's lives, whether we realise it or not, that word is "FEAR," yes fear!! The fear of taking myself back into the world of pain, that my sub-conscious mind has been trying to protect me from, without me even realising it.

I've read somewhere that the sub-conscious mind is the biggest liar in the world with its duty to protect us from all manner of dangerous things and situations. Mine has done a really good job doing just that but now its time for my conscious mind to override the sub-conscious and face my demons once again. Yes those demons that chip away at your mind and life, even when you don't realise they are doing it.

You have to understand, that for me to open my mind again to the reality of what went on in my families' life, is going to be very scary and hard to do, because to put everything across in a way for you all to understand and even to feel a fraction of the pain and reality, means opening ME up to a whole heap of pain and I must be crazy doing it on the eve of a New Year. But there again, for me to continue on this journey that I took when starting this book, it has to be seen through to the end regardless of any pain that I'll feel.

This story has to be told and read for me to continue on the path I chose to follow a few years back, people have to know the devastation that can ensue, when a deviant predatory bastard decides to follow his perversions, with no conscience, feeling or cares for the pain and suffering he will create in so many people's lives. This is made even worse by the fact it happened to him as a child and him knowing how it affected him! IT is the few words that at this moment are so hard to say but say them. I must, feel them. I must and those words are, *"CHILD SEXUAL ABUSE" "CSA"!!* See the fear of saying it out loud in my conscious mind was there but once said it wasn't so painful. That's something else for me to learn, the fear of fear itself is what's really holding me back all the time.

That animal killed off so many childhood dreams and shattered so many childhoods, to pursue his filthy perversions and all under the guise of a caring uncle, brother and brother in law and in the meantime pulling the wool over so many adults' eyes and particularly mine. *"Oh how fucking stupid, naïve and trusting was I?"*" Despite so many red flags over the years, that's been my cross to carry and will be forever and a day. It's all up to me how long for and how heavy my load.

I have to use what I've learnt to put into something positive, i.e. writing this story, training to be a counsellor, so I can work with families that have suffered the same traumas as mine and hopefully writing a follow up, filled with positive things about myself, family and how we all came through this and survived.

Because SURVIVORS WE ARE!!!

I'm going to end today's writing with the positivism it was started. I've just rang Marisa and read out what I'd written today. That's when the lump appeared in my throat and a few tears flowed, regardless of how hard I tried to stop them. Seems another lesson just learnt is, *"it doesn't hurt too much writing but the reading out aloud for someone else to hear, is the real killer."* Just maybe knowing somebody else is hearing, sharing or reading my pain as well.

*I started to date my writing from this point on, which is something I wish I'd thought to do from the very beginning. The dates may jump around but it is only when I added something or my own comments.
I am seeing from how I was writing, that once again I was quite close to the edge but as I say, *"try walking in my shoes these last years and I wonder how many people would have stepped over the edge."* *

Saturday 3/1/04 1.23am
Not exactly a good time to be writing this before going to bed, once again the fear tried to stop me, telling me that I shouldn't be facing demons before going to bed, my mind might open up, in turn allowing all kinds of things to haunt me as I try to go to sleep. Unfortunately this has been the only time I've had to do this and the other thing is FUCK THOSE DEMONS!!!!!!!! I'll face the bridge of not being able to sleep later.

3/5/05
*As you may have noticed I was a little angry when I wrote that last part, having re-read a lot of this story now, its made me realise how much of an angry man I was for so very long. It's hard to believe in many ways for me because of how different my life and I am now. With saying that though, *"I couldn't be who I am today, if I hadn't been who I was yesterday"* and who wouldn't be angry after what we went through? *

After a week or two of uncertainty and the mixed emotions that were spread throughout the family, we all became content in our own worlds that before long the beast would either die naturally, or the life support machine would be switched off.

Lillian was the only one it seemed to affect badly. I heard that she'd started hitting the bottle harder and had even phoned work saying she was too upset to come in because her brother was dying. I did find it confusing but tried to understand why she was behaving like that. I suppose a part of her was grieving the loss of the brother he was and the closeness they'd shared a long time ago, before he turned into a monster and the beast that he became!

Lillian did try speaking to me on the phone about how it was affecting her but I had to shut her out of my mind and feelings. My top priority was my kids and how it was affecting them. Lillian had already caused so much devastation in all of our lives and I couldn't afford to be dragged into her new drama, over her perverted brother. I didn't admit as to how much all of this was affecting me as well, watching for signs from the kids and in a crazy way even scared that if he did die, could he have enough evil in him to haunt us in some way. I apologised to Lillian and said I could understand her to some degree but I had the kids to concentrate on and had to look after their needs. She seemed to understand and didn't try and unload anymore on to me at that point.

She had her new circle of drinking buddies as far as I was concerned; she was going to have to rely on them for any emotional support that she needed. I knew then I'd passed a major milestone within my own recovery, because I hadn't automatically jumped into my role of rescuer for Lillian, my co-dependent behaviours of the past were at last diminishing and I really knew deep inside me, that something had finally changed.

The older kids couldn't understand why it was affecting her so badly either and they too couldn't offer her any support.

Time went by and Michelle hadn't called me back, which troubled me every now and then. I kept assuming she'd fallen out with me for not meeting her at the hospital on the first night she'd found out. Lillian's brother Neil hadn't rung me to let me know anything either.

Looking back I can recognise the fact that my fears stopped me from following things up, It also has to be said that life was rolling along nicely, chaotically as always but a totally different chaos than that of the past. Christmas was around the corner and we were all making plans for it. We all wanted to make it extra special this year because of the chaos and hurt that Lillian had caused the year before.

Lillian dropped a bombshell on me one morning about 4-5 weeks before Christmas. She said, *"The beast had been coming into her mind a lot around that time and she'd phoned the hospital but they'd told her that they hadn't any record of him being there"?* My head started spinning and going a hundred miles an hour, replaying what people had been saying around the time we'd found out and I was struggling to make sense, because of all the things I'd been told by them. Then the penny dropped, *"which hospital had she been phoning"?* I asked and she replied, *"the Royal Infirmary."* My mind came back from space, when I realised and explained it was Hope Hospital he was in. She then said she'd follow it up the next day and I was content to let her, as I felt she should be the one to enquire about him, again being honest with myself I felt a knawing fear deep inside again.

She hadn't called me back for two days and I'd realised she'd obviously changed her mind and rang her; she said she would phone Neil straight away, as she thought he'd know what was going on. She rang me back and dropped the bombshell; the last Neil had heard was about a week before, *"the beast was making progress and why was she so interested all of a sudden?"*

What was I hearing, it couldn't be. How could he??? The doctors had said if a patient didn't recover after the first four days, then they wouldn't. He was brain dead, there was no signals coming from the brain etc? Then I remembered something that had confused me weeks before when Michelle had said, *"he is breathing for himself."* If he was breathing for himself then surely the brain was working to some degree. I knew I'd felt it at the time but had chosen to ignore it and I'd tried not to read too much into it because it was taking me away from my hopes that the beast was finally on his way out. How foolish I'd been once again relying on information from other people, once again not following things through myself and finding out for sure what was going on.

What an idiot, a scared idiot I'd been, too scared deep down to visit the hospital pretending to be a concerned relative. The doctors and nurses wouldn't have known the loathing I had for the beast. They wouldn't even be aware of what a monster he was. FEAR, FEAR, FEAR and wishful thinking again that things would take their own course and I could once again bury my head in the sand. It was almost Christmas and I couldn't let the kids know, what could I tell them, *"Oh by the way the beast is making progress,"* after I'd assured them he was on his way out, like I'd assured them he'd go to prison, assured them we'd get justice. Come to think of it I was sure of a lot of things concerning the beast and was so very wrong so many times.

5/1/04

Once again it seems the devil protects his own and it certainly seems the beast gets through a lot of scrapes, or of course the reverse could be true, the flip side of the coin and in reality the beast has suffered an inward pain, a form of dying slowly, maybe. Hmm I sense definitely the life of fear! I can still see the fear in his eyes, thinking back now to our last chance encounter. I'm starting to feel a little more optimistic with that thought.

What if in reality the reverse is true? What if in reality while in his comatose state his mind was really full of torment, memories flashing through his brain day in and day out? What if this really was just another form of his punishment of his life on earth? I don't know what progress means, it could mean so little progress in his recovery, what might his level of recovery be? What will his quality of life even be?

There's only one way to find out and that means me plucking up the courage very soon to find out. I have to weigh up all the pro and cons of that one first, or being truthful finding the guts to do it! Stop making excuses to avoid it! Such a small thing to do picking up a phone to ask a few questions but in reality a massively daunting thing for me to do, again the fear factor!! Tomorrow is another day so they say.

Thinking back, so many people wanted to do the beast damage in the early days of finding out. One guy who I'd only met once was begging my friend to give him the beasts address, he wanted to knock on the door and start cutting him up, this my friend assured me he was capable of doing, without even batting an eyelid.

Another guy came out with a statement of wanting to sew a rat up his arse. I think he was only saying that at the time but he again wanted to damage the beast. So many others had heard and wanted to do something. It would have been so easy to be in a crowded room surrounded by witnesses whilst he was severely damaged or even killed. One of the things that really stopped me was the thought of him prospering from it, by getting money from the criminal injuries board. I wouldn't let anybody near him, or give the go ahead. And now this is what would probably happen, he'd get a big payout and be on disability for the rest of his life and happy to feed his addiction to the booze daily.

Now I'm being pessimistic and must find out for sure.

*I remember this next part so well and wrote it as I felt at the time but once again so very close to the edge. *

6/1/04
Feeling sick and short of breath, had to open all of the windows in the house, as there is a smell about. Feeling like I have to cleanse the house with fresh air, cleanse me. The wind is picking up and blowing a cold draught on to my head,

don't much care at the moment; even if I have to sit here with a hat on. I need the air to blow through the house.

The moment picked itself earlier today. Lillian had asked me yesterday if I'd phone to get an appointment with her doctor for her. I too needed to see my own doctor as the eczema on my face and head, seemed to be spreading and getting worse lately, stress related, even though I don't seem to feel stressed much at all, inside I obviously was.

I made both calls and then picked up the yellow pages, not expecting the hospital the beast was in to be covered by my area. I was wrong there it was in black and white right in front of me. What do I do now? I had to go shopping first and then make the phone call later my mind told me. Can't make the call and then go about my day, I told myself. I just sat there, staring feeling a bit sick for a few minutes, then I decided to just go for it.

Coughed first, then my eyes seemed to get a film over them blurring my vision, I couldn't even see the numbers, that's it, leave it until later I told myself. I cleared my eyes and thought again for a second. No it has to be done now or never, as I took the phone off the receiver mechanically punching in the number that I could now see as clear as day. It started to ring and I took a deep breath thinking of what I could say. Would I get any information if I said I was his brother in law? Saying brother in law made me want to vomit. What if they tell me he's already been discharged?

The phone rang forever, for so long I thought I'd misdialled or the number must have been changed, wanting to put the phone down because it was taking too long. Surely it's a sign, that now is not really the right time to make this call, feeling sick and oh so nervous inside. All the time reassuring myself that now is the time and if I have to wait minutes with this phone in my hand, sooner or later somebody would answer it, they had to, it was a hospital for God's sake. Then a voice answered and that was it. I went into auto pilot trying to sound like a concerned relative and said *"Hello I've just come back to Manchester to visit some friends."* (Couldn't say family in case they got on the fact family would or should have already informed us? Ready with an explanation that my wife and I have no contact with her family normally,) *"and have been told that my brother in law has been admitted to your hospital."* (Really trying to show concern in my voice at that point.) Then I had to say his full name to sound more authentic. I held my breath and waited for her reply, a little voice inside trying to keep me calm, another voice saying, *"he's been discharged and you don't really need to know all this, what's the point in keep dragging it up?"* Her voice came back to me saying, *"Yes he is on one of our wards I'll put you through now."* Once again trying to compose myself to say the same things, only this time it would be the nurses I'd be asking, the ones who'd been looking after him. What if he'd told the staff if I phoned, not to tell me anything? (I was getting paranoid now.) What if my saying brother in law wasn't a close enough relative? Had to counteract that one by saying my wife has had a breakdown and can't ring for the information herself, would that swing it?

Once again a voice came through the phone line to me and again auto pilot kicked in, *"Hi I've come to visit friends and have been told my brother in law has been admitted to your hospital, somebody said he'd been beaten up."* She told me that he was with them but she had no idea of the patient's condition. Is that it? My mind was saying, is that as much as I can get out of them? Is this as much as I was going to find out? I then heard myself asking, I hadn't consciously thought it but it was my voice, I could hear calmly and politely asking *" Is there anybody else there who could tell me how he is please?"* She replied, *"Well I could go and ask one of the nurses for you."* I wasn't even talking to a nurse. *"Thank you very much I'd appreciate that."* Once again knowing I'd have to ask one of the nurses closer to him.

The nurse came on and again I asked the same questions trying to show concern, then came the bombshell I was dreading, *"Yes he's fine, we have a meeting on the 14th of January to discuss how we are going to discharge him but he is up and walking around."* Then I was starting to get a bit fuzzy. *"I was told he'd been beaten up and had a blood clot removed form his brain."* She replied, *"You can come and see him on the ward if you like."* *"So he's able to talk then?"* I asked. *"Oh yes he can talk but you can visit him yourself between 2-8 pm."* I could tell she wasn't going to say anymore and to have asked anymore, would have been suspicious, so I said, *"I'll have to come down to see him then, thank you very much for your time."*

Putting the phone back on the receiver, my head was once again spinning. I wanted to get sick. "HE'S BEING DISCHARGED! YES HE'S WALKING AROUND! YES HE CAN TALK!" None of this was what I'd wanted to hear!! Then my brain snapped back and replayed something she'd said, *"He is going to be discharged but we have to decide where we are going to discharge him to."* What does that mean? Sounds like he hasn't made a full recovery, or could it mean that as he was homeless they had to find some accommodation for him. Still so many more questions needing to be asked and answered.

Why is it when it comes to the beast there are always so many question, so many questions that only he has the answers to?

I just had to go downstairs for a glass of water, the house is freezing and it has numbed my head and face as I was going down the stairs.

The smell has gone and that clammy stifling atmosphere has also gone. It feels fresher but so cold. I've switched the heating on but I can't bring myself to close the windows yet, even though my fingers are going numb with the cold.

Struggling to type now as well, its odd but I hadn't noticed before, I'd got up to get a drink, how cold it really was.

(Must have been trancelike whilst typing this, haven't even checked anything I've typed yet either, just kept pummelling the keyboard. There will be plenty to correct, I think.)

After a few minutes of sitting there, playing everything through my mind, I decided to just go shopping and work out what to do later. On deciding, a thought sprang into my mind, *"Only one thing for it, I'm going to have to go visit him. I have to find out for myself what state he's really in, it's the only way I'm going to know."* But that thought filled me with dread.

I had to get out, had to get away from the house, had to go and do something. I felt numbness all over me whilst driving, even after getting out of the car and walking amongst people. I felt like I was in a world of my own, trying not to dwell too much or even think about the phone call too much but the voice in my mind kept saying, *"You'll have to go and see for yourself."* I knew it was the only way to find out for sure,

"I WILL HAVE TO GO AND FACE THE BEAST ONCE AGAIN"!!

I've faced him so many times, so many times had him by the throat or intimidated him. Why oh why does it feel so different this time. Could it be that my mind had accepted he was going to die and that was it for him. I'd never have to see him again. What has happened to me, that I feel so much dread and fear lately?

I walked around the supermarket picking things up, looking at people and thinking, *"they have no idea what is going on in my head."* People just going about their business and me like a zombie trying to hold myself together.

I bumped into an old friend of mine, a friend I'd known since I was 7-8 years old. Normally I'd have shaken his hand wishing him a happy new year etc. Today all I could mutter was, *"Hi how are you?"* He seemed as distracted as me replying, *"There's no point in complaining."* At that point somebody else approached him and shook his hand, I just muttered, *"see you around,"* and he slapped me on my shoulder a few times as if to say take care mate. That was it, one of my oldest friends that I hadn't seen for more than two years and between us the best we could do was mutter a few words and go our separate ways. I hadn't even managed to say I was sorry to hear about the death of his step Mum months earlier. She'd been a friend of mine as well. I hadn't even shown my respects to him, which made me feel guilty. I looked around for him as I continued shopping but it was too late, that moment of opportunity had passed.

I drove home still on autopilot and unloaded the shopping, feeling hungry but knowing I couldn't eat, feeling guilty as I was supposed to prepare a casserole dinner for later. I couldn't even look at food let alone eat some.

I decided to just come upstairs switch the computer on and type away without thinking. Just type my feelings and get as much down as possible and that is the last few pages you've been reading. I've done my best to express how I felt, so you can begin to imagine and feel the reality of the whole experience for yourself.

In between all of this, the kids have come in and I've managed not to let them know anything different is going on at all. I've been smiling and sorting out our clean clothes with them.

How the hell am I going to tell them and when?

Seems to be a few coincidences occurred today, although I haven't been able to write since earlier on this afternoon. Michael phoned and actually caught me in at an unusual time; he talked a while but wanted to avoid talking about the past, he seems quite positive and that was good for me to hear.

Lillian my soon to be ex wife phoned as well to tell me she'd received a letter from her solicitors, informing her the decree nisi had been accepted by the court and the decree absolute would be on the 26th of this month.

Seems to be few loose ends getting tied up, me going ahead with phoning the hospital and the divorce finally coming through.

Lillian seemed a bit down when I saw her yesterday but I still felt the timing was right to at least ask if she still felt strong enough to follow through with phoning the hospital. But when I asked her if she was going to phone to find out about the beast, her face said it all, before her mouth even moved to answer, *"No John I haven't got the strength."* Whilst turning and walking away I admitted to her, that it scared me too but I'd do it soon, I just didn't think it would be as soon as this.

She sounded a bit more positive within herself earlier, so I didn't want to burst her bubble and tell her what I found out today about HIM.

Once again having to keep so much to myself, carrying the burden and the

BEAST HASN'T GOT A CLUE WHAT ANYONE ELSE GOES THROUGH.

14/1/04
Haven't been able to do anything since last week because I caught a flu virus that put me on my back from Saturday until Tuesday. Once again the timing has gone against me, not being able to continue with my writing and delaying me from getting to the hospital to confront the BEAST. Tomorrow IS ANOTHER DAY.

Saturday night Sean came up to sit with me for a while in my bedroom, I'd drank a few hot brandy toddies (purely for medicinal purposes ha) whilst we were laughing and talking he mentioned the beast. Before I knew what was happening it had slipped from my mouth. *"I phoned the other day."* I put both my hands to my mouth and threw my head upwards just like a child would, if something had slipped out. I stared at Sean for what was only seconds but seemed like minutes, trying to read his face. Inwardly I was panicking and looking for a reaction from him. He seemed to smile and shake his head, like he was trying to make sense of what I'd said. I felt something in my guts and knew immediately that this was the time, something in his face, his voice I have no idea but my 15-year-old son was ready!! So young in age but so grown up and so very, very brave.

I explained how I'd found out weeks before Christmas. How guilty I'd felt for hiding things from him and gave all the reasons for my decision to bide my time before telling him. I reeled everything off and he sat listening and absorbing, paying particular attention while I explained. I didn't think the BEAST could have come through without some form of brain damage. Occasionally he'd interrupt me to ask a question but his voice was steady and now and then a slight smile would appear on his lips. After what seemed like an eternity, I'd said as much as I could and sat back realising how well the whole scene had fell into place and at the perfect time. He shook his head and said, *"Well Dad sometimes living can be so much harder than dying and this is how it's meant to be."*

We both hugged and once again my son had made me so very proud of him.
We talked about so many things, occasionally bringing the beast into the conversation but the beast had lost because he wasn't in the forefront of anything that we were sharing that evening. This was a father and son bonding yet again, even closer than before. We both agreed to bide our time before telling Paige though.

His parting words, as he kissed me on my head, before going to bed were, *"I'm going to write some new lyrics Dad."*

Sean had been expressing his thoughts through his music for the last year or two now, he'd been writing his own lyrics and one of the most expressive sentences that had been very prominent to him was, " *The Horror Through My Eyes.*" For him it was the words that summed up the horror he'd seen and had experienced in his short time on this earth. I could fully relate to these particular words, as I knew to some degree what he meant, even though I'll probably never know the full extent of what the BEAST did to him, I could still feel how hard hitting those words were, by the way they came across.

Amongst his circle of friends and other circles, Sean had become known as Ovill or Mr Ovill the rapper, that was his nickname. The story of how it came about is this. One night him and his friends were about to walk under a railway arch when somebody commented that his head was the same shape as the arch and they all fell about laughing. The original nickname was Oval but that seemed too derogatory and was changed to Ovill. He was quite happy with this nickname because he'd been getting stick for some time about the shape of his head; a lot of people had been calling him egghead, especially in his earlier days when he'd suffered at the hands of bullies. As always, Sean turned the situation around and dealt with it positively.

He'd been rapping for his friends for a while now and one of them had told me he was the best he knew for his age. One of the youth clubs they all went to, had some people coming in, to work on music with the kids. Sean did a bit of his rapping one night and the guy who was running it said he couldn't believe how good his lyrics were and he suggested to Sean, that he continue writing lyrics as much as he could because in his opinion, he was really talented and could do something with them in the future.

A few weeks later Sean and his friends went back, the same people had obtained some government funding to do more work with the youth club. When he saw Sean he was ecstatic and said, *"hey it's the kid with the wicked lyrics."* They did some work with him and over the next couple of weeks recorded a CD. Sean was exhausted with it all, learning how to flow properly with the words, working on the timing, all the time these guy's were pushing him to his full potential, making him stop and do it all again, over and over again, they even brought a female backing singer in to sing the chorus with him. It took weeks to get right and on the last night they put it all together. The main guy gave Sean a choice, he could take the CD as it was or he could let him take it away and apply for some more funding to put it together properly in a studio. They'd been working in a kitchen with all the kids outside the room being really quietly, so noises weren't picked up. Sean opted to let him take it away. We are now waiting for it to come back and listen to it properly, then decide what he wants to do with it.

In the meantime his cousin who is a DJ gave him some music that he himself had put together (known as beats in the rap world) and Sean is now writing enough lyrics to do an album.

Time will tell at this stage but that son of mine has words to say and a talent to tell them. The beast can never take that away from him, another line he has written is *"Now beast its my time to feast."* I think that expresses how Sean is now feeding off him and his experiences at the beast's hands. Another line that springs to mind is, *"I am a SURVIVOR, I have earned the CREST but I am one of MANY."* What a powerful way of reaching so many young people out there, who have also suffered at the hands of the monsters that have invaded their worlds. Who knows how many lives might be changed by his words, how many kids might speak up knowing that they can and that someone will listen!!

Last but not least how something POSITIVE can come from all of that pain and chaos of his childhood, there is HOPE because Sean is living proof of it. HE IS A SURVIVOR who is LOUD AND PROUD, he no longer carries shame!! He's given that back to whom it belongs, THE BEAST!!

Chapter 4

Decisions

16.1.04

On the 14th I had to take Paige to the hospital to have her wisdom teeth checked out. We did what we always seem to do in public and that is laugh together. Paige is a very giggly person when she gets going. The more I became aware and actually looked deeper into the playful behaviour that goes on between us in a public place, the more I realised that she wants people to notice us and hear us laughing together, as she said when people gave disapproving looks. *"What's wrong with a father and daughter laughing and getting on so well together."* I've realised that she feels safe at those times and likes to let herself go a little more than she normally would, in turn having a sense of pride in the close relationship we have together and it also has to be said, maybe a bit of showing off.

I fuel her laughter with the odd gesture of surprise, pulling a face or pointing a finger in mock horror, that she is embarrassing us, then she sets off in squeals of laughter and the tears roll down her cheeks. She tries to stop laughing and of course I make her worse. All in all considering that we are visiting a hospital, it feels like a day out for us and a great bonding experience for us both. She doesn't laugh that loud but a grumpy miserable looking old man, turned round to give us both the most disapproving look ever then turned away. That was it she was off again. I also realise that in many ways the inner child of my own comes out to play, I too spent a lot of times as a child attending hospital appointments. I was very accident-prone and suppose I wish my visits had been as funny and bonding with my parents.

We left the hospital and were driving towards Elizabeth's. Paige needed to use the toilet and will never use a public one. Elizabeth's was close by so we decided to go there.

We reached a certain point in the journey and I heard, *"I wonder what's happened to him?"* I froze and came back down to earth with a bump. We'd still been laughing and then wham she dropped that question on me. I turned to her and asked, *"What made you ask that question?"* As light-heartedly as I could, once again reading her face, trying to read her mind and testing for her reactions, also letting my paternal gut instinct kick in. *"Hmm I don't know but this road always makes me think of him when we drive down it and I was just wondering,"* she said. She looked ok and had spoken quite spirited, considering it was the beast she was asking about.

I had to take the bull by the horns and be honest with her and yes I decided not only was this the right time, it had presented itself whilst she was on a high and we'd bonded so closely in those few hours. I explained all the things I'd told Sean, including how he'd asked only a few days earlier. She commented that, *"It had been a long time since we'd heard anything and she'd started to suspect something was wrong."* Then the words came out. *"Hmm so I will still get a chance to face him then."* I didn't even have to look at her because I knew what those words meant. She was very different to Sean, she wanted her pound of flesh and the BEAST had a formidable enemy in Paige!! He wouldn't get off so lightly with her!!

When we'd first told her about Sean and myself bumping into the beast, she was surprised that Sean hadn't wanted to do anything physical. She laughed a little coldly at the time but very confidently said, *"Oh, I'd want to jump all over him, if I saw him. I'd want to batter him."* Who could blame her? He robbed her of her innocence all those years earlier. I feel in some ways that what was as bad if not worse than that was the fact that she'd punished herself for years because she hadn't protected Julie our granddaughter, her niece, when he made her leave him in the Wendy house alone with her. She would be standing up for her nieces as well as herself and needed her own form of closure!!

Her comments reminded me of those months earlier, Paige had been playing up a little; her and Sean seemed to be arguing all the time. She was constantly having mood swings and wanting to stay at her Mum's a lot. I kept watching her behaviour and was getting more and more concerned about her but feeling powerless and confused as to why she'd changed so much. One night she came and sat on my bed. She told me that for the last couple of weeks or so she'd been having nightmares and wasn't sleeping very well. My first thoughts were that things must be coming to the surface and she needed to speak to someone. She wouldn't speak to her Mum because she didn't trust her; and she seemed to have very little respect, if any at all left for her Mum.

The main reasons she used to stay over at her Mum's house were because a lot of her school friends lived near her and she sometimes needed to get a little space from Sean and myself. I wanted her to go back to see her child psychologist and felt this should be worked through with a professional. Paige was totally against that idea but she did admit that she felt comfortable enough talking to Marisa and had spoken to her on a lot of occasions when she was upset etc, or generally fed up with Sean and myself. Marisa would then talk to me and I could work towards resolving the situation or problems at the time. It worked well all round because Paige could get her points of view across and Marisa had a better way of making me understand how a young girl's mind worked. This was a totally different ball game though. We were talking about disclosure regarding sexual abuse. It would be a lot for somebody to listen to and be able to take in, also adding the fact that Marisa was emotionally attached to Paige and treated her like a daughter. They'd both developed a strong relationship together, which had been a Godsend to me considering Lillian's behaviour over the last year or so.

Would Marisa be strong enough to listen though? I had to weigh it all up.

I phoned Marisa and discussed it with her, she being the rock that she is agreed immediately. I told Paige and left things to take their own natural course, in turn allowing her to speak when she was ready.

A week or so later Paige came to me and felt upset, we talked for a few minutes and once again I mentioned counselling and waited for her reaction. Surprisingly she agreed immediately and that lifted my spirits. The next day I got in touch with the psychology department and Jan immediately made an appointment for us to come in the following week. I was elated when I told Jan that Paige had agreed herself to come in, because she'd been very reluctant to go in the past and we both felt this was a significant breakthrough.

That week went by and towards the end of it Paige was wavering and changing her mind about going, once again we were·being cheated by timing. If I'd been able to get her in there, the next day for example, she'd have been open and would have talked more about how she was feeling at that moment but so much can change in a week and her moods had lightened.

The war we go through daily and the battle plans that have to change at any given moment. That's exactly what it feels like sometimes a constant battle and occasionally you are under very heavy fire. You then have to dig in and make plans to find a way to get out in one piece.

Then came D-day, the appointment.

Whilst driving there I told Paige how much it meant to me her going and how Jan could help her work through things better than Marisa or myself. I tried explaining how a trained professional outsider looking in and not emotionally attached would be better all round for her. She of course was saying how much better she'd felt lately and how she didn't need, or want to talk to anybody etc. All I could do was hope the appointment would go the right way and she might just open up.

She sat and talked about a whole heap of things from school to home life, Jan dropped in some key questions throughout the meeting and Paige answered them all, openly and honestly. It made me realise how far we'd really come, since the last time we'd been there. Also how much my daughter trusted me as her parent, how much she'd grown up and how tough she really was.

Jan explained that sometimes something could trigger the old memories and feelings, in turn making people who'd been coping and moving on ok, feel vulnerable again. She then asked, *"Has anything happened that might have triggered something?"* I sat there and the penny dropped like a ton of bricks on my head, I felt so stupid. *"Of course, mine and Sean's encounter with the beast."* I went on to tell her how it had all come about. That was the answer to why she'd been having the nightmares. It was like a delayed reaction that had crept up on her weeks later.

Paige sat and expressed how much she would have liked to be there when we saw the beast. Jan explained how it would have been a form of closure for her and the nightmares and feeling uncomfortable would diminish once Paige had come to terms with things for herself.

Jan summed the whole meeting up by saying how many changes she'd seen in Paige and myself. How we'd both managed to let go of Lillian and accepted Lillian was now in control of her own life and what she decided to do with it. She mentioned how much closer we'd become as our family group and she trusted Paige that if she had any problems, she would reach out for somebody when necessary.

It made me realise that I was being over protective and my daughter was capable of making her own decisions about her life but if things changed we could always come back again.

All in all it was a positive meeting, I didn't get exactly what I wanted but my baby was ok and that was all that mattered to me.

22/1/04
This time last week the beast seemed to be in my mind so much, I was feeling inadequate because I kept putting off the visit, I'd convinced myself I must do. Determined every night going to bed that the next day was IT and the next day I was definitely going. The next day would come and I didn't even want to get up. Yes! I had the flu, yes! It takes a while to get over it, no! I hadn't slept well the night before. So many different reasons or excuses but I'd said it so I must do it. I had to face him, it was the only way to know for sure how bad, or even how good he was really doing.

Friday came and this was it, this was my last chance to go and I was determined now.

I had to wait for somebody that day to come replace some tiles on my roof. The builder had said he'd be here between 12-2.30. That was ok because once he'd been I could go to the hospital. I decided to do some writing while I waited. I did a fair bit as well. My mind seemed so much lighter and my writing seemed to flow so easily.

Earlier I'd had a few thoughts; do I really need to go? Would I do better to just let it go now? Look how much better we've all been! The last time I was in the beast's presence I felt tainted somehow, something I'd carried for a while after every encounter. Am I thinking these thoughts because of one of life's biggest cheaters again, FEAR? Will it do me more harm that good seeing him again? Instead of dismissing these thoughts, I could just put it down to fear. Or, maybe because I'd said it, I would now have to do it. I decided to just let the thoughts drift in and out of my conscious mind.

2.30 came and went and the builder was a no show. I had to laugh at that thought because I was so sure he'd be early and I'd have plenty of time to get to the hospital and back before the kids came in from school. They'd be back by 3.15.

My mood still seemed so much better and it felt like I was already letting go. I was re-reading what I'd written and feeling so good about the way things seemed to be coming across lately. Even the day that had felt like my world was collapsing and I had all the windows open, it had even seemed to flow freely then. That was it, in the next thought I'd decided, " *I wasn't going, I didn't need to go!!*" Why should I jeopardise myself anymore by facing the beast, jeopardising my sanity even? He wasn't worth it, what would I really achieve by seeing him, what would it really do for me or us. *"I didn't have to go and wasn't going"*

I felt the weight of the world lift off my shoulders in that final second of deciding and it had absolutely nothing to do with fear!! It was to do with self-preservation and survival and I felt damn good for making that decision as well!! Whatever will be, will be with him! What goes round has come round and I have faith that fate is already at work in his life. I need to find closure for myself regarding him and I don't have to see him for me to do that. I need and am doing exactly what I need to do and that is finishing this book once and for all.

Now I have another decision to make. Do I leave this as it is and do a bit of filling in, starting at the beginning? The thoughts of reading this from the beginning are a bit daunting though, as I haven't read it through for over a year. This is my family's whole life, in black and white in front of me. So much pain, anguish and raw emotion have gone into this writing. Four years of my life writing it and re living it over and over again. I was such an infant in my own recovery and understanding of the aftermath of child sexual abuse when I first started this. I only started writing to improve my typing speed and skills in the first place. It seems like a lifetime ago and in some ways a whole different life altogether.

154

I don't seem to have a problem in writing it anymore, almost like a form of detaching myself, sometimes I don't have a problem reading it to myself but the odd time I have read aloud for Marisa, it kills me and I choke up with tears. We've all changed so much these last four years. So much about me has changed and especially the way I express myself now. To change the beginning could in many ways take away the whole reality and rawness of emotions surrounding the moments that it was written. There were times during these last four years; I was so close to the edge there was a real danger of me falling over it.

How easy it would have been to just curl up in a ball, giving up on life and this hurtful world, I'd found myself thrown into because of the beast. So many times wanting to die just to escape the torment, so many other times holding on to life, fearing death and the thoughts of my children being left alone to cope without me.

Losing hope of ever seeing that light at the end of the tunnel but then again another day the light was shining brightly and we were all moving towards it. But with this newfound way of expression, it may well help to put things across better if I change it.

I'll have to think long and hard on this one.

24/1/04
I still feel I made the right decision last week; once again the beast has still not managed to be in the forefront of my mind. It feels like since deciding not to go and face him, for the first time in a long time I AM LETTING GO, I'm finally letting go properly.

I needed these extra few days to make sure and it's only by writing these last few lines, that's made me fully realise anything. At last I'm coming to my senses and realising it's not for me to go round like some kind of avenging angel, or vigilante.

By allowing him into my mind so much was keeping me locked into him somehow, in many ways creating my own inner torment and indirectly allowing him to win.

Sooner or later when the time is right, somebody will let me know how he is. Or there again another chance encounter may well happen. Who knows but for the first time in a long time I FEEL WHOLE? I feel like a complete person and in control of what I think and do now. No longer standing looking over into that precipice, that bottomless pit of horror, sorrow and despair.

Today is the beginning of the rest of my life!!! We will still face problems in the future but they can never ever be as bad as the problems of the past, nothing could ever compare to that.

Elizabeth phoned me yesterday to tell me that the baby she is carrying is a boy; I'm going to be a Grandad again in four month's time. They are the future of my family, the grandchildren. Nobody will get to them through secrets and secrecy and we are all that much wiser now. I especially have more wisdom to pass on as they grow and I'll sit as an old man telling stories that will pass from generation to generation.

I did it; we all did it!!

We broke through that cycle of sexual abuse, WE ARE TRUE SURVIVORS AND WE SURVIVED.

GOD BLESSED US ALL.

THE END

(OR IS IT?)

29/1/04

How quickly the bubble was to burst!!

How quickly somebody was going to let me know!!

The very next day I got a call from Michelle telling me that she was due to appear in court on the following Tuesday. She was looking at six to twelve years for street robbery and was really worried this time. She put her Mum on the phone to speak to me. She was saying how a few days earlier Michelle had phoned to say she felt she was slipping on the methadone programme she was on and could she come and stay for a few days. Michelle had also signed up to do a counselling course. This sounded really positive, rather than waiting until she'd slipped, she reached out before she did.

Her Mum had done such a lot for her since she came back into her life and I felt happy for them both. The drawback was because she was staying at a hostel. She could only be away until the next day otherwise she'd be deemed as not needing the place and my first thought was that she might not go to court.

Her Mum seemed so sure that if things were explained to the judge properly and how since they'd both been in contact with each other, Michelle's life was turning around and how positive Michelle's life was becoming, he might not pass a custodial sentence. I found myself getting carried along with this same train of thought and although I felt it was wishful thinking on her Mum's part, you never know and there is always hope.

I said I'd go to court with them to offer some moral support. They were both ecstatic at that and thanked me saying how much it meant to them both.

I let the conversation flow and then subtly asked Michelle about her Dad. She said, *"he's a mess, he couldn't walk or talk properly and had to be re-taught how to read and write etc."* Then came the words that cut through my heart like a knife. *"He has no memory of the past. He thinks my name is Mitchell and I'm a friend. He doesn't realise I'm his daughter."* My heart felt such pain, not only had he survived to haunt us all again, he couldn't even remember what he was, or had done!! The Beast had cheated us again!!

She carried on talking oblivious to what was going through my mind. From what seemed like a great distance away I could hear her saying *"Yeah after six days the doctors at the hospital took me into a side room and asked if I 'd give permission for the machine to be switched off. I couldn't agree to that and I visited him all the time for the next six weeks. One night, while I was sat talking to him, he suddenly opened his eyes. He opened his eyes while I was there!"* My mind snapped back slightly realising that if she'd agreed to what the doctors had asked, he'd be dead and buried now. I felt like shit and a sudden jolt of anger towards her! I quickly quashed the thought knowing how she felt about him, despite what he'd done to her.

She carried on, *"He's been moved to another hospital now for rehabilitation and he thinks his brothers and Mum have visited him."* Again my brain was coming out of the mist and a little more aware of what she was saying. *"His Mum and brothers?"* I asked. *"Yeah he said they'd visited him, so they can't be dead. He can't accept that they're dead and he thinks they're still alive. Yeah and his memory is slowly coming back. Looking at him, he looks just like a? I don't know? Just like a boy again, yeah just like a boy again."* Bingo I was back now; she was trying to protect him still!! She'd slipped up but I couldn't let her know I'd picked up on it. She wanted me to believe he was totally helpless and couldn't remember anything. We ended the phone call and I sat there drained and confused, trying to make sense and playback the conversation. I grabbed a piece of paper and a pen and wrote down all the key points, trying to unscramble them in my mind.

The words *"He can't remember anything,"* kept jumping out at me, he must remember! That's it now, once again that's it, I'll have to go now, I'll have to remind him, I'll have to look into his eyes and see for myself if he does remember. I lay down with so many different thoughts flashing in my head; I was heading back to the precipice again. I wanted revenge all over again and was feeling so very different to the thoughts of only a few days ago.

After what seemed like ages, I got up and made dinner keeping myself occupied and trying to put the mask of normality on in front of the kids, even sitting down that evening to watch a film with them.

He was in my head again. Once again fate had intervened and my feeling of freedom and peace within myself was short lived.

Later that night Michelle phoned me, it was like listening to a child, the people at the hostel had let her use the office phone because she was so upset. She was really worried about going to court and maybe prison. She really felt she'd reached a turning point in her life. I did my best to support her but once again finding myself getting dragged back into the world I'd fought so hard lately to break free of.

Tuesday morning came, I woke up and didn't want to go and I mean, I really didn't want to go to a courtroom again but because I said I'd go, meant I had to. I couldn't let Michelle down because she was too important to me and I think deep down I knew this could well be the turning point for her and just maybe the start of a whole new journey in her life.

While I was getting ready Michelle phoned me, panicking because they still had a train to get from the hostel into Manchester and was worried they wouldn't make it on time. I said I'd meet them at the station and get them to the courts. It was added pressure for me but again it had to be done. I found I was getting dragged in deeper emotionally as well. I hadn't seen her Mum for donkey's years and wasn't sure how we'd react to each other. It was going to feel strange none the less.

As I pulled up to the road leading to the station my phone rang. Whilst answering I jumped out of the car and was looking out for them. It was Michelle on the phone and as I looked around I could make out two shapes in the distance. Once again I felt by instinct as opposed to being able to visibly see, that it must be them. I laughingly said *"I'm sure I can see you but not positive as I haven't got my glasses on."* One of the shapes turned in my direction and set off running towards me, with the other one following slightly slower.

The kid ran and jumped straight into my arms and was hugging the life out of me. Her Mum Bernadette followed and with a big smile put her hand out to say hello. We shook hands and then we both kissed on the cheek. It didn't seem that strange after all. We were both looking at each other and she was saying after all these years we meet again. The kid (because that is what she became for those minutes, a kid again) was in the back seat chatting away excitedly saying over and over, *"doesn't he look well Mum, doesn't he look well?"* I could see she was delighted to have us both together. I knew then that my coming was worth the effort for her.

We rushed to the courts and I dropped them outside as we were late and drove to the car park. By the time I got to the foyer they were already gone, obviously to whatever courtroom she was to appear in. I checked the wall with all the listings on but couldn't find her name on any of them. I then went to the main desk to enquire, the lady told me they'd already gone upstairs to the second floor.

As I got up the last flight it seemed to darken before my eyes and then the realisation dawned on me, *"It was the same floor I'd been to, over and over again when the beast was appearing or supposed to have appeared."* Memories starting flooding back, I felt nauseous and out of breathe. Trying to regain my composure and push the memories to the back of my mind.

I turned the corner walking towards the courtroom we'd been in, so many times before. The weirdest thing was I couldn't see Micelle and her Mum. I was walking towards the same room past all the other rooms. I was re-visiting days gone by in an almost trancelike state. I could see the police officers jumping out of their seats to stop me getting to him. I could see the bastard as clear as day sat next to his brother, eyes fixed like a rabbit in a spotlight, as the officer in the case was trying to hold me back and saying, *"John you can't be up here, you have to stay downstairs."* I was still walking forward as they were walking backwards, my eyes fixed on him as more of them tried to stop me. My answer to that was, *"But I'm not a witness anymore remember, I can be up here now."* It was said so calmly still moving forward. Then the officer said, *"Please John your family need you downstairs with them, please go downstairs to the witness suite."* I looked at the beast one last time and snapped back to reality and turned away to go back downstairs without saying another word.

Only this was now and not then, the beast wasn't in there this time. I was there for Michelle, even though she hadn't been there for us the last times I was in these courts.

I turned around and realised that I'd walked right past them, not even noticing them sitting on my right.

That was a freaky experience and I've just totally relived it whilst writing this, I hadn't even noticed how dramatic those moments were, when I wrote this part the other day

I walked up to them, Bernadette told me there'd been a mistake and the case had been put back again. None of us had needed to even be there at all. Bernadette was saying how she'd been up travelling since 5.30 am, Michelle looked kind of relieved and I thought to myself, *"No way will she be able to stay straight until the next case"*

We went to the restaurant for a drink and sat talking. Michelle commented that her prescription for methadone hadn't been there for her that morning. I asked how she was feeling and she said she was fine. A little shocked I replied, *"Oh well that's good if you feel ok."* My guts told me something else though but I suppressed it.

They both suggested going for a drink together, looking at my watch and it was only 11.30am, I declined the offer with the excuse I had things I could be doing.

I dropped them at a bar close to the train station and went on my way, with the full intentions of writing all about the last few days.

I got in and Marisa phoned. I told her everything and she asked if I was ok? *"Yeah of course I am,"* I replied, not realising that I wasn't and wouldn't be.

Bernadette phoned a bit later on and stayed on the phone for two hours, for two hours we were reminiscing and she was pouring her heart out. I could tell she'd had a few drinks but it obviously helped her to relax enough to talk so openly. She then started to go in deep about the past and the reasons she'd had to leave her kids. She told me many personal things that I promised her I would keep to myself.

I realised how bad her own childhood had been and she'd then married a deviant.

One of the things I will tell, as she hadn't asked me to keep this one to myself is this.

On their wedding night he pulled her to one side at the reception and told her that the night before on his stag night, he'd gone into the toilets with a man and allowed the man to masturbate him. She said she was so shocked and naïve she didn't know what to think, or say and spent her wedding night alone in her bed. This didn't come as a shock to me because I knew a long time ago he was bi-sexual.

I felt like I was holding a counselling session and giving her the opportunity to get a lot of excess baggage unloaded. After two hours though I was feeling totally drained, because it was unearthing so many unhappy memories for me

160

as well. I was glad when my mobile phone rang and I was able to use it as an excuse to get off the phone.

I was trying to make sense of so many things when the phone rang again. This time it was Michelle to let me know her new court day was in April and thanking me for going earlier. She was talking away freely about how she'd checked into a hotel near the hospital because she'd visited her Dad. I let her talk. *"Yeah he knows who I am now and was going mad at me because he thinks I'm neglecting him. He said I don't come and see him often enough and when I go back on Friday he wants me to bring him a pair of trainers to wear. But I worry in case he tries to get to the pub."* Whilst she was talking I couldn't help thinking, *"Sounds like him, totally selfish and he'd know she'd have to sell her body to buy them for him. Hmm he can't be in that bad a way then was the thought that passed through my mind."* Then I realised I'd heard the pub!

"What the pub?" I asked calmly. *"I thought he couldn't walk properly."* *"Yeah he can walk up and down the corridors without help."* She then realised what she was saying and changed the subject quickly.

It was then I asked about her prescription again, she answered, *"No, it's not my fault it's their fault. They didn't have it ready so it's their fault. So I had to get a little something for myself."* I tried not to judge and was in no way surprised. That's what my gut had nudged inside me earlier; she'd had Heroin before she came to court.

Her Mum had told me she'd lent her £15 after being to court, which meant she'd gone back out onto the street selling herself to buy more gear and pay for the hotel. £15 would have only got her enough to get through the afternoon. The cycle of destruction was back in motion, she was a Junkie and three month's is a lifetime away for her to try and stay out of trouble.

Marisa phoned me; once again I brought her up to date and explained I was again considering visiting the beast. She listened patiently (as she always did/ does) and then asked me to consider what I was doing to myself, after deciding only the other day that I didn't need to see him ever again.

As always I assured her I was ok and as always believing I would be.

Yesterday the depression set in. The dark thoughts were taking over again, seeing him over and over in my mind. Now I was back at the edge. I'd run towards it this time and felt those old familiar feelings. I could feel it; I was sinking and drowning, going under!!

How was I? Why was I? Not again!!!!

161

*4/2/04
I needed to take some time out from this for a while. *

The How Was This
Michelle and her Mum had phoned me, which meant I felt obliged to go.

As it happens her Mum asked me a question during our long conversation, *"Why have you always been there for Michelle? "* The answer is because I love her. At one time it was partly due to the guilt of not being able to protect her when she was younger, from what the Beast was doing to her. I've managed to work through that aspect though, because I know that I was asking questions back then and had I been given any inclination from Lillian that sexual abuse was even a remote possibility, I would have been on it and followed everything through until I knew for sure either way. And in our case so many children could have been spared the horrors of what was going to happen to them because of the beast's perversions and Lillian's silence! But the Beast was so cunning and powerful; he'd managed to silence so many children who then became silent adults.

I don't really do much for her other than when she needs me to. She picks up the phone to connect with someone who loves her unconditionally and wants nothing in return, other than the odd phone call to let me know she is OK. . Bernadette then went on to tell me how much my staying involved with Michelle had meant to Michelle and she always speaks about me and loves me a lot.

The Why Was?
Because I love kids, always have and always will.

Every single one of the people involved with this whole drama, that was created by the perversions of the paedophile I call the beast. I've known them all since childhood including his first victims, his siblings. Although they are mostly all adults now, I am the only father figure any of them had in their lives. The whole of my ex-wife's side of the family are totally dysfunctional.

I've said it before and say it again, *"The Beast and I are like two sides of a coin. I love and protect children whilst he is a defiler and abuser of children."*

As long as I have breath in my body, anyone of the survivors in this family, or any family can come to me and I will be there for them as much as I can.

Not Again!
Comes from my feelings of helplessness when I allow myself to get dragged back into his world, i.e. trying to think what is going on in his head, or what

162

is really happening to him etc. The thoughts of revenge, knowing how much he can never be aware of how much pain and damage he created in so many peoples lives. Its almost like I feel the pain of everyone, with the pain comes anger and with the anger I implode, because I can't explode at the Beast.

What Have I Learnt From This New Experience?
That I cannot allow myself to become too emotionally involved, because then I'm no good to anybody, especially myself and my youngest children. They're the ones who live with me and saw the emotional damage that was done to me last week. I can be there for anybody needing my help but have to learn to separate a little to be effective.

Neither Michelle nor her Mum have been back in touch since last week, so obviously my job was done for them. My problem was, I stayed in the whole drama whilst they carried on as normal, or as normal as they can be.

Michelle will be back on the streets selling her body and her Mum will be doing her best to make up for not being there whilst Michelle was growing up.

I learnt a valuable although painful lesson once again on this journey of mine and hopefully I'll remember it for the next time.

I had my entire family round for dinner on Sunday including my Mum and her husband. There were four generations of my family in one room together, my Mum as head of the family, myself, Marisa, my kids and my grandchildren. We laughed a lot; we ate together and had a thoroughly good Sunday afternoon as a family unit.

I love my family so very much.

My divorce came through this week, which gives me a sense of freedom, a feeling of moving on from the past and new direction in my life.

Lillian seems to be taking things quite well herself too. Our marriage was a massive victim of what the beast did to our family but we had our time together. Now it is time for us both to move on and forward as two separate people. We had a lot of good times together and shared a lot and I have to forgive her.

We brought wonderful children into this world and I've a lot to be grateful for.

THE END

(OR IS IT?)

Chapter 5

Will It Ever End?

21/6/04

How time flies and it still wasn't going to be the end, how many ends will there be to this book? How many times will it feel like we're moving on and things will be ok, or cannot get any worse? Are my family and I cursed? One major crisis after another, is this normal, do things like this happen to other people as well? Probably yes, yes I think it does but maybe different circumstances. Where do I begin this time?

Just over two months ago I'd been for my own counselling session and a few things were opened up in me. For no real reason, I decided to take a drive around the area the Beast had been spotted in only the week before. A friend I'd happened to bump into for the first time in quite a few years had spotted him. Suppose it's worth mentioning how it came about, especially when we look at the way fate and destiny have intervened in so many aspects, of this journey I've been travelling.

I went to meet a friend in a pub one Friday night. As I walked in I spotted a guy called Terry, who'd been a friend of my ex's family since they were kids. We chatted for a while and he shook my hand saying, *"I'm glad the beast got his just deserts and I believe you had something to do with it. Fair play to you John."* I was a bit shocked but smiled inwardly, knowing that I didn't directly have anything to do with it at all. I suppose a lot of people would assume I did though and no amount of denials by myself would change that train of thought. Being totally honest, how many people would have looked down on me for not doing anything physical, to such a monster that had hurt my family. I was content to let him keep his thoughts anyway.

The following week I went back to the same pub and he was there again. He came up to me and said, *"I can't believe it, after we were talking about him only last week, and I saw him in Hulme while I was working. I wanted to give him a dig but there are a lot of security cameras in the area though, John and I was in my work van so could have been identified."* What a coincidence I thought and I couldn't help asking how he looked. I 'd been curious for a while now. Terry said, *"He's a mess. He was just shuffling along like an old man and looked like a tramp."*

That was how it happened and once again I had a lead on where he might be and had to follow it up.

Whilst driving I'd noticed a few down and out looking guys, I pulled over to have a chat and see if they could give me any idea, of where the beast could be staying. Remember that no matter how low peoples lives can go, or in which manner they decide to live, i.e. alcohol or drug addicts, *"nobody but nobody likes child molesters."* I explained why I was looking for him and what he'd done. They were more than willing to help me, even saying that if they found out who he was, they to would give him a beating. Once again I had to protect the beast and explain, I didn't want him hurt because from what I'd been told he was a mess anyway. I just wanted them to tell him, *"John said HELLO,"* nothing more than that. I wanted him to know I'd found him again and that was all.

I saw a few more guys and the story was the same with them but they directed me to where they thought he could possibly be staying.

I drove to the place that I'd already thought of earlier but hadn't known its exact location. I pulled up at the gates and looked down the driveway, where I saw a group of men together. To the left of them was a lone figure squatting against the wall; he then eased himself up in a wobbly manner. I focused as he straightened up and shuffled towards the ramp and handrail that was at the entrance to the building. It was he; I knew it was he, even though my eyes were letting me down from seeing him clearly. I knew it was he and could sense it in my guts! He gripped the handrail and turned towards me, staring right at me for what seemed like ages. We seemed to lock on to each other. I knew it was impossible for him to see me clearly from that distance and the car I drove was different to the one he saw me in last time, which coincidently was within yards of where he was now.

It seemed like minutes but could have been only seconds that we were both looking in each other's direction. He then turned and shuffled inside the building.

I'd seen for myself what had become of him and he was a pathetic shadow of his former self. He looked old even though he was only a year older than me; he was thin, very scruffy and unshaven. How far had he fallen, what goes round had certainly come around in his case and it left me with a great sense of satisfaction, that some things are worse than death!! Maybe we hadn't been cheated after all!

Over the weeks if I was in the area I'd drive past, just on the off chance I might bump into him, knowing that I probably wouldn't but you could never know for sure. I didn't and was quite content with the fact, I at least saw him that one time.

Chapter 6

27.6.04

THE NIGHTMARE
Lillian phoned me a few weeks ago to let me know the car I'd given her had gone missing. She started crying and saying there was more to it though and I should come over to her house, then she'd tell me what had happened. She was really distraught and sobbing her heart out.

I rushed over with feelings of dread as to what she was going to tell me. She was upstairs in her room when I got there, crying uncontrollably. I let her compose herself and then asked what was wrong, she started off with the car." *I got caught drinking and driving last week,"* she said. My heart sank and I felt sick to my stomach because I'd known for a while that was coming! I hated drink driving and she'd promised me when I gave her the car she'd never do it. She said, *"the police made me leave the car on a busy main road when they arrested me and when I went back the next day the car was gone. I went to the compound but it isn't there either. I think it must have been stolen."* She then burst into more sobs saying *"But that isn't it all, I was raped. I was raped the other week. That's why I went back to the club, I was raped."* She wasn't making sense to me and I was fighting to make sense of the things she was saying, at the same time not asking or saying too much, through fear of making her worse than she already was.

To be continued at a later date.

29/4/05
*I've decided to fill the gaps in on this part, obviously back then it was so very confusing and too traumatic for me, because I missed so much of it out. Have to admit to not knowing why I didn't finish it off back then. Or why I came back on two separate occasions and still didn't finish it. Just re-read what I wrote on the 30.7.04 and obviously I'd found out, as usual there was always more to do with anything in Lillian's life, than it would first seem. Obviously I decided to come back and write it at a later date but didn't get round to it.

*Have read what I wrote on the 5.7.04 and it's becoming a bit clearer to me. I started off explaining my emotions and then went off on a tangent completely, as to why I was so messed up over the whole thing. Am going to leave the writing of those two dates as they are. You as a reader will probably get confused because I certainly did but to take them out would detach the enormity of the affect she had on me. I'm going to jump past and write it all as I feel now. *

30/7/04
Been a while once again but that's the way it is. I've been reading through this last bit about the rape (funny how easy it was for me to write that word rape

then.) It was so very hard to go into this part of the writing back then. It would be so much easier for me to do it now because of how far forward I've moved. The thing is that I don't want to write about this at this stage, preferring to leave this where it is for now and come back to it at a later date. Once again it will become clearer when this part is finished and again she is not a priority in my life anymore.

5/7/04

So many things have changed again since this last part was written, seems to be the story of my life things changing by the week, day, hour, minute or even second!! Light humour here *"But this is the story of my life."*

So many things seem to happen and change, I could do with writing continually. The only problem is, it's so painful to write and requires a lot of energy, which seems to be getting drained from me constantly, so I don't have the time or the energy to write. It's a vicious circle to which I have to find a means of breaking and recreating to give me more time and energy. Even now I will have to leave soon to pick Paige up and its already 9.07 pm, this is hardly a subject you want to be writing before you go to bed but HERE GOES ANYWAY.

Continued

I felt the usual man thing of wanting to ask how, where, who and a hundred other questions. I was also struggling with those old thoughts of revenge. *"This is it now, the final straw, I can't let another person get away with hurting somebody close to me."* Even though we're divorced she's still the mother of my children and of course I had to deal with that deeply ingrained, misguided sense of loyalty that was instilled in me from childhood. *"I'm the protector which makes me responsible for everyone's welfare around me."*

What misguided sense of duty and honour did my father inflict upon me. There again he was born from another era and never had the chance to finish his form of programming on me. If he had lived, surely he'd have adapted and been able to take away and minimise some of the damage he'd done to me by the way he brought me up. It's for me to adapt and minimise the damage done, for me to deprogram myself from thoughts of duty that are so unrealistic.

Fortunately as the events unfold while I'm writing this next part, it seems the enormity of what I have just realised is fully sinking in, whilst writing those last few lines without really thinking too much about it. I've already been putting into practice those very words and changes within myself subconsciously for a while now.

6/7/04

Its up to me to now to break all contact with Lillian, it's the only way for me to survive. I flicked through a few pages that were written at the beginning of the year and once again I've realised how easily I get dragged back into her dramas. No matter how many times I take two steps forward from detaching myself, I realise I then take one step back which means, I'm still not moving as far forward as I need to do, or anywhere near as fast as I need to. Just maybe if I moved further and faster, the younger kids may then follow. The older kids have managed to detach so much more than the younger ones but with saying that, the older kids have their own families now and the younger ones need a Mum so much more.

Events will unfold and this next part will make so much more sense as it is getting finished but I for the moment have to ramble, divert and put pieces of my own thinking down, to make sense of the rest as it happened and in turn affected us all. Also how just maybe, this will be the catalyst to making all the changes and pieces of this whole puzzle, or story fall into place and flow easier and constantly.

I certainly hope so.

29/4/05
HAVING PUT THE PIECES OF THE PUZZLE TOGETHER
She was lying on the bed sobbing uncontrollably and yes my instincts were to want to hurt whoever had hurt her but at the same time that other side of my mind was picking up on things that didn't add up. I remember looking down on her with a sense of loathing (I have to be totally honest there) and disgust at her. I suppose part of that was due to the fact she'd lied to me about being raped years earlier and in turn the devastating affect it'd had on me back then. I couldn't even put my arms around her to console her, which made me feel guilty and even worse.

She was crying and saying, *"they drugged me and held me down but I can't remember what they did to me. I woke up in the morning with my knickers on inside out"*
I asked where it had happened? She replied, *" It was near Northmoor road but I don't know. I think it might have been Rusholme. I just ran out and got into a taxi."*

(That didn't add up and I suspected why)

I said, *"Surely you remember where the taxi picked you up."* I was trying to stay calm and not rush her but was trying to work out where it'd happened so I'd be able to find out who it was. *"I don't know but I think it was Rusholme."* I knew then it was the Northmoor road area. I also knew she was trying to throw me off the scent, which was typical of Lillian!

(No matter how bad a situation was, there would always be lies)

168

I knew people from around there, so it wouldn't have been that hard to find them and Lillian knew that.

She'd been out a few weeks before and I'd noticed bruises all over her upper arms and asked what had happened? She told me she'd got into a fight in a club and went on to explain this big story of how it had all happened.

I then realised the bruises had come from being pinned down but couldn't work out why she'd lied about it.

I let her cry for a bit and then said; *"Now calm down and tell me as much as you can remember but take your time."* She then looked up at me with pitiful eyes, a similar look I'd seen in the hospital bed all those years before and said, *"John please I want to come home, I want to come home and back to my family. I hate my life. Please John, I want to come home."* She started sobbing again and I had to back off.

After a few minutes she calmed down and started to tell me what had happened, she said, *"I was in a club with Carol but we got split up at the end of the night. I'd been talking to these guys earlier and they offered me a lift in their taxi. They said one of them would drive me home in his car when we got back to their house. We went into the house to get his car keys, he gave me a drink of water, I thought it tasted funny and I don't remember anything after that"* She started sobbing and saying, *"John I don't even know what they did to me but I'm so sore."*

(I again had to pull myself away for a few minutes on hearing that)

I've decided to stop writing about what she told me and continue with what I later found out and worked out for myself about the whole thing. Once again she told so many lies, once again my gut instincts knew deep down she was lying.

She and her niece Carol went back to a house with three young Asian guys after being in a club; on the way they picked a bottle of Vodka up from a restaurant. Back at the house Carol went upstairs with one of them, which suggests that they already knew them. Lillian stayed downstairs with two of them and they must have put a date rape drug into her Vodka. At some point Carol came downstairs and saw Lillian without her jeans on and covered her up assuming she'd just had sex with one or both of them and fallen asleep afterwards. She then went back to bed. This was the norm I suppose, because they went out together picking men up all the time.

She didn't want to tell me too much in case I found out the truth, I have no doubts that she was raped; the really sad thing is that she felt the need to make up lies.

I found out a few weeks later she got picked up in a club again by an older guy and got into a car with a total stranger, who luckily for her drove her home that time.

From the day she told me about the rape, I'd gone through so many emotions, it haunted me for such a long time. I kept going over things in my mind all the time and in many ways torturing myself over again. I wanted her to seek justice but she wouldn't involve the police. I was really saddened because it probably wasn't the first time they'd date raped women, or even the last time it would happen. Which would mean even more unsuspecting victims.

I wanted revenge because it felt like a form of lashing out, at everything that had happened to my family. Somebody else had abused her and she didn't deserve that!

I felt guilty because as much of a mess as she'd made out of her life, I couldn't bring her back home and into our lives because I felt sorry for her. My co-dependency again, trying to fix the alcoholic. She'd been part of my life for twenty five years and even taking into account how much pain she'd put us through, part of me still had a form of love for her.

I ripped myself to pieces all over again and within a few weeks she threw it all in my face and continued on her self-destructive spiral downwards.

8/7/04

For the last few months' Paige has wanted to move in with her Mum and her sister. She's reaching an age where she needs to be around other females. Unfortunately for Paige most of her school friends live near her Mum's and she only has one friend living near us. Not for one minute did I want that to happen but did agree if Lillian would give up drinking. Lillian had promised Paige at the beginning of the year that she would stop drinking and get help for herself. Paige put a lot of energy into that belief but as time has gone by she was to end up bitterly disappointed.

Seems Paige is already detaching, because her Mum phoned earlier and Paige asked when she would be in because she wants to collect the rest of her stuff, her stuff being personal things she took over for her bedroom at her Mum's house. I've known for a while she was slowly moving out and despite how much that thought scared me, I had to let things take there natural course. Seems my patience and letting things develop without becoming the heavy-handed parent has paid off.

Paige came to me the other night and said, *"Dad I'm not staying at Mum's anymore because it too painful for me."* As much as I was saddened to see her so upset and disillusioned with her Mum because of the way she was living her life, its also been so nice to see how happy she's been this last few days. It's almost like she now knows she's at home and finally accepted that it is indeed her home. In fact I commented earlier this evening how she has a glow about her and an energy I haven't seen for a while. With that innocent comment I just wrote, has come back a memory long ago forgotten for me and it's taken me back to the times when Lillian would just up and leave us. We'd sit all weekend (it always seemed to be weekends) trying to make sense of it all, be positive and look to the future. Towards the end of the weekend we'd all liven up because we'd had so much quality time together. That was then and so many times Lillian came back for the whole thing to start over again. Not this time, we all have to let go.

I feel it will be a while yet for Sean but in some ways he's been letting go for quite a while already. Things have changed quite a bit and he'll feel the need to stick by her, for a while longer yet because of his co-dependent behaviour. He too will come to his senses in his own time.

With saying that, *"Who knows, she might just sort herself out?"* Is that wishful thinking on my behalf or just a hint of my own co-dependency? Time will tell and she'll have to do it for herself, I've taken three steps forward with no intention of taking even one step backwards this time!!!

Chapter 7

Freedom

30/7/04
The Day My Grandson Was Born On The 12.6.04
Sean wanted to stay at Anthony's that night, after visiting Elizabeth and the baby at the hospital. I'd arranged to visit later on that evening with Marisa, when things had quietened down a bit for Elizabeth.

I had so many things to do that day including dropping Sean off and then going on to shopping. Whilst driving towards the supermarket I came to a set of lights. That suddenly made me realise, the route I was taking would be right past where the Beast was staying. I could so easily have taken another route but that would be running from the unknown, in turn never knowing!!

Mixed thoughts came into my head. *"Not today; I don't want anything to spoil today! Ha don't be silly it's a chance in a million you'd bump into him today, almost impossible odds."* I felt tingles of anticipation fluttering in my tummy none the less, though. The thought of how ironic it would be for me to see him today, of all days was in my mind. Gut feelings, knowing it's possible; it is going to happen because it's meant to happen. And today of all days!

Shit how will I react? How will I deal with it? Is it going to spoil what should be one of the happiest days of my life? My grandson was born today and he and Elizabeth were fine, even though Lillian had scared the life out of me because of a bad dream she'd had, that they both died whilst Elizabeth was giving birth. So many things flashing through my mind but I was excited at the thoughts of the encounter, the encounter that was about to happen in the next few minutes, the encounter that was going to change something within me forever, how did I know all these things, was I going mad?

All the time getting closer to my destination, knowing he would be there!

Before I knew it I was turning the corner, looking down the driveway to the building in which the BEAST WAS STAYING, HIS LAIR, HIS DEN OF SQUALLOR AND INIQUITY.

THERE HE WAS, HE WAS SAT THERE IN THE SUN WITH HIS BROTHER. IT WAS A NICE SUNNY DAY AND THERE HE WAS, SAT WITHOUT A CARE IN THE WORLD, OBLIVIOUS OF THE CAR THAT HAD PARKED A FEW YARDS DOWN THE ROAD. NOT A CLUE AS TO WHO THE GUY GETTING OUT OF THE CAR WAS. NO IDEA THAT THIS COULD BE HIS LAST DAY,

THE DAY HE MAY DRAW HIS LAST BREATHE.

HAD THE MAN REACHED THE END OF HIS TETHER, HAD HE GONE OVER THE EGE IN HIS MIND, TO WHICH THERE WAS NO RETURN, OR THERE WOULD BE ONE OF TWO OUTCOMES, TO WHICH THE MAN HAD NO IDEA HIMSELF, BECAUSE HE WAS NO LONGER FULLY ATTACHED TO WHO HE WAS. HE'D WITHDRAWN INTO HIMSELF AND WITH PRIME EVIL INSTINCTS, HE COULD ONLY FOCUS ON THE BEAST, HIS PREY HIS QUARRY. THE ANIMAL HE'D HUNTED FOR MANY YEARS OFF AND ON.

I was smiling to myself and feeling giddy, once again even a bit of fear, looking around to see if there were any witnesses. Very aware of the fact the police station was across the road, inwardly not really caring anymore, stomach still turning and tingling as I walked towards them both.

Would he even know who I was? How would I handle it if he didn't?

They were sitting on the steps, the brother first and the beast on the other side of him, a few steps lower. I was drinking the whole scene in, as I got closer to them.

He was looking past his brother, looking past the man approaching him; he was looking past me without a flicker of recognition, or awareness of the presence of anyone!!

As I passed his brother and was almost within touching distance of him, there was a flicker in his eye; a slight wince in his face, so very minute but it was there, it was fucking there!! He knew who I was I could smell it, taste it and sense it within my very being. I was running on animal instincts at that moment, all my senses acutely working, with my prey within striking distance, when I heard the words, *"DON'T PRETEND, YOU DON'T KNOW WHO I AM MALCOLM."* With almost a hint of laughter in the voice, *"don't pretend, you don't know who I am."* It was my voice I could hear and that was it, I was back. I'd even used his name. The hint of laughter wasn't insane laughter; it was more a hint of 'don't be so fucking ridiculous, nonce' and the really strange thing was, *"I didn't even feel angry."*

He looked towards me as his brother said, *"Hello John how are you doing?"* I was standing right in front of him, this pathetic looking creature, unshaven, unkempt with a can of beer in his hand, that was shaking as he was looking up at me. He knew who was stood over and in front of him. But how much would he remember flashed into my mind, as I unconsciously started talking, not fully aware of what prompted me to open the conversation with the words. *" I've had a grandson born today, a grandson that you will never, ever be able to get near.*

You will never ever be able to destroy his life, as you have so many others." He sat there staring blankly saying, "*I don't know what your talking about,*" in a slurred and quiet voice. His brother then added *"John he is…"* as he moved his fingers backwards around his temples, to indicate the beast was a bit slow or backward. But I was looking into the beast's eyes, the windows to the soul, his blackened soul and I saw something different there. He knew what I was saying; the beast was mesmerised and unable to look away from me.

I felt so powerful at that moment but so calm and in control of everything. I was feeling, seeing and saying. I was feeling peaceful inside, with no hint of rage or anger.

I went on, *"You know what I'm talking about, all the kids you've abused and you know what you are and what you've done. How could you have done all of that, knowing what its like to be abused yourself and how it affected your life? What about the time you came to tell me what had happened to you as a kid and I tried to get help for you."* His brother spoke, "*I didn't know about that John.*" I kept my eyes on the beast the whole time and answered him, *"Oh yes he was abused twice as a kid by different people and I tried to help him, when all the time he was abusing and raping kids."* The beast was pointing to a scar on his head and saying, "*I had an accident.*" I cut him off sharply saying, "*Yes somebody beat you up, because you are a nonce. I know about that. You were in a coma but you survived.*" He was looking at me like I should pity him.

My next words shocked me but changed everything. *"I want you to know MALCOLM that I bear you no more malice, I wish you no more harm, because what I see before me is worse than death."* He nodded his head in agreement but his eyes expressed his own inner torment and pain to me. *"I will not hurt you or harm you ever again, I'll never lay a finger on you."* His eyes shifted, unsure whether to believe what I was saying. He then relaxed slightly as the realisation of my words sank in. I still felt calm and peaceful, like a massive weight was being taken off me, I was letting go, at last this overwhelming weight was being lifted off my shoulders. A millstone I'd been carrying for so long was disappearing from me, as I was speaking.

I wasn't forgiving him but I was letting go of the anger and hatred inside me that had been dragging me down for so long. He was pathetic and as I said *"Wishing you ill is coming back to cause me ill in my life."* The realisation in my own mind, was *"HE WAS NO LONGER A THREAT TO ANYBODY."*

He sat before me drinking in everything I was saying, without that fear in his eyes, replaced instead with the relief that came from believing my words. I'd been haunting his mind, he'd lived in fear of me turning up in his life for many years now, never sure of how things would go between us. He'd suffered

174

enough from me now with that side of things; the rest was up to fate. God or whatever? I was letting go.

With our eyes locked together I gave my final delivery. *"One day I want you to sit down with me and tell me whom you abused, how you could do it and why."* His eyes once again said so much more than his words. *"Yes I will but not today because my heads battered. When can we do it? How can I get in touch with you?"* His eyes were saying to me, *"yes I want to, I need to get it out of me."* He even seemed eager to tell me.

As I turned to walk away I said, *"God will decide when we next meet."* I was a little shocked to hear myself say that but it felt appropriate at the time.

I got back into my car and phoned Marisa, I couldn't believe how well I felt and so much calmer than I could have ever imagined. Marisa was delighted at the way I'd handled it and we were both buzzing about going to the hospital later, then out for a meal afterwards. I went shopping feeling great and with my spirits lifted.

Chapter 8

Wanting To Conclude Things Now

2/8/04

Feeling a bit saddened and a little fearful of what's to come, or what to do next about this story. All the way through I had no doubts, or very little anyway that the News of The World would want it. Imagine my shock this morning when I finally plucked up courage to ring them, as I'd had no reply to emails I'd sent, to be told more or less that this is "old news." Unless he is re-offending there won't be any interest. This has taken years of painstaking typing (due very much to my speed) and gut wrenching hard work. The other thing he mentioned was, because only Lillian's case went to court we only had proof of that one, they couldn't name him through fear of being sued. Have to admit that I was so shocked at getting knocked back and that I didn't prepare myself properly meant I wasn't able to come back with, *"this isn't about naming him, it's a story about a family that have gone through so much and still are because of a beast."*

Never mind, next time I phone it will be different and I'll be better prepared. He also said that if I get it published I should get back in touch with them.

The publishing side seems a lot more difficult than I initially thought it was going to be but once again I'll find the angles to get round that as well. I spoke to a lady at one publishing company who was very helpful and gave me some advice; she also mentioned that they'd be having a publishing competition next year and maybe I should consider entering it.

I'm trying to be optimistic without being unrealistic and although I strongly believe things will work out ok, I still feel a bit scared that they might not, based on what's happened today. That thought is scary to me because this whole book idea was going to be totally life altering and the thoughts of not making a difference with this whole experience is very daunting for me. I've looked ahead at my life as it is and, I'm feeling a little bit more pessimistic.

What will be will be so they say and my famous words *"Tomorrow is another day"*

I AM GUTTED AND AFRAID THOUGH!!!

11/10/04

Once again its been a long time since I've been back to this, never mind I have to just accept it for what it is and the only way it can be done it seems.

Where to begin? The last weeks have been a challenge once again and once again the challenge has been met. Even though in reality it wasn't even a challenge, just one more episode of pain and self-destruction, that is part and parcel of the aftermath of the Beasts perversions. If I were reading this story myself, without any understanding of CSA, I wouldn't believe it possible for things to have such far reaching and downright traumatic, even tragic consequences, whereas, in reality, I am in it. I do live it and yet can still manage to keep a seal most times now, on what seems to be a trapdoor located in my lower gut, that seems to be so well barricaded, nothing seems to be able to open it. To let the real pain and agony of the whole ordeal penetrate it, to reach my inner core, my inner core that may just feel the most horrific pain ever, resulting in a complete and utter mental shutdown/breakdown for me.

Does this make me some kind of superman/super Dad, or am I just an ordinary person and people in general can/could cope with similar circumstances, in their everyday lives. I somehow suspect it'd take a rare breed of person to cope in reality though.

Maybe I've just managed to duck and dive with the blows, as and when they've been launched at us as a family unit. Whatever/however the truth of the matter is that we do and will cope as long as we have breath in our bodies; we are survivors and will survive.

I thank God now, for some of the input my Dad put into me about being strong, family loyalties and the fact that our bloodline is as a strong as an ox. Just maybe he was right and maybe in the book of life/fate whatever, I have been prepared to overcome anything. This is my destiny and my one chance to turn this whole tragic situation around, so my next generations can live a totally different kind of life, so much safer and even somewhere near normality. This is survival of the species/bloodline and I'm the head of this family, so have to stay strong, focused and knowledgeable of everything going on around us, also learning how to minimise the fallout and devastation that could ensue by not knowing enough. This is like being in a war zone, its like terrorism that can and does strike without notice or forewarning.

14/10/04

Having read back a few pages, I've decided to now start from the beginning. What a very daunting task that seems to be. So many things have once again been going on and even this morning back in child psychology with Paige, a very long story that I may or may not add to this whole saga.

I have toyed with the idea of leaving this whole story the way it is and going back to just change names etc.

So here goes, I'm going back in time, way, way back, for the first time in a long time. Wish me luck.

29/4/05
Well it may have taken six months to do it but I've managed to read through and make some changes.

What a coincidence that I got as far as this point? Michelle phoned me for the first time in ages. She's managed to stay off the drugs and although she still drinks, at least she doesn't have to sell her body and risk her life to feed that addiction.

She's also going abroad on holiday for the first time with her boyfriend who has recently moved in with her. They've been doing the house up together and she sounds really happy and positive, which is so lovely for me to hear.

She did mention the beast and apparently he's still in the hospital. They can't find anywhere to take him because he still drinks and is incontinent. He sits in the smoking shelter outside the hospital all day, begging money off people to buy alcohol. Doesn't seem like he has much of an existence does it and I wonder if he ever thinks about, what brought him to the place he's at now eh?

Seems some things are "definitely worse than death"!!!!!

After speaking to the guy at the news desk of the News of the world, it did give me the idea of sitting down with the beast and asking him questions whilst recording what he was saying, to use as proof of what he is/was and has done. Even though it wouldn't stand up in a court of law, it would at least be an admission of guilt from him. Have toyed with the idea ever since and I might just do that, if I can stand the thought of sitting and listening to him? Maybe it would be a great way to finish this whole story off, with him finally admitting to the world what he is!! Maybe he still wants to get it all off his chest, like his eyes told me month's ago.

I've got a few weeks left before the publishing competition to decide what to do.

2/5/05
Well it didn't take a few weeks to decide after all. After talking with my brother David last night, I've decided to do it this week and tomorrow seems as good a day as any to me. I'm going to phone Michelle later to double check that she's told me the truth, before I drive up there looking for him. Just got a cold shiver run up my back as I read these last few lines but hey, *"nothing ventured, nothing gained"* so they say and I feel so much stronger and ready to do this now.

5/5/05

As always things don't go to plan, I haven't been able to get hold of Michelle until today. She's just rang me and I've explained to her that I need to speak to him, to put a final end to this book, almost like putting old ghosts to rest. She made me promise that I won't hurt or scare him and of course I promised her faithfully I wouldn't. *"I gave her my word."* No guarantees that he won't be scared when he sees me, in fact there are no guarantees about anything really but because I've given her my word it does put restrictions on me, which I'm glad of. I haven't told her I want to record him though. With saying that I'm not sure it will be possible to do it. We'll find out tomorrow.

I'm going to carry on writing today and try and put tomorrow to the back of my mind and trust in God that things will all fall into place, because they're meant to go that way and if they don't, then maybe it wasn't meant to be.

6/5/05

Tonight is my Paige's prom night, I've just phoned her to listen to the excitement in her voice. She's at her friends getting ready and I'm going over to see her dressed before she leaves. She wasn't going to go to her prom because she's been depressed and angry for so many reasons, these last month's. With saying that if the truth was known she's been depressed for a long time now.

I'm writing about Paige first because it was the thought of her and tonight that has got me off my bed just now. She flashed into my mind and I got a rush of energy that kicked me up my arse to get on this computer and start writing about today. Paige is a remarkable kid and such a very strong character; she has to put so many restrictions on herself because a lot of the time there is a real danger of her going the wrong way.

She is a rebel at heart and a very disturbed kid who tries to deal with her own issues and not reach out for help. Thankfully these last few weeks she's been reaching out to me more and more and our bonds are becoming stronger.

She hasn't slept properly for weeks, many times she comes to lie on my bed for a while, to get some comfort. There have been a lot of tears lately for her and a few for myself being honest. Its so hard having such a troubled child and feeling so useless and defenceless, because you can't do much more than love them unconditionally and be there for when they fall. Always being ready to hug, love and dry those tears when they come.

My Paige has been having terrible flashbacks these last few weeks; she's remembering small details, even down to the fact the beast wore a brown leather jacket. She remembers him telling her Mum that he was taking her and Sean to his house to play. She remembers him coming into the bathroom and splashing water on her and her Mum leaving her in the bathroom alone with him. She won't tell me any more than that at the moment but we don't have to be geniuses to work out the rest do we.

If she remembers the small details, then she obviously remembers the traumas of what he did to her as well. She will come to me in her own good time, of that I'm quite sure. Paige has been testing me for quite a while now and I have to say, I think she knows how much I support her and how my love is unconditional.

For tonight I'm going to leave her in her own happy little world of her prom, despite her asking me straight out what had I been up to today? I looked at her and said, *"Nothing."* Her reply to that was, *"Dad I can tell by your face you've been up to something."* She is such an intuitive child and can see right through me sometimes, she's her father's daughter after all. She didn't push for an answer, which is very unusual for Paige but if I know her, she'll know it's got something to do with the beast.

The reason I wrote about Paige first was because of how drained I felt earlier. I've just typed and not even looked at the screen and will correct any typo's later.

Why am I so drained?? Because I've spent time in the presence of the beast and it's kicked the living shit out of me!! But that was earlier on and this is now, so here goes, with how it all went.

Interview With The Devil
I knew it was going to be today and didn't sleep too well last night; I saw Sean off to college and drove Paige to school. I just wanted to go to sleep when I got back and lay on the bed. I suppose part of me wanted to go asleep because that part really didn't want to follow through, with what I knew I had to do today.
I got ready on autopilot and set off to Ashton. My mind started to fill with the *"What ifs?"* all the way to my destination. What if he isn't there? What if he won't speak to me? What if he'd deteriorated since the last time I saw him? Once again I decided that what would be would be!!

I parked up and started looking on a notice board for his ward number and the building it was in, I only had to walk in a straight line for a couple of hundred yards to it. I started walking, feeling a little sick and nervous inside. I spotted the sign for the building before I noticed the shelter outside it, where I saw a forlorn figure sat in the far corner, staring aimlessly out of the window in front of him. Just by looking at him it was obvious. It was what he did every day, hour after hour. My immediate thought was, *"how sad and what a life?"* Both at the same time! I knew then it was on and it was meant to be.

I walked into the shelter and he looked up at me and said, *"hello"* as he probably did to everyone that walked into the shelter. He looked so old; his teeth were orange and rotten. I smiled at him and said *"hello"* back. It felt so easy to do, which surprised me. He looked up at me again and I said, *"Do you not recognise me Malcolm?"* He looked at me again and smiled and said, *"I do recognise you but can't think where from."* I told him that I used to be married to his sister. He looked at me and came closer. Then he said *"Lillian."* I could smell his breath and couldn't help but keep looking at his orange teeth with disgust.

He then asked why I 'd come to see him. I told him because I'd promised I'd come back one day for him to speak to me. I asked him again if he recognised me and he said, *"yes"* and even said my full name. That was a really good sign and I felt more optimistic, he then carried on talking about Michelle and how she comes to see him every few weeks with her boyfriend and the dog. These were all positive signs, although his speech was slurred and sometimes it took a few seconds to get certain words out. He knew what he was saying.

He then mentioned that Michelle had phoned the ward but he'd been in the shelter having a smoke when she rang. She'd tried to warn him that I was coming, which was something that had crossed my mind, when I was first getting in the car. I couldn't blame her because once again she was torn between her love for me, loyalty and love for her Dad.

Some other people came into the shelter to smoke so we went outside. We stood outside the shelter; there was a barrier for the cars and lorries that had parked up with the engines still running. I knew the tape would be useless because of all the noise and was trying to think of a reason to get him to my car, when he asked if I wanted to go upstairs to his room. As much as the thoughts of going into his room filled me with disgust and loathing, I knew I had to follow it through; it was a perfect situation with peace and quiet to record what he was saying.

I expected it to be smelly and dirty and knew I wouldn't be able to sit down, because wherever I sat would have been a place he'd sat.

My mind flicked back to a few years ago when I'd gone into his old house, I planned it beforehand because I wanted to get my hands on his statements to the police. At the time he was in prison on remand and it was my chance to see what he'd said in his statements. It was illegal for me to do it of course but I didn't care at the time.

I went round to the back of the house and the back door was open. Michelle was asleep on the settee and some other guy was there too. I woke her up to tell her what I wanted to do and she said it was ok to look around and fell back into a drug-induced sleep.

The living room carpet was saturated and water oozed around the soles of my boots. The place stank of cats and I wanted to be sick because the smell was that bad. I knew then how badly it must have affected Anthony, the time he'd been in to look for the beast and I remembered how much he gagged when he came out of the house.

I was now in the animal's lair and it stunk to high heaven, nothing could have prepared me for that smell. I felt contaminated with everything I touched, I searched all of the downstairs and then went upstairs. As I was going upstairs the smell got worse and I had to pull my sweatshirt over my nose and mouth but the smell was still getting through.

There were clothes strewn all over the floor and the beds were unmade. This was where he slept and I was feeling physically sick moving his things around, looking for the statements.

I looked in one of the bedrooms and there were kittens playing on the bed. My mind went back to a time when Michelle told me he had kittens and used to persuade the local kids to come in to see them. He was still up to his old tricks then. He always had she cats and bitch dogs that were forever having puppies and kittens. There was cat shit all over the bed and carpets.

(In my stomach it feels like I'm back there now, my face is wrinkled with disgust as I'm typing and feeling sick)

I had to lift the mattress to check underneath it in case they were there. How the hell did people live like this and how far had the beast fallen. He used to be so house-proud and was always smart in his appearance. Oh yes his life wasn't so nice anymore, that was obvious from the way he lived.

I searched everywhere and found nothing, I went back downstairs and said goodbye to Michelle and got outside as quickly as I could. I was sick next to the car and kept breathing deeply to try and get the smell out of my nostrils, mouth and right into my lungs and stomach but it wouldn't go for ages.

I got into the car and drove home to find Lillian had left us again. She knew where I was going that day and she still left us. Imagine having been through all of that and then having to deal emotionally with her leaving, at the same time being strong for the kids.

We walked towards the lifts and the beast was chattering away to the best of his ability, his mind seemed slow but I could see that he was wakening up and remembering things.

We walked along the corridor and I was feeling a terrible dread about going into his room. When we walked in I was surprised because it didn't smell and was tidy. It was a hospital after all and I realised that I hadn't taken that into account. Maybe I'd expected the worst because of all the smelly homes we'd had to go into when we were looking for him.

He started talking straight away and said he wanted to be in heaven with his brothers and his Mum. He sat on his bed and looked so very sad and I'm sure he was on the verge of tears, when he said, *"my Mum and brothers visit me sometimes when I'm upset. I've told all the staff that I don't want to be here, I want to be with them."*

I then switched the Dictaphone on and had the microphone just sticking out of my jacket pocket.

He started talking about how much money he had and how it was restricted because he was only allowed so much. He pointed to his head as if to explain it was compensation for what had happened to him. That was one of the reasons I'd never let anyone beat him up in the past.

I said, *"So you'd rather be in heaven then?"* He answered an emphatic, *"Yes"* and started talking about Michelle again.

Somebody came into the room to clean the table next to his bed. I tucked the Dictaphone in my pocket quickly. His next words froze me and made me wonder why he'd said them. He turned to the lady who knew him by name and said, *"this man here used to be married to my sister and he has loads of children."* She looked at me confused and repeated, *"loads of children"* and then said, *"Right."* I looked at her and smiled but it was the look on her face that made me wonder if she knew his history.

Maybe it was my paranoia, or maybe because children would visit patients in the ward, then surely the staff would have to know what he was. She smiled and left the room and I turned to him and said, *"Yes that's right I've got loads of children, do you remember them?"* He sat there staring and thinking and said *"Anthony."* I repeated, *"Anthony, yeah that's right."* He smiled at me like he was pleased with himself for remembering and was quite comfortable with my reaction, almost like he wanted to please me because he was remembering.

He then said, *"Annette."* Once again I repeated the name and said she was Janet's daughter. His next words troubled me because he said, *"You had two boys."* It disturbed me because he mentioned a boy first and that I had two boys, I knew his preference for boys and how it was all about rape with boys, the same way it had happened to him.

I told him I had three boys and he said in a very loud voice, *"Michael"* and repeated his name and asked how was he was? I told him he was ok.

I said Michael, Anthony and was waiting for him to say Sean but he didn't and mentioned Michelle instead. He again stared in front of him trying to remember and then said *" Denike, Denike."* I said, *"Denise"* and he said, *"yeah Denise."*

This was better than I thought it was going to be and as horrible as it was to hear him say my kid's names, I had to stay focused on why I was there and how important it was to keep him at ease and for myself to stay completely calm and focused!!

He then said, *"What is the other one?"* I said, *"Elizabeth"* and he said, *"pretty Elizabeth who is the same age as Michelle."* I said yes that's right. He was starting to remember small details now because he then said, *"they were born in the same hospital."* I asked him if he could remember how many hours there was between them. He looked and said *"two hours!"* I told him it was seventeen and he said, *"Is it?"* He looked so relaxed, with absolutely no idea how much loathing I had for him, or how stomach churning it was for me to be in his presence!!

He mentioned Lillian again and said, *"you don't live with her now do you?"* I replied, *"no not anymore."* He looked at me for a few seconds and in a whispered voice asked, *"Why?"* I told him we'd ended up divorced, he asked why a few times and the best I could think of was, *"we just didn't get on anymore and ended up splitting."* Not that all the devastation and pain you'd caused could have anything to do with it of course, passed through my mind.

I then asked him if he remembered my younger kids? He said Anthony again and then Denise, he then asked, *"how many kids did you have?"* I told him six all together and named Michael, Elizabeth, Anthony and Denise. I then said, *"two young ones, little ones."*

He then asked, *"What happened to my Stuart"?* I explained that he'd put Stuart into care when he was sixteen and he said, *"Yeah,"* like he understood and then asked me if I ever saw him. I said, *"no but I have heard he's with a good family and is twenty-nine now."* He then asked how old Michelle was and I told him she was twenty-six.

He then said, *"I was born in fifty seven in Ireland wasn't I, and I've been over there haven't I?"* Now that was some very good details for him to remember and I had it all on tape. If he could remember details like that, nobody could try and say he didn't know what he was saying, whilst he'd been talking to me. I was feeling so much better about how promising this was becoming and how could I get him to say some other small details to show he was sound of mind!!

He then told me I looked really smart and asked why I shaved my hair. I said it was because I was going grey and to hide it. He laughed and said, *"I'm not, look!"* And took his hat off to show me. I said, *"Your Dad Fred always had a good head of hair didn't he?"* He thought for a second and said, *"It was grey."*

I asked if he remembered living next door to me and he immediately said, *"yes we lived next door to each other, yeah. We both had dogs and you had a black one."* I said yes a Doberman; he jumped in and said, *"Yeah your one ran away didn't it?"*

I then asked do you remember his name? I was still fishing for details, he said *"Sheba"* and I said *"No Apollo."*

He then mentioned his white dog and started waffling about taking it to hospital. The white dog was the one that used to carry the chocolate and I can still see my Sean walking back from the shop in his red shorts and yellow and white T-shirt, with the dog walking in front of him carrying a bag of Maltesers. I'm pretty sure that's the same day the beast told Sean he'd kill me if he told us anything.

He then said he remembered what had happened to him the day he got hit. He and his brother Stanley were walking out of the gates to the hostel they were staying in, when a white guy kicked Stanley to the floor and a black guy that was with him hit the beast across the head. That was all he remembered. I wonder if it was a random beating or had someone pre-planned it. Maybe word had gone around about what he was?? It sounds like it had been planned to me, though.

He then started talking about the man in the room next door who constantly calls for the sister and all about his routine in the hospital, the times of his medication etc. He then pointed at a closet and said, *"All the clothes in there are brand new, that I've bought and paid for."*

I asked him if he remembered being in prison and he answered, *"Yes, yes, two prisons,"* straight away. Then I asked if he remembered what he' been in prison for? His reply was, *"yes but I didn't do anything with children. I didn't do anything like that. I had women, I had women, I wouldn't have done anything like that"* He was getting a little bit excited and aggressive by then. I'd obviously touched a nerve.

I stopped him and said, *"the last time I spoke to you, you wanted to speak about it and get it all off your chest."* He said, *"I told you that I didn't do anything to my*

185

daughter or my son, I never done anything like that, I had a girlfriend." I stopped him there and said, *"So all those kids that have come forward and told me what you did are wrong then?"* He said, *"they must be because I would never do anything like that with children, I had women that I went out with."* I then said, *"Even Michelle said that you did."* He stared at me and said, *"Michelle told me that you made her say it and when I came out of prison she said that I hadn't done any of the things I was supposed to have done. I wouldn't have messed with children because I had women"*

(Its amazing listening to the tape now as I'm typing, his speech is getting clearer as he's trying to cover up for what he is. He is still a dangerously clever beast!!!!!)

He then said, *"If you think I've done those things then you should have battered me. I would never have done anything like that with children. I had loads of women out there."* That was obviously what he'd been saying to the police, solicitors and barristers all along. *"I would never have done anything like that to children! I have loads of women out there."* I wonder how many of them looked at him and knew exactly what he was? Yet still defended him!!! Yes he did have quite a lot of women back then but that doesn't mean he wasn't a predatory paedophile!!

He then went back in time and started talking about dancing and picking up girls in the pop in, which was a youth club he used to go to when he was young. He then said, *"If you think I done that then you are completely wrong."* His speech was slipping again.

I said, *"So that means that there are an awful lot of people, that are now grown up and have got it wrong? I've spoken to all of these people and I believe them! Do you know what? I really thought that you would tell the truth."* Then I reminded him the last time we'd spoken he'd told me he wanted to tell me the truth and had even asked me when we could do it? I then said, *"You even said please come and see me again. I told you the time will work itself out and God will decide!! You said you wanted to tell me the truth; it was when you were Stanley in Hulme."*

He said, *"If you think I've done anything like that, then take me to your car and batter me. If you think I've done anything like that, then you are confused. I've never done anything in my life whatsoever,* (his speech once again improving) *done anything to children."*

I remembered him putting his coat on, in his house the night David and I first confronted him. I knew back then he wanted me to beat him. Could it be possible in his twisted mind that he thought a beating was punishment enough for what he'd done?? How twisted paedophiles minds are!!

He then started talking about us both taking it in turns to take our kids to school and whatever people said and whoever they were, they were fucking disordered (he used the word disordered.) He then said *"John, while you're stood there, do you think I would ever do anything to children? Well I never and I would never do anything to children."* Whom was he trying to convince? Himself, or me? He said, *"I used to look after children, I used to mind your children."*

(His next words chilled me to the bone, where was his head at when he came out with this?)

He said, *"You used to borrow my children and I used to borrow your children."* My mind flicked back to when his brother Alex who was also a paedophile used to bring his girlfriends daughter down to the beasts house. I'd heard he used to still visit the beast when he'd moved from next door to me as well, with the same little girl. His brother in law used to also visit with his daughter and I have to admit that as the years have gone on and the more I've learnt about paedophiles, it had crossed my mind a few times that they may well have abused each others children and in the beasts own words, *"BORROWED CHILDREN"*

Elizabeth had flashbacks about two people attacking her in a bathroom; one of them was tall and blonde. I'd always suspected the beasts brother in law of being involved because he was tall, blonde and my gut instincts looking back.

8/5/05
(I'm sitting here now trying to think how did I cope listening to all the things he said? It seems so long ago and I feel more detached as each day has passed since Friday. I must have switched myself off and detached from the enormity of it all.

In an hour I'm taking Sean to the studio to record another track for his album, he's getting so much better with each track he records. That son of mine is a true survivor and with his determination, he'll make it in whatever he does with his life!! For the time being it's his music keeping him going and he is a "lyrical genius"!!

As much as I don't really feel up to it today, I'm about to switch the tape back on and listen to the beast again.)

I then said, *"I know you've done it because I've spoken to enough people, that you've done things to. I've read statements made to the police, I've listened to Lillian tell me what you did to her when she was young. I've listened to my own kids, I've listened to Annette and I've listened to Carol. They've all told me."* He then said in a drained voice, *"Well your wrong!"* I said, *"you told me last time you wanted to tell me the truth but obviously you don't."* I kept trying to get him to re-connect with himself the day he looked into my eyes and said, *"yes, when can we do it."*

He said, *"I've told you the truth."* I stopped him there and said, *"that's not the truth, we both know, that's not the truth but if that's the way you want to leave it, then that's fine by me. That's the way you want to leave it, then that's up to you. I'll go now because there's no point in me speaking to you"*

I wanted him to think this was going to be his only chance to tell the truth and that I was prepared to walk away but inside hoping he'd grasp on to it and see it as a chance to cleanse himself somehow.

He then said, *"I didn't do anything wrong."* Once again I butted in and stopped him speaking by saying, *"people like you don't think its wrong, you think its normal, you think its ok to do things like that. You even think that the kids want you to do it, that's what happens with people like you. You believe the child loves you and you can do things like that. You don't see it, as being wrong but it is wrong! It happened to you, do you remember? It happened to you when you were young."* He said *"no."* He was being so different and I knew I was getting through to him! I said, *"do you remember somebody getting you when you were young?"* I paused for ages. He sat thinking and then said, *"I don't remember that no."*

I reminded him, he'd come to me and told me that somebody had abused him when he was young and it was one of his friend's brothers. And it had happened another time when he was younger, in a house they lived in, in the country. I said nothing more for a few more seconds and once again he was thinking to himself. I then said *"Clayton something or other, Clayton."* I let him think about it, at the same time willing him to finish the rest, to prove once again that he was competent. I said it again. *"Do you remember where you lived as a kid, Clayton something or other?"* He moved his lips and I read what he'd said, I had him because it was an unusual name, his lips formed the words, *"le moors."* I was so calm and said, *"that's the one yeah."*

I'm listening to my own voice at the moment and I didn't give anything away, even though I knew deep inside he was walking right into a trap and digging his own grave.

"What was it Clayton what?" He finished it, *"Le Moors."* I said, *"yeah that's it, Clayton Le moors."* He repeated it again. I said, *"you told me it happened again when you moved to Moss Side, it was one of your friends brothers, his big brother."* I let him think again, you could almost see his mind searching itself, by his eyes.

He changed the subject then and said, *"What have I supposed to have done?"* I said, *"I don't know, I thought you were supposed to tell me. You said you wanted to tell me. I know what you've done through talking to so many people but I thought you wanted to tell me yourself."* He started to get excited again and raised his voice and said, *"I'm trying to tell you now!"* I said, *"No, what your trying to tell me is that you didn't do anything and you know that's not true. I definitely know that's not true but as I say that's your choice. I can't make you say anything and if you don't..."* he interrupted me and asked, *"why was I in prison so long?"* I told him he'd been in prison because he kept running away before the court case and sentencing.

He then said, *"John what's your second name?"* I told him and he repeated it and then said, *"John what is happening to me now, what are you going to do to me?"* I told him, *"Absolutely nothing. I only came to see you because the last time I saw you, I said we'd sit down together and you will tell me whom you hurt and why? And I asked you if you would apologise for doing it and you said yes I want to. I want to tell you the truth but I can't do it today because my head is battered. That's what you said and your hands were shaking because you were scared of me and I said you had nothing to be scared of. You and me can sit down and you will tell me the truth, then I will go away and tell all those people, all those children, that you said you were sorry for what you did to them. Because it had happened to you and you knew how much it had messed your life up. That's why I came today because I believed you when you told me you were going to tell me the truth and this was just one way for me to go back to those kids and say listen he's not happy about being alive, he's had a bad accident and he doesn't want to be around anymore, he's not happy with his life but he said he's sorry. He said he's sorry for what he did to you. I thought that was what was going to happen today. Nothing more, I'm not going to do anything to you. There's no point in me doing anything to you."*

He said, *"Alright then, alright then, how many people have I done, done confronted?"* I knew he was going to say, *"how many people have I done things to?"* But he changed it to confronted for some reason and his speech seemed to get worse. I said, *"How many people what?"* He repeated, *"that I confronted."* I said, *"I don't understand you, what do you mean?"* He then said, *"Who did I desire"?*

(I've only just heard what he said whilst listening to the tape but he said, *"WHO DID I DESIRE?"*

I said, *"Who did you what? Sorry!"* He then said, *"Who did I do something to?"* I repeated, *"Who did you do something to? I thought you were going to tell me, that's what I asked you for. I mean I know some of them but I wanted you to tell me yourself."*

He said, *"Alright then I will say I'm sorry but I don't remember."* I said, *"So you don't remember? Ok!"* He said, *"but I'm sorry."* I stopped him and said, *"but that is no good because the sorry only counts if you remember and if you can remember Clayton Le Moors and you can remember what school you went to and you can remember what street you lived on. You remembered Lillian the minute you saw me, you remember your Mum, you remember Alex, you remember so many things, and you even remember your little white dog. You remember my Doberman. If you remember so many things, then surely you remember whom you abused. You used to have she dogs that used to have puppies. Do you remember you used to always have puppies and if you remember all of these things, yet your telling me you don't remember!"*

He then raised his voice and almost shouted, *"I don't remember please, look at me I would not have molested anybody, when I was going out with women."* I said, *"Ok, ok, that's fine if that's what your sticking to but I know a lot of children that would call you a liar and I know a lot of children that are suffering now and have tried to kill themselves and have had to go and see counsellors, their lives are a mess because of what you did to them when they were little."*

He said, *"You are wrong."* I stopped him and said, *"well there you go, it makes no odds to me whether you admit it or not but I know what you are and I know what you've done because I live it. I live it every day with the kids you did it to and I see what they've gone through, so I live it every single day, so to me it doesn't make any odds if you admit it or not, it doesn't make any odds if you lie or tell the truth? That's your choice but you're the one when it comes judgement day, when you go before God and he turns around to you and says, you had an opportunity to tell the truth and get all this off your chest and cleanse your soul but you lied and you left all those people behind and they are never going to hear you say I am sorry for what you did to them! They are never going to hear it."* I was really getting to him now and said, *"my Paige wanted to come and see you herself and stand in front of you but I didn't think that was such a good idea. She wanted to see you for herself and see what's become of you and I think she wants to hear you say, your sorry for what you did to her because you messed all of their lives up. They're all doing ok but they'd have done a lot better. Like I say you can remember the minutest details throughout your life and yet your telling me you can't remember something like that and yes you did have a lot of women. There was a lot of women that were into you because you were a good looking lad, you were a smart dresser and you had the gift of the gab but you had an illness and that illness was that you liked children and you've done some terrible things to children, Malcolm, you have done some terrible things to them. You've given them nightmares and you've hurt them, you've hurt them badly just like you were hurt when you was a child. Somebody hurt you, because you came and told me and I tried to get you help, somebody hurt Alex, you hurt Lillian. Do you remember your Mum's boyfriend Joe"?*

I paused, I wasn't letting up now because he was staring at me and replaying things in his own head I said, *"Joe hurt Lillian as well."* He was thinking and then he said, *"Joe."* I repeated it and said, *"He hurt Alex. He abused Alex as well. Alex told me that and he told me you abused him when you were kids as well. Alex told me himself before he died. You were ill Malcolm, you were sick."*

I stopped talking and waited, after a few seconds he said, *"do you want me to die?"* I said, *"I don't want you to die, not at all. I just want you to be honest with me that's all."* He shouted, *"but I am telling you the truth."* I said, *"ok then that means Alex's lying then, Lillian's lying, Michael's lying, Michelle's lied, Anthony's* lied, Elizabeth's lied, Annette's lied, Carol's lied, Denise lied, Sean has lied, Paige has lied, Christina, Michelle's friend has lied!! All these people have lied then and nothing really happened to them, is that what your telling me?" He shouted, "yes," and I said "Ok that's fine, on your head be it, its your soul mate, its your soul and you won't be going up there where your Mum and Robert are that's for sure. You'll be going down there mate (as I pointed downwards.) You'll be going downstairs. They don't let people like you up there!! If you believe in God then you believe in the devil! Do you think for one minute if there is a heaven that someone who's hurt so many people, is going to go to heaven? Do you think that, do you really think that?" He said, "I will go to heaven." He was looking worried by then and I said, "Will you? Right! I don't think you will mate. I know you won't."

He was getting angry again and then he said, "You've only come down here to torment me haven't you?" I said, "no I haven't come to torment you no; I've come to see something through to the end. I came to speak to you because you told me you wanted to tell me the truth the last time I saw you. That's why I'm here and do you know what? I actually believed you at the time! I believed you! I believed you! I believed you but I can see that same look in your eye."

He was glaring at me by now and I said, "you haven't lost any power, you are still powerful, you're still powerful and you still know what your doing." He asked "where" and I said "in your eyes I can see it in your eyes the way you're looking at me. I've seen that look before. I saw that look the first time I ever confronted you! You look like years have come off you now." The transformation was amazing he had been staring right into my eyes and trying to intimidate me, the same way he'd tried when I confronted him the first time. He even looked younger again and yes he still had power in that fucked up shell that was now his body! He knew what he'd done and he knew what he was! And he was trying to intimidate me again! I said, "A minute ago you looked pretty fucked really but not now, not now! Anyway its up to you, its your choice because I'm going to leave now and you won't see me again. I won't be coming back again, I came for the last time today to give you a chance to tell me the truth"

He said in a pleading voice, "I'm telling you the truth." I interrupted him in a slightly more dominant voice and said, "it doesn't matter. I'm going to leave now because you wont tell the truth. So I will leave but I wont be coming back again. This is your last chance because I'm not bothered either way, because I believe all the kids. I believe what everyone has told me about what you've done. I believe them and I don't believe you! I don't believe you and you know you're the one that will carry it mate! You'll carry it! You'll be the one to carry it! I was just a fool for believing you wanted to tell me the truth" I was grinding him down again. He shouted, "I've just told you." I stopped him again and said, "your shouting now aren't you, your shouting now, you're a liar!"

191

We stood there staring into each other's eyes for what felt like ages, he was challenging me with his eyes and trying to break me down! Maybe even reaching deep inside, to that little frightened boy inside of me that had also been hurt as a child.

I could feel my own anger building up because he was now confronting and challenging me with his eyes. I was trying so hard to appear strong but not to frighten him at the same time. If I was to unleash how I really felt inside, my hands would have been round his throat and I would have tightened them slowly at the same time seeing the panic in his eyes, as his life force was slipping away. But of course I couldn't do that, although how many people could have shown such restraint I wonder?

I said, *"you're still Malcolm, you've not changed. Your fucking body might be knackered and battered but the old Malcolm is still there! You're still sharp, you might not be able to talk or walk properly but the old Malcolm's still there! I can see it in your eyes."* He was getting really angry by then and said in an evil voice, *"I'm looking at you."* I said, *"Why are you looking at me? Go on what are you thinking while your looking at me?"* He said, *"I'm looking, thinking,"* and then he screamed, *"you."* I said, *"Go on what are you thinking?"* He sprang forward and raised his arms and I have to admit I recoiled from him. He was looking straight at my pocket with the microphone sticking out. I'd seen him glance at my pocket a few times earlier; I'd looked for something in his eyes to show he'd seen it, this time he stared. I covered it quickly with my hand. Then he said, *"You used to do it when you were drunk."* I said, *"pardon, I don't know what your talking about."* He said, *"You might have been doing things! "* I said so very slowly, *"no, no, no, no, no, no, you and I are the exact opposite to each other! The exact opposite!"*

He looked me straight in the eye with a twisted evil look and said, *"You and me used to be partners."* We used to be like that and crossed his fingers to show we were close. I said, *"oh yes! We were friends at one time, until I found out what you were."*

I paused and then said, *"anyway you're not interested in telling the truth, so I'm going to go and I just hope you live to be an old man."* He said, *"no."* I said, *"It's not a very nice life is it?"* and waited for a reaction. He was thinking again and I was praying to God for him to admit it.

(Being totally honest those prayers were answered within moments!! He started to look so deflated! I kid you not, it was happening before my very eyes)

He sat on his bed and I asked him, *"Do you want me to give you a few minutes to think about it?"* His voice altered then and he said, *"What do you want me to say?"* I said, *"I just want you to say sorry to them all and mean it! I want you to tell*

192

the truth and mean it! That's all, nothing more." He said, *"Tell the truth to what?"* I said, *"About what you did, nothing more than that, just tell the truth and say you're sorry! That's all I'm interested in. I can go back and tell all those kids, that you said you were sorry"*

I knew I had him now he was opening up he'd become aggressive and abusive, that hadn't worked; now he was wearing down, prayer can be a powerful weapon!

The next part was really weird and I did wonder if he'd seen the microphone because he said, *"My name is Malcolm Hunt and I will tell you the truth, it must have happened."* He asked, *"Is that alright?"* I said, *"It is the truth, it's happened."* He said, *"alright I just said it then."* I said, *"no, you've just said it must have happened." There you are that's because I've said it! I want you to tell me, I want you to admit it! Not that it must have happened! Do you remember? Be honest do you remember? I'm not asking you to go into details! I'm not asking you to name them all! I'm asking you to tell me if you remember what you did to them."* He said, *"I don't."* I said, *"you don't well that's fair enough, I don't believe you but that's fair enough! I don't believe that you don't remember! Yet you remember so many other things! But if that's what you're saying, then that's it then! If that's what your saying then, that is it then! I can't make you say something can I"?*

He was thinking again and I kept quiet for a few seconds and said, *"Only you can do that Malcolm."* He then said, *"Alright then I apologise for what I must have done."* I said, *"Must have, or did do!"* That was it. That swung it because he said, *"DID DO!"*

I then said, *"So are you telling me now, that you did abuse children,"* and he said *"I DID, right."* I asked if he remembered who and he said, *"no."* I said, *"You don't remember which ones?"* And in a weakened voice he said, *"no."* I said *"but you know you did?"* And he said, *"yes."* I asked, *"Do you remember that you were abused as a child,"* and he said, *"no!"* I said, *"no, so you don't remember that."* He answered, *"no."*

I said, *"Do you remember abusing mine?"* And he said, *"no."* I then said, *"what about Lillian, when you were younger,"* he said, *"no, not to my sister."* I said, *"That's what you were in court for! That's what you admitted being guilty to! That's what you pleaded guilty to,"* he said, *"my sister."* He started thinking again and I repeated, *"you pleaded guilty for Lillian."* He paused for ages and then said, *"What I ever did,"* and then paused changing it to, *"what I must have done, must have done, must have happened."* I said, *"It did happen Malcolm."* He said, *"I'm telling you"* and I said, *"you're telling me what?"" And he said, "What I, what you said I did."* I asked, *"Do you remember it now? Do you remember it, you know its true but do you remember its true? Is that what your saying?"* He said, *"yeah."* I said, *"you tell me, just say that to me! John I did abuse those children."* He said, *"John, I abused them children."* I said, *"you did"* and he said *"I did"* and I asked, *"and do you remember now? Be honest now! You've been honest this far! Just say it, yes or no."* He said *"yes"* and I said, *"you do remember."* He said, *"yes"* again. I said, *"Right, are you sorry for doing that to them now?"* He said *"very, very much."* I said, *"Do you regret it Malcolm?"* And he said, *"I do remember it and I am sorry."* I said, *"so you do remember and you're sorry?"* And he said *"yeah"* and I said, *"I will tell them that now and I'm sure that they'll be glad to hear that."* He said, *"I must have abused them."* I said, *"yeah you did."* He said, *"I'm telling you the truth, I abused them."* I said *"you did, I know you did and you know you did but I will tell them what you said now and I thank you for telling the truth."*

I was still trying to open him up some more when he said, *"I'm telling you the truth John,"* I then asked *"do you feel better for telling the truth?"* He said, *"what I did, I'm telling the truth! What I did was wrong! "* I repeated *"what"* and he said, *"it was wrong what I did, I was wrong."* I said *"thank you"* and a part of me meant it, I felt relieved after all this time, it was like at last he'd admitted it and probably for the first time he'd said it! It also meant that now the News of The World might be able to print the story.

He then said, *"I will say thank you for coming to see me and telling me what I did was wrong."* I said, *"There is no court case now, its nothing now, its just two men in one room and that's it! But at least I can go away and tell people that I gave you a chance and you apologised! You admitted it!"* He said, *"Thank you very much!"* I said, *"So you do remember now?"* He said *"yes."* I said, *"You remember why you were in prison"? And the court?"* He said *"no."* I said, *"police station?"* He said, *"I can't remember that."* I asked if he remembered the names of those he abused and he said *"no."* I said, *"You just know that you did it."* And he said *"yeah."* I didn't know what else to say and just said, *"Right ok."* I stood there a few moments then said, *"You hurt them you know! You hurt them badly."* He said, *"I?? For what I did?"* I couldn't make it out and said *"what?"* He repeated it and said, *"I forgive for what I did."* I repeated him and said, *"what you forgive yourself?"* He said, *"no! what I've done."* I said, *"I can't forgive you, I can't forgive you because I'm living with all the people you've hurt! I have to see them every single day! So I can't forgive you! That's not for me to do"* He wanted me to forgive him!! What did he think? That I could absolve him for all his sins!!

He may well have escaped man's justice but will he escape God's?

He then said *"I'll see you down"* and I said, *"I knew you'd remember though! I knew you'd remember! I saw it the last time I spoke to you, that you remembered."*

He pointed to his head and asked, *"Was I like this?"* I said, *"Yes, I could tell that you knew! Maybe I will come and see you again, maybe I will. Maybe you'll have remembered more, or maybe you'll want to speak some more. Who knows?"*

He said, *"I don't want to see you no more."* I said, *"Why is that? Am I a reminder of what you've done?"* "He said *"yes."* I said, *"So you don't want to remember what you did?"* He said, *"I've given you what I remember."* I said, *"right ok fine"* and turned the Dictaphone off.

10/5/05
I said goodbye and walked out the door and down the corridor, he was trying to keep up with me but I wanted to get as far away from him as possible!

I needed to see how much time was left on the tape because I'd panicked towards the end, in case it ran out whilst he was talking. I shifted my body to the right so I could slip the Dictaphone out of my pocket and look at the tape. I was right, there wasn't much tape left.

He shouted my name as I turned around and he said, *"Wait for me."* I thought he might well want to tell me more. As we walked to the lift he said you taped me! I said, *"How did you know that?"* He said, *"I saw you take it out of your pocket."* I admitted I had and said, *"listen I did that so I could play the tape for everybody and they could hear you say your sorry. I told you this isn't about the police or getting you to court anymore, because you are fucked! There isn't a court in the land going to put you away because you're fucked, look at you. This is about them and me now, In fact I've written a book about you. You are going to be famous for what you are."*

He then asked me, *"so you don't think I'll go to heaven then?"* I said, *"no you won't go to heaven, your Mum may be up there but I doubt that your brother is, because he was like you."* I'd got through to him by mentioning heaven, after him talking about wanting to be with his Mum and brothers.

The time I first confronted him after his accident, he had the look in his eye of a man who wanted to cleanse himself and confess everything. For all I or we know, he may spend most his waking hours praying to die. Death would be too easy for him though!!

Part of me really wants to go back and try again; maybe I've awoken something in his mind. Maybe so many bad memories of what he is and what he's done have come flooding back since he saw me. Just maybe!! Could I manage to do it again, or would it do me more harm than good?? I'll have to give it some more thought, after I've re-read the conversation as I typed it. I don't think I can bring myself to listen to the tape again though.

12/5/05
Just when you think its safe to go back into the water, that great white shark

called life jumps at you from nowhere and bites a massive chunk out of your emotions, confidence and the strength and hopes that you've been building on for so long. All the time thinking "things can't get any worse now, we are going in the right direction etc" I had everything all mapped out and far as I could see nothing could distract me from my writing, oh foolish me once again.

The night before last Sean and Paige came to see me in my room. Once again Dad's guts told him something might be wrong with them I'd gone into Sean's room to speak to him and Paige, without really realising it I said, *"why don't you come and sit with me and we can talk."* Sean looked up at me and said, *"You're such a great Dad."* My reply was, *"why because I asked you to come and sit with me."* He said, *"No for always knowing when to suggest it, you're such a great Dad."* Although I felt it was a strange thing to say, I wasn't too perturbed by it because Sean often tells me I'm a great Dad. A title I don't really think I deserve but one Sean wants to bestow on me, so yes I am.

After a few minutes they came in and sat down, the old triangle back together again, we'd been sitting like this for a little over four years by now. I asked Sean what was wrong with him? He looked at me, shook his head, looked downward and said, *"I can't even say it Dad, Paige will you tell him."* Paige looked at me and said, *"Sean has got someone pregnant, Dad."* I looked at him with disbelief and asked Sean who it was. He said, *"Dad I didn't want to tell you because I knew you'd be so disappointed in me. It's Roxanne, from across the road from my Mum's. I didn't even do it properly because I realised it was wrong. It didn't feel right at the time, so I stopped."* *"But you didn't use protection Sean! You always told me you were going to be the condom king after you'd seen how your brothers lives have been affected."* He said, *"Dad, I know and I'm so sorry I'm an idiot"*

My head was again sent spinning as all my thoughts were coming in together. The first thoughts maybe the baby isn't his because the girl has been known to sleep around. Second thought she's sixteen and had a baby only five months ago.

Sean was so upset and as angry as I was, I didn't have the heart to shout at him. Paige assured me that Roxanne wasn't sleeping around, because she'd have known about it and because Roxanne really liked Sean, so most definitely wouldn't have slept around because, she thought he might go out with her after they'd had sex. I was so very disappointed in Sean and felt that he'd taken advantage of the girl!!

I started thinking hard and of course my writing and getting published will make a difference and told Sean, *"Don't worry we'll work it out, we have seven month's to prepare for this. You keep writing and recording your lyrics and I'll keep writing because now either you or me have to make it before December. Sean you have*

196

done something so very stupid and now we're all going to have to pay the price and suffer the consequences"

I haven't even been able to come back to this because of how deeply it's affected me and put me into such a depressed state of mind. I really believed on Monday night when I said to a whole group of people, *"that at last I think the worst is over and its not what life throws at you, its how you deal with it, is important"!!* Oh how much did I think I was in control of my life once again and only the next night, I would be shot down in flames! It is true though, its how you deal with it that counts and although I feel very weakened at the moment, at least I'm typing again and within a few days will have caught my breath enough to start fighting again and focus on this story and the strategies involved to get it published first and then sold. It was really important before but now it's taken on a whole new urgency, for a child that's not even born yet. Not just any child but my son's child and my grandchild!!

I have to stay focused on my goals!!

14/5/05
Well it's a Saturday and the day before my birthday, hmm 46 yrs old tomorrow and only 4 yrs away from 50! Lets face it with how chaotic the last 46 yrs have been, surely I'm entitled to find some peace in the coming years! It would be unrealistic to not have bumps in the road but hopefully no major boulders eh. We still have to face the problems the birth Sean's baby will bring but for now I have to put that to the back of my mind, to be dealt with at a later date.

Last week Lillian told me that she wanted to go and see the beast for herself. I understood and said when she was ready, I'd tell her where to find him. Yesterday she mentioned it again, I said I'll take her because I'm hoping that seeing her may trigger his conscience enough to admit to more of his atrocities and get a much clearer confession without it sounding like I'm forcing him or putting words in his mouth. So hopefully I can/will, find/have the strength to go through it all again.

Obviously this never happened, she never did find the strength and eventually I stopped mentioning it.

5/10/05
Bringing It To A Finish
I have to end this now because I cannot do it any longer, the only way to describe it is, *"my pain threshold is weaker now."* I can't separate the feelings or need for closure from my everyday life anymore. I need some time out for me now before my next projects and can't keep coming back to add more to this story. I've accepted it's happened but keep re-living it whilst finishing it off. I'm

going to write a quick update now and END it once and for all, after the final edit which my friend Jo is doing for me now.

My kids are all doing as well as can be expected, Sean will have his album finished soon and the college record label manager predicts great things for him. Lillian finally sought help with her drinking a few weeks ago and was in a detox unit; so far she has managed to stay off the alcohol. Michelle has stayed clean from the drugs for six month's now and in my opinion is a "True Survivor" for accomplishing it; she also wants to train as a drugs counsellor.
There is still a question mark surrounding the dates of Sean's baby, we are going to keep an open mind until the baby's born. If the baby doesn't look like Sean, we will have to have a paternity test to know for sure before we take the next steps. If the baby is Sean's it will change all of our lives and he and I will take full responsibility for his or her upbringing.

Michelle and a friend of mine have asked me to write their life stories and I plan to write a recovery book of my own, once I've done more research and learnt even more about coping with the aftermath of CSA.

Well I was lucky enough to find a publisher who is genuinely interested in helping me get this book into print at last. As always so many other things have gone on in the last six weeks since I last wrote anything, but hey such is life eh.

When I got up yesterday morning Paige had left her bedroom door open, a sure sign that she's had a bad night sleep because of nightmares. I went to close the door gently so as to not awaken her when she almost jumped out of her skin because I'd startled her that much. She then said *"He is going to die soon dad, I can feel it. He is going to die in the next few weeks and I want to see him before he dies."* I wasn't surprised and said *"You go back to sleep baby and we'll talk about it later."*

Having given that last few lines a little thought, I think I too feel something may happen to him and I did react very calmly when she said what she wanted to do, almost like it is meant to happen before I finally finish this book. Either way we'll find out on Saturday because I'm taking her to where I last saw him to see if he's still there.

Jan the psychologist that Paige used to see did say that one day Paige may want to see the BEAST to bring about her own form of closure. Marisa phoned me yesterday and came up with a very good theory, being that Paige may still be picturing the beast as he used to be in her own tormented little mind, as opposed to how he really is now which is a shadow of his former self and a very sad, forlorn and pathetic looking creature.

I'm not going to rely on him just happening to be there or maybe even sitting on the steps this time. I'm going to go in and enquire because for the first time ever I can honestly say that "I AM ABSOLUTELY NO DANGER TO HIM AND IN TURN TO MY FAMILY AND MYSELF" because all of my anger, hatred and rage towards him has gone. I know wholeheartedly he is safe from me, or should I say *"The me that used to be. Thank God!!!"*

I discussed things earlier with Paige and she said she needs to see him one last time, she said, *"Dad I want to see him in front of me and spit in his face."* She will be safe from him because I'm there; I just hope it doesn't have a worse affect on her afterwards. One thing I'll have to be very careful and aware of is the power that is still behind those eyes of his. I'll watch for that and intervene very quickly if he tries that with her!! I have looked into that monsters eyes so many times over these last years and despite his very weakened physical state his mind is still fully aware and the evil still so very strong within his inner being.

14/12/05
The following weekend both Paige and I geared our selves up to face the beast. We dropped Sean off at the studio and went to the hostel the beast is living in. I left Paige in the car because I knew it would be too dangerous a place to bring a young girl because of the type of people staying there. I had full intentions of bringing the beast out to the car for her to confront him. I walked down the driveway with a mixture of emotions, none of which were fear or anger it has to be said. The place was closed up and a notice at the side of the door said, "**No visitors allowed at weekends and not to ring the bell**". I was gutted but had no choice but to turn away, when I told Paige she didn't really seem to be bothered but I said we would find time to come again during opening hours. She hasn't mentioned it since and it's getting too close to Christmas now. Maybe she decided just going was enough and she has been so much happier and content lately. Either way once again I have to wait for her decide and approach the subject. Personally I hope she never does want to go but have to leave that as her decision and will support her either way.

The baby was born last week and looks very much like Sean, she is absolutely beautiful and already I'm a doting Granddad. It's not the ideal circumstances to bring a baby into the world but as always we will do what has to be done as a family unit. We had her over on Friday evening, all day Sunday and I'm picking her up tonight for a few hours. She will be able to stay overnight soon which will be fantastic despite changing nappies and night feeds ha! She will be surrounded by love, which is important, and a firm foundation to bring her up.

This weekend is pre Christmas Dinner for all my family; my kids and Grandkids are coming over for some of dad's home cooking. Everybody is doing their own things this Christmas for the first time but I couldn't resist having an excuse to get them all together under one roof before the end of the year. Of course the baby will be guest of honour and surrounded by her family for the first time in my home.

Thank you for coming on my journey with me, I hope you found it enlightening. I also hope that if you are a fellow survivor, you got inspiration and if necessary realised its ok to reach out for help when you need to and most importantly there is always HOPE! If CSA hasn't ever touched your life, I sincerely hope to God it never does but you may be a little wiser and better informed as to how traumatically it does affect people. Just maybe you will find the strength to join the battle to get the government to pour more resources into the recovery of survivor's and stiffen sentences for the offenders. The main aim is to raise awareness and for people to realise its not a taboo subject, its ok to talk about it and it is really going on in REAL LIVE'S all over the WORLD..

Take care,

John

The End